P9-DWH-851

CRITICAL ACCLAIM
FOR *TRAVELERS' TALES*

"The *Travelers' Tales* series is altogether remarkable."
—Jan Morris, author of *Journeys*, *Locations*, and *Hong Kong*

"For the thoughtful traveler, these books are an invaluable resource. There's nothing like them on the market."
—Pico Iyer, author of *Video Night in Kathmandu*

"This is the stuff memories can be duplicated from."
—Karen Krebsbach, *Foreign Service Journal*

"I can't think of a better way to get comfortable with a destination than by delving into *Travelers' Tales*...before reading a guidebook, before seeing a travel agent. The series helps visitors refine their interests and readies them to communicate with the peoples they come in contact with...."
—Paul Glassman, Society of American Travel Writers

"*Travelers' Tales* is a valuable addition to any predeparture reading list."
—Tony Wheeler, publisher, Lonely Planet Publications

"Like having been there, done it, seen it. If there's one thing traditional guidebooks lack, it's the really juicy travel information, the personal stories about back alleys and brief encounters. The *Travelers' Tales* series fills this gap with an approach that's all anecdotes, no directions."
—Jim Gullo, *Diversion*

Adventures in Wine

TRUE STORIES OF
VINEYARDS AND VINTAGES
AROUND THE WORLD

T R A V E L E R S ' T A L E S

Adventures in Wine

TRUE STORIES OF
VINEYARDS AND VINTAGES
AROUND THE WORLD

Edited by
THOM ELKJER

Series Editors
JAMES O'REILLY AND LARRY HABEGGER

TRAVELERS' TALES
SAN FRANCISCO

Wine is earth's answer to the sun.

—MARGARET FULLER

Table of Contents

Part Four
IN THE SHADOWS

Part Five
THE LAST WORD

Adventures in Wine: An Introduction

by Anthony Dias Blue

Wine is a great adventure, even if you never leave the comfort of your favorite armchair. You don't need a tourist visa or a matching set of luggage to discover the world of wine, although having a decent atlas and a good wine merchant within driving distance wouldn't hurt.

Wine is a passport to the world. Since I was eleven years old (yes, I started early), when my father took me to Burgundy, I have used wine as a window onto places, cultures, and times in my life. On that first trip to France my dad let me taste some top Burgundies out of the barrel. That sensory impression has stayed with me my whole life. All my impressions—the taste of the French food I'd never experienced before, the ripe, earthy smell of the air in the wine caves, the sight of the famous vineyards, the emotion of being in such a special place—flood my memory even today when I taste fine Burgundy.

Getting to know wine is getting to know the world. More than just a complex and delicious drink, wine is history, geography, the very soil from which the grapes are grown. It opens us to life on a deeper level and it enriches and enhances our days.

Thom Elkjer's compendium of fascinating and addictively readable tales brings together a wide array of wine experiences, and suggests that wine is perhaps the closest thing the planet has to an elixir of life. As Jim Harrison so matter-of-factly puts it in his moving reflection on the nature of wine: "The simple act of opening a bottle of wine has brought more happiness to the human race than all the collective governments in the history of earth." I say amen to that.

This is the best kind of travel book—one in which we learn

from those who have been there before us. We visit wine's sacred sites, such as the mountaintop on the island of Santorini, where Stephen Yafa relates the ancient Greek legend of wine's divine origin. We are initiated into its rituals of power and privilege: Peter Mayle takes us to the Hospices de Beaune auction, where great Burgundies flow like lemonade at a Sunday picnic, and Tony Aspler brings us a coveted invitation to dinner at Bordeaux's Chateau Mouton-Rothschild.

But, as we discover along the way, wine also inhabits places entirely unexpected. Thom Elkjer reveals the charm of wine country nestled in the desert near Tucson, Arizona. Robert Holmes describes his photography assignment at a kosher winery in Israel. Tim Russo finds political symbolism in a glass of wine in the former Soviet Republic of Georgia.

We also see wine from all its social angles. I wonder which wine tasted sweeter on their respective palates: the house wine of Domaine de la Romanée-Conti served to the exhausted grape-pickers in Michael Blumer's harvest story, or the jug wines that Laura Higgins's shotgun-toting Georgia redneck relatives sampled under the tutelage of her sophisticated Parisian fiancé? I couldn't hazard a guess.

The point is that the geography of wine is as much an emotional landscape as it is a physical terrain. The writers in this volume not only take us around the globe, they also explore the subtle complexities of our innermost responses to wine, the psychic *terroir*, as it were. Witness Jim Harrison breaking out his best remaining bottle of Margaux as he contemplates the near death and miraculous recovery of his beloved English setter, Tess. And sometimes—can it be?—we may even tire of too much wine and, like Richard Sterling, slip off into a Chinatown honky-tonk for a soul-cleansing gin and tonic.

Whatever stage you're at in your appreciation of wine—rank novice or auction-house maven—you'll find bottles to savor, ideas to contemplate, and stories to retell in *Adventures in Wine*.

PART ONE

ESSENCE OF
WINE COUNTRY

STEPHEN YAFA

Sipping with the Gods

All wine country is the same country.

THE SHEPHERD'S NAME WAS STAPHYLUS. THE NAME OF HIS GIDDY
goat remains a mystery. Modern Greeks know their mythology, and
trust it to impart profound truths about the nature of man at his
most heroic and lamentably human. That's why Kostas Antoniou
tells me the tale of the shepherd and the goat with a solemnity usually reserved for religious canons.

On the Greek isle of Santorini, we are standing high up at the
edge of a thousand-foot cliff that drops straight down to a spectacular crescent-shaped caldera in the Aegean below. Kostas, short,
trim, middle-aged, black hair brushed straight back, wearing a
heavy gold wrist chain, perfectly pressed pants the color of butter,
and a matching sweater woven with metallic threads, takes his time
in the Greek manner. There is day, night, tide movement, earth
rotation. You don't hurry them; you receive them. So, too, with tales
well told.

The shepherd Staphylus, he explains, took his goats to pasture
each day and noticed that one was late, always, to rejoin the herd.
Not simply late, but gleefully late—joyous, says Antoniou in a
thick accent that imparts yet another dimension of ancient wisdom
to his recitation.

3

One afternoon Staphylus spied on the grazing goat and discovered he preferred a certain plant. What plant gave such pleasure? Staphylus decided to find out: he pressed the small round fruits growing on it, and brought its juice to Oeneus, King of Aetolia, his homeland.

The king sipped, smiled, sipped again, and lent his name to the joyous liquid— *oenos.* Wine.

Since Staphylus was a mere mortal, the thankful ancient Greeks could not legitimately worship him. There were rules. But not to worry, the shepherd was reputed to be the son of Dionysus, sired by Zeus himself. Much like the CEO of a large corporation taking credit for the invention of a minion, Dionysus went into the books (or onto the tablets) as the discoverer of wine. He'd already invented theater, and as Antoniou suggests with a sly smile, this was a most felicitous pairing, since spirits seem to bring out the flair for dramatic oratory in all of us.

As if to confirm they knew all about the true effects of *oenos*, libation of the gods, on human behavior, ancient Greeks gave Dionysus the mind of a man and the instincts of a beast.

The god Dionysus or Bacchus is best known to us as a personification of the vine and of the exhilaration produced by the juice of the grape. His ecstatic worship, characterized by wild dances, thrilling music, and tipsy excess, appears to have originated among the rude tribes of Thrace, who were notoriously addicted to drunkenness. Its mystic doctrines and extravagant rites were essentially foreign to the clear intelligence and sober temperament of the Greek race. Yet appealing as it did to that love of mystery and that proneness to revert to savagery which seem to be innate in most men, the religion spread like wildfire through Greece until the god whom Homer hardly deigned to notice had become the most popular figure of the pantheon.

—James G. Frazer,
The Golden Bough

Now, four thousand years or so later, Kostas and I raise a glass over the wine-dark seas in praise to all things Dionysian, glorious indulgences that the lucky ones among us live to regret time and again.

Kostas and I may appear to be old friends recycling past memories, but in fact we've only just met. Kostas owns the Antoniou Winery, and when I arrived on this balmy afternoon an hour or so ago, I was an American guest, a lover of wine, or just another pain in the neck: it remained to be seen. A formal man, Kostas Antoniou greeted me with a stiff handshake in the main hall of his modern glass-enclosed winery, with its breathtaking views of the glittering Aegean spreading out in all directions. A jeweler as well as a winemaker by trade, he surveyed me like ore of uncertain character; with typical Greek reserve and civility, he offered me a taste of his half-dozen bottlings, then turned to leave me in the hands of an assistant who began to pour generous samples.

I asked for a spit bucket.

The assistant looked at Antoniou, who was walking away. He stopped, turned, shrugged, and the assistant disappeared into a back room. I noticed Antoniou casting a different look at me now—appraising, even curious.

A spit bucket is not exactly an odd request in a winery, but when the assistant returned with one that actually had dust collecting on it, wiped it down, and set it on a tray with the glasses, Antoniou moved to the table where I sat and silently watched as I swished, gurgled, and spat. On the flat vineyards surrounding his winery Antoniou was growing the island's most popular and prestigious grape, the white Assyrtiko, mixed with lesser amounts of Aidani and Athiri. The miracle of Santorini is not that it produces a splendid white with pineapple and licorice overtones, but that it can produce any grapes at all. Its soil is pumice, lava rock created nearly four thousand years ago when Santorini, home to thriving Minoan and Mycenean civilizations, blew its top. The erupting volcano transformed a round island into a crescent surrounding a huge sea-filled hole, the caldera, about five miles wide, and covered the entire remaining terrain with dense layers of inhospitable, brittle, cooled lava.

In time, wily nature found a way to create a grape varietal that flourished in this poor porous "soil." Like the Greeks themselves, who have survived innumerable hardships during occupations over the centuries, from the Venetians to the Ottomans to the Germans in World War II, yet through it all have still preserved their essential nature, these Assyrtiko grapes have struggled and survived with integrity against long odds. They have had help from ingenious local vineyard managers. Old Assyrtiko vines, whose roots were often planted more than sixty years ago, are hand-woven into ground baskets, called *stefani*, that protect the grape clusters against fierce summer winds. There are no trellises in an Assyrtiko vineyard; instead, you gaze out over an expanse of desert scrub covered with green vegetation and fruit bundled inside low-lying nests of vine cane that look as though they were built by a colony of prehistoric birds.

The conditions are primitive, and while the resulting wine can be elegantly layered, it's not the sort of manicured estate-grown environment where sterling silver spit buckets catch the glint of crystal goblets while ladies in ruffles cavort. You want to spit out wine on Santorini, try the dirt beneath your feet. Yet Kostas Antoniou didn't appear to be offended as I tasted from this glass, then that glass, spat, made notes, and bit into a cracker to cleanse my palate.

"You do your work slowly," he said at length. I took it as a compliment. "Which of these speaks to you?" I pointed to glass number two; I had asked for a blind tasting, so I did not know its name, only its qualities. "You experience the unforgettable," Kostas said. He did not smile. Smiling, for Greek men, represents submissiveness in business or among male strangers. But he seemed pleased.

He snapped his finger. The assistant arrived with the bottle in its bag. Kostas removed it and read from the back label: "There is only one Aegean…and one Santorini, the black diamond of the Aegean. And there is only one superior wine: Antoniou. Experience the unforgettable."

He looked up. "You choose the one I make myself. Ten percent Athiri, to give the softness." He gestured out the side window. "Only from six rows."

A limited estate bottling. In Napa or Australia's Barossa Valley, the label would go on about harvesting dates, oak fermentation, pH levels, soil composition, and microclimate variations. But not here on the black diamond of the Aegean. None of that was any of your concern. You liked it, you didn't, end of discussion.

"You still spit?" Kostas was holding the bottle out to me; an empty glass had magically appeared before him.

"Not this stuff!" I rejoined.

The last tourists were leaving. He waved for the door to be locked as he poured me a full glass. The year on the label was 1999. Everything else was in Greek, bordering a splendid watercolor of village dwellings. Kostas lifted his glass. He toasted in Greek, we drank, and he gestured for me to follow him. I held up my hand to take another sip. This thing in my glass, this wine, it had apricots in it, even citrus like a Sauvignon Blanc, but also anise, and then, too, something quite distinctively its own, an elusive tropical puckerish fruit under a few high notes of lemony acid, and...

I took my glass with me. Five minutes later we were standing inside the cliff that formed the foundation for his winery. I'd followed Kostas down a narrow winding staircase to an abandoned tunnel that sat directly below a large banquet room on the winery's bottom floor. Large dark chambers carved out of pumice with towering ceilings rose up on either side of the passageway we entered, which was lit by dim bulbs. A small door opened into each empty chamber. Feeding out of the bottom of the chamber was a hose that ran along the center aisle to a sliding panel at the opposite end of the tunnel. The scene was part cathedral, part Edgar Allen Poe, with a touch of Alice in Wonderland after she'd fallen through the looking glass. I'd never stood inside a mountain. As he walked along, Kostas told me that after World War II, when there was still no electricity on Santorini, the island produced table wine for mainland consumption. But transporting the wine down the steep dangerous paths by donkey to the port below was impossible, and so the former winery owners had devised a method of letting gravity do the work. The fermented wine was pumped into these cool, lined chambers, thousands of gallons at a time, where it sedimented out; when ready, it was fed through the hoses out the rear of the winery, down the side of the caldera, to holding tanks below, and from there onto cargo ships.

Opening a door above the sliding panel, Kostas led me outside. We were at the lip of the cliff, high above sea level, where the abandoned hoses still ran down in a straight perilous drop to the port far below.

Peach and violet ribbons, backlit by the fading sun, streaked across the sky. A warm wind enveloped us. At that moment I knew why the gods decided to take up residence in Greece, as opposed to, say, Poland. There was no other place on earth, at this moment, that any sane person or deity would rather be.

As if reading my mind, Antoniou asked me, did I know how wine came to Greece? In my ignorance, I pondered sailing vessels capsizing in the Dardanelles, and migratory albatross carrying their jettisoned cargo across the straits, where errant grape seeds took root and gave birth to the Greek wine industry. But Antoniou was about to entrust me with historical information on a much more Olympian plane. He deemed me capable of listening, and perhaps understanding. Something about the slow way I tasted wine apparently sat right with him. He must have sensed that he could take all the time needed to tell me stories that took all the time they needed to get told—a very Greek perspective.

When he launched into the story of Staphylus, King Oeneus, and Dionysus, he did it in a way that implied a depth of common, shared experience. For the first time I understood the power of those ancient gods to forge a bond of friendship between two men from distant lands, and gave silent thanks for letting one of them be me.

Stephen Yafa has written about wine for San Francisco *and* Diablo *magazines. He is the founder and executive director of the Digital Story Center in San Rafael, California (www.digitalstorycenter.org), and lives close enough to Napa and Sonoma to indulge a chronic home-winemaking habit of more than two decades.*

MICHELLE RICHMOND

⋆ ⋆ ⋆

In the Valley of the Beautiful Women

Wine is life, death, and love.

My husband and I had come to Hungary in search of the ultimate new beginning. Our time together had been spent in New York City and San Francisco, our conversations punctuated by the honking of taxi drivers' horns on Central Park West or the clattering of the 37 Corbett as it labored up Market Street. About our life there was an aura of noise and familiarity. It was thus in January of 2001 that we chose Hungary for our honeymoon. Hungary was foreign and far away, a place where neither of us knew the language or the lay of the streets, a place where we were unlikely to run into other American newlyweds.

My husband had been there in 1989, long before I met him, just after the fall of the Iron Curtain. I had gone in 1995 as part of a whirlwind backpacking jaunt through Europe. Both of us remembered a certain grand hotel in Budapest that we had been unable to afford on our earlier solo trips: the Hotel Gellert. As a backpacker I had picnicked atop Gellert Hill and watched with envy the well-dressed tourists lounging by the outdoor thermal pool. My own place of lodging was across the river—not a hotel but a hostel, where I shared a bathroom, cold showers, and a smelly dorm room with dozens of other backpackers.

Six years later, on the first night of our honeymoon, I stood on one of three private balconies in our suite at the Gellert and looked across the street to my previous picnic spot on the hill. From that vantage point I could also see Liberty Bridge, its lovely green iron-work stretching over the Danube, uniting Pest and Buda, old and new, the grandeur of the past with the bright vigor of the present. My husband was lounging at the massive Communist-era desk in the sitting room, sipping complimentary champagne, dressed in the plush white robe that he had found hung over the heated towel rack in the bathroom. We both felt that evening as if we had indeed found what we were searching for—an unfamiliar place, a quiet room, a temporary peace in which to share the first heady days of our marriage.

That week we toured the State Opera House, shopped for hot sausage and folk art under the gleaming tile roof of the Great Market Hall, climbed the crooked streets of the Castle District, and had espresso and *turo suti* at Gerbeand. Afternoons we took the waters at the Hotel Gellert, donning the plush white robes and riding the ornate hand-operated elevator down to the spa. The pictures I had seen in the guidebooks didn't do justice to the marble columns, the stained glass roof through which sunlight streamed onto the steaming water, the Majolica tiles that gave the indoor swimming pool an ethereal appearance, a shade of turquoise more brilliant even than the warm waters of the Caribbean.

If the water itself was soothing, however, the experience in its totality was not. The women's locker room teemed with naked bodies and was manned by matronly women in blue uniforms, shouting orders with about as much gentility as a squadron of army commandants. On my first day I innocently paid for a massage, and moments later I was stripped bare by a rotund woman with wiry hair who proceeded to shove me onto a cold metal table beneath a glaring yellow light and hit me with her fists for half an hour.

After the first flush of excitement, my husband and I couldn't help but notice that the bus came to a screeching halt just outside our window throughout the night, and that the garbage truck arrived every morning before dawn to wrest us from our hard-won slumber. One morning we sat down for breakfast in the hotel's dining room, and my husband glanced up at the buffet table to see a co-worker from his office in San Francisco. We had come a long way from home, but we hadn't come far enough.

So it was on the fifth day of our honeymoon that we found ourselves on a bus bound for Eger, winding through the gentle foothills of the Bukk Mountains. Our waiter at a small, out-of-the-way restaurant in Pest had told us we couldn't leave Hungary without visiting this beloved town in the Northern Uplands. After pouring a light Hungarian beer to go with our hearty goulash, he confided to us that wine was his true passion. "Promise me you will go to Eger and sample the Egri Bikavér." As if to make sure we wouldn't forget, he took a napkin and sketched the outline of Hungary, and in the northeastern region of this crude map he penciled in a bottle of wine. On the label of the bottle he made a miniature line drawing of a bull.

Passing through the low, rolling hills, we felt at last the

Imagine the delight of Magyar tribesmen who rode into the Roman province of Pannonia in the late 800s and discovered a land covered with vineyards. They promptly settled down and became the forerunners of modern-day Hungarians, whose country ranks just out of the top ten among the world's wine-producing nations. The big star is Tokay (also spelled *Tokaj* and *Tokaji*), a sweet, perfumed white wine which comes from a norteastern part of Hungary near Ukraine and Slovakia, called Tokaj-Hegyalja. For centuries, the wines of this region enjoyed such a high reputation that vintners in other lands appropriated the name "Tokay" for their own wines.

—TE

tension of the city slipping away. Vineyards dotted the hills, but these were nothing like the lush green vineyards of Napa Valley, which had provided a pleasant backdrop for our day trips from San Francisco. These vines were brown and gaunt, struggling against the hard winter. On the bus, people spoke quietly in Hungarian, a tongue so unique that modern linguists still debate its origins. I was just beginning to breathe deeply, to feel completely at ease, when, across the aisle from us, a teenage girl turned up the volume on her headphones and started moving her head slightly to a song I vaguely recognized but couldn't name, an American tune that had been popular in the eighties. She was drinking Coca-Cola out of an oddly shaped plastic bottle, and I was thinking that there is nowhere in the world where one can entirely escape America, no land to which my husband and I might retreat and find ourselves truly alone, truly at rest, truly other.

From the bus station we wandered through the quiet streets, past the beautiful wrought iron gates of the county hall and the imposing, bright yellow Eger Cathedral, crowned with gigantic statues of saints. Twenty minutes later we arrived at the Senator Haz, a quaint two-story building on the edge of Dobo Square. The concierge greeted us cordially and handed us a key attached to a heavy wooden cone bigger than my hand, then showed us upstairs to a small room with dormer windows overlooking the square.

We had planned on spending only a night or two in Eger, then traveling east to the Lake Balaton region, but something about the unassuming little town drew us in. It was as if we had been placed under a spell. Whereas in Budapest we had tried to do everything, in Eger we succumbed to a deep and lengthy sleep. After a long dreamless night in the dark little room, we would wake each day around seven A.M. and climb the steep cobbled lane of the castle, from the top of which we could see the town stretched out and slumbering, the Matrá hills rising up in the distance. Then we would leave the castle and wander the streets, getting lost in narrow alleys. Here and there we would pass a group of ruddy-faced children walking to school, or an elderly woman in a long dark coat hurrying to market, an empty cloth bag tucked under her arm. Paris and Venice could not begin to rival the romance of Eger in the early morning, with its Baroque buildings and iron gates rising over cobbled streets, the little stream meandering past tree-lined avenues and stone houses, the somnambulant notes of the cathedral organ peel-

ing through the crisp air. Around nine we would return to the inn
for breakfast, go up to our room, and immediately fall asleep.

Most days we slept until about two, then went out for lunch and
wine, returned to our room, and slept again until midnight or so,
when one of us would wake the other up, and we would eat cheese
and salami we had purchased earlier at the market, drink a bit more
wine, and read English translations of the nineteenth-century
Hungarian poet Petofi Sándor, who wrote many lyric poems celebrating nature and love before his 1949 disappearance in a battle
against Russian forces. At some point in the night one of us would
go to the window and open the shutters to see the moon shining
down on the empty square, casting an icy glow over the twin spires
of the Minorite church. Then we would lie in bed talking about
married life, which seemed a grand affair indeed, a magical cycle of
drinking, eating, and sleeping. We were so lazy, in fact, that we didn't
even visit the famous Szepasszony-volgy, the Valley of the Beautiful
Women, until the day before we had to return to Budapest.

That afternoon, we bundled up in scarves and mittens, put on
comfortable shoes, and began walking south from the Senator Haz.
After about a mile we came upon the enticingly named valley,
where dozens of cellars were cut into the soft volcanic stone. The
facades of the cellars were made of wood, concrete, and stone.
According to our travel guidebook, summer afternoons found hundreds of tourists sitting at outdoor tables, getting drunk to the music
of violinists who roamed the hillsides. It must have been the weather
that kept both the tourists and the violinists away on this particular
afternoon. The valley was so quiet that our footsteps seemed a sac-
rilege. We walked the winding little road, past one closed cellar after
another, until we heard voices from behind an iron door. Upon
entering, we found two locals sitting at a table and talking to the
proprietor, who greeted us in Hungarian and urged us to sit down.

The air was cool and damp, the ceiling low, and the place smelled
vaguely of mold. The floor sloped downward from the entrance,
and the walls were decorated with stone cuttings. The proprietor
wore a dark sweater, a gray wool skirt, and heavy boots. With one
hand she held the bulbous end of a long flute above her head, and

with the other she expertly guided the dark liquid into our glasses. We decided to stick to the reds. The first wine we tried, Médoc Noir, was rich, sweet, and so dark that it turned our tongues black. Next came the robust Egri Léanyka, "the girl of Eger." Finally we asked for a liter of Egri Bikavér, the famous wine that had been recommended to us by the young waiter in the restaurant in Pest. Upon hearing this request, the proprietor nodded in approval, poured the liter gallantly, and retired to the table in the corner to talk to her friends.

My husband's voice was lower than usual, slightly drawn out, as he recited the legend of Egri Bikavér, a story he had been saving for me ever since he read it in our guidebook on the bus ride from Budapest. Egri Bikavér, or Bull's Blood, got its name some 450 years ago, when 2,000 Hungarian soldiers defended Eger Castle against 100,000 invading Turks. In most accounts of the siege, the boiling oil and pitch that the women of Eger poured from the castle's ramparts onto the invaders play second fiddle to a far more civilized weapon—wine. The valiant István Dobó served his vastly outnumbered soldiers large quantities of this fiery local delight in preparation for battle. The soldiers fought so bravely and their beards were stained such a deep, unsettling shade of red that the Turks believed the Hungarians derived their strength by imbibing the blood of bulls.

As I sat with my new husband in the Valley of Beautiful Women, a fuzzy hat pulled low over my ears, I felt anything but fierce. A welcome lethargy settled over me. Earlier that day I had left him alone in our room at the Senator Haz and walked to the Turkish baths at the Archbishop's Garden. Although the baths of Eger lacked the opulence of the ones at the Gellert, they were less crowded and therefore far more relaxing. On Wednesdays, the thermal bath was reserved for women only, and I had relished those few minutes away from him, alone in a foreign country, immersed in the curing waters that traveled from some ancient inner place to gurgle through the earth's crust at that particular point on the globe. Because I could not understand the words that rose and fell around me, they made a kind of music.

The same music echoed within the walls of the cellar. I don't know how many hours my husband and I passed contentedly in the low light of the cavernous room, listening to the muted conversation of the three Hungarians. The wine, the words, the memory of the steaming waters, lulled my mind and limbs. I thought of the soldiers who had fought from the castle ramparts as the Turks pressed forward, both sides bloodthirsty and bent on victory. My head swam with the wine, my bladder was ready to burst with it. I couldn't imagine defending a castle in such a state.

My husband leaned forward and kissed my hand. I had known this man for five years; never had he seemed more relaxed, more at ease in the moment. In that dark cavern in Eger we had finally found our beginning, our place of solitude, our lovers' respite. Within the cool earthen walls no city noises reached us—no buses, no trains, no random scraps of American songs. The locals paid us no mind, and the proprietor left us alone until one liter dried up, at which point she would bring us another. The air was damp and cool, the wine warm on our tongues, the marriage itself as solid-seeming as the wooden casks that lined the inner reaches of the cellar. Traveling cross-country and over the Atlantic had not been enough, nor had the grand old hotel in Budapest, or the bus ride through the Bukk Mountains. No destination had taken us far enough, until, at last, we marched to the valley floor, shunned the sunlight, and descended into the earth. For a moment I imagined going deeper, into the massive wooden casks themselves, into the fiery red warmth that was said to have saved a nation. I imagined how the bulls' blood must pulse within the intimate darkness of the casks, that warm elixir pumping through the secret heart of Hungary.

After leaving her home state of Alabama in 1992, Michelle Richmond lived in six states in as many years before settling in San Francisco. She received the AWP Short Fiction Award for her story collection, The Girl in the Fall-Away Dress.

KAREN MACNEIL

Arriving at Wine

The most important wine knowledge is personal.

As a young woman, for reasons that remain inexplicable to me today, I not only liked the taste of wine, I liked the very idea of it. Wine, it seemed to me, symbolized our deep connection to the land, to seasons, and to each other. Wine wasn't something you owned like a stereo, it was something you took into your body. Moreover, you didn't just drink your wine while someone else drank theirs. Everyone shared the same wine, a communal act that has remain unchanged for thousands of years. Even today when I hear some whiz marketing director suggest that what the wine industry really needs to do is package wine like cola in single-serving containers, I think to myself, that person is missing the whole point.

And so in my early twenties, pulled as I was toward wine, I decided to try to understand it. And that's where the going got rough. Unlike food (I loved food and had become a food writer by then), wine was overwhelming. My mind ached just trying to remember things like the difference between Meursault, Macon, and Muscadet. It seemed not only impossible to sort these things out, but there was seemingly no way in, no learning path. There were wine experts and then there was everybody else, and I was most definitely an everybody else.

So, as only one who is young and naive can, I decided to hang around the experts. As a food writer, I could sometimes wangle my way into wine tastings and in those days, the late 1970s and early 1980s, New York was full of wine tastings. On any given week, the entire *consorzio* of Chianti Classico producers might be in town giving lectures and pouring their wines for wine writers and restaurateurs to taste, while across town there would be a tasting of top Bordeaux or vintage Ports.

And so I would beg to be invited, then sit in the back of the room (usually I was the youngest person and one of the only women), and listen as the wine elite espoused this view or that. If I understood 10 percent of what they were talking about, it was a good day for me. Sometimes I felt like I was making headway; more often than not, I left the tasting with more questions and insecurities than I went in with. Worst of all, there was no one to whom I could ask those countless basic questions most of us have when we are starting out. It was a different world then. You didn't stand up in the ballroom of a posh New York hotel and ask why red wine is red.

Still, I was hooked. For all the frustration, wine was also incredibly intriguing. It wasn't ever perfectly knowable like, say, onions, and that was in part what made it so compelling. Wine was a mind trip. Knowing even the smallest scrap made you want to know more. Slowly I began to feel as if the dark room I'd been in was getting lighter—faintly. Though I didn't realize it then, I'd begun to teach myself about wine by piecing things together. I still didn't use professional terms, but I was finding my way. I knew that Bordeaux was more like Anthony Hopkins than like Robin Williams, and that was a good place to begin.

After about five years of this, I screwed up my courage and proposed a wine article to the editor of one of the magazines I wrote for. To my amazement (and terror) she said yes. The piece was on California and so I flew out, rented a car, and drove to the Napa Valley. In my eagerness, I didn't even think about appointments. I just showed up at the Mondavi Winery and (amazing to me now) Bob Mondavi took me around and talked to me about his wine. At Beaulieu Vineyards, the late André Tchelistcheff, considered one of the greatest winemakers California has ever had, made me follow him up and down through stacks of wine barrels, drawing out this and that, making me taste and tutoring me along the way. It was the same everywhere. California was in the first stages of a golden age and it seemed like every vintner in the whole state was gripped by a compulsive desire to share his or her excitement with anyone who was interested.

What I didn't know then was that this deep-seated sense of hospitality, generosity, excitement, and community is at the very core of the wine business everywhere in the world. You can knock on the door of winemakers from the dusty hills of Australia to the storybook villages of Alsace, France, and the same thing always happens: the wine-maker stops what he or she is doing, you are welcomed in, wines are opened, a conversation begins and so does a friendship that, often enough, lasts forever. If all of this sounds a little romanticized, let me tell you that I truly don't know of any other industry in the world where people are so giving, and it's one of the things that binds together people who love wine in ways that are both powerful and primal.

The article I wound up writing was not your typical

André Tchelistcheff's impact on the California wine industry was immense. He effected a major boost in basic quality simply by his insistence on sanitation. As a second-generation devotee of the nineteenth-century microbiology pioneer Louis Pasteur, he understood the presence of an invisible world of microbes that had to be managed just as much as the vineyards. His introduction of temperature-controlled fermentation helped make white wine a viable commercial product in California for the first time. And because white wines could be delivered to the marketplace earlier after the vintage than reds, the flow of cash to wineries and growers increased dramatically, enabling further widespread improvements in vineyards and wineries.

—Rod Smith, *Private Reserve*

wine article, but then I wasn't a wine writer. I was more like the reader, a wine drinker just trying to figure things out. I have to make a small diversion here. As you can undoubtedly imagine, trying to sell a story idea to a magazine editor is far from a piece of cake. It's pretty easy to have a batting average of, say, twenty rejections for every acceptance, and that's if you're pretty good (when you're starting out, you can pretty much wallpaper a small room with rejection letters). So you can imagine my shock when, after the publication of my first wine piece, several editors from other magazines called me asking me to do wine stories for them. I was floored, but I wrote the stories.

What happened next was pivotal. Sitting in my office one day, I got a call from the organizers of one of the major wine competitions in California. "Would I be a judge?" they asked. They would fly me out; the judging would happen over three days. I was ecstatic. This, I felt, was my big chance to break into the professional wine arena. Out I went.

There were thirty judges: me and twenty-nine men, most of whom were nearly twice my age. We were put in white lab coats and asked to draw slips of paper from a hat. My scrap of paper said: Cabernet Sauvignon. I was to be part of the Cabernet panel; our job was to taste and evaluate 125 Cabernets that day. All I could think of was that I hadn't prayed hard enough for Riesling.

The way the judging worked was this: There were six teams each made up of five judges. Each team, sequestered in a different room, would concentrate on just one variety. The judges were seated next to one another at a long table facing a moderator standing at a huge blackboard to record scores. Ten glasses of wine at a time would be brought to each judge. We were to silently taste each wine (no discussions were allowed) and then decide on one of four evaluations: gold medal, silver medal, bronze medal, or eliminate. We had no idea what the wines were other than that they were all Cabernets from California. When all the judges were ready, the moderator would ask for our decisions which we were to announce aloud. For wine one, the judge sitting in seat number one would give his vote, then the judge in seat two, then judge three, and so on. The person who had to go first changed with each wine. So for the first wine, the judge in seat one went first, but for the second wine, the judge in seat two began the process. I was in seat two.

For three hours that morning, everything went smoothly. All of us on the Cabernet panel gave the wines more or less the same evaluations which, incidentally, were not high. In fact, we'd decided that most of the wines should be eliminated, meaning that they didn't deserve medals. Unbeknownst to us, the organizers of the tasting were aghast. How could so many famous wines (the organizers knew what the wines were) be eliminated? The Cabernet panel, they decided, was too tough.

We were puzzled ourselves. Independently, each of us was also wondering how it was possible that so many wines were so, well, *uninspired*? Then it came. Wine number seventy-five. It was my turn to go first. Here it is, I thought to myself: finally, a great wine. "Gold," I said unhesitatingly to the moderator. She went down the rest of the panel, who voted: eliminate, eliminate, eliminate, eliminate.

I could have crawled under the table. Every fear I had about not knowing enough about wine came flooding to the surface. I looked out of the corner of my eye, expecting each of those men to be stifling a laugh or at least smirking. In fact, none of them showed any reaction whatsoever, for they understood something that I, as yet, did not. In the course of the next hour, the same phenomenon occurred with every single judge on the panel: voting gold when everyone else voted eliminate, or voting eliminate when everyone else voted gold. As my fellow, more experienced judges knew, despite all of the objective criteria we're supposed to bring to bear in thinking about what makes great wine great, there's no escaping subjectivity. There will always be a wine you love beyond reason even when everyone else is thumbs down, and there will always be a wine you wouldn't give a dime for no matter how highly regarded it is. That's the way wine is. And probably, that's the way it ought to be.

Though my understanding of wine was growing and my appetite for learning about it had become rapacious, I was still pretty inexperienced. Most of my knowledge had been accrued during tastings in hotel banquet rooms. I wanted to see the world. The same year of my first judging, I learned that the Sherry Institute of Spain was going to take fifty writers to Sherry (known as Jerez in Spain) to learn about the city and its famous beverage. Knowing little about Spain and nothing about Sherry, I wanted badly to go. I called the institute and asked to be considered. A week later they called me back. They had made up their list of invitees based on those wine writers they considered most important. I was number fifty-one. I was going nowhere. Then, two days before the trip was to begin, journalist number fifty had to cancel. I was going to Spain.

Sherry could not have been more of a culture shock. A remote and fiercely proud part of Spain, it also lives in its glorious past. It was from Jerez that Christopher Columbus sailed for America, and it seemed as though no time had passed in the cathedral-like bodegas that smelled pungently of old wood. I'd never seen a winemaking process so complex or labor intensive. Actually, I'd never drunk Sherry before, and now here I was, drinking (or at least tasting) about fifty glasses a day. By day three I considered writing an article called "Death By Sherry." I was learning, all right—learning to hate the stuff. My whole body yearned for a glass of white wine that wasn't fortified with brandy, as is all Sherry.

That night, one of the bodegas was hosting a black-tie dinner to begin about midnight (quintessentially south-of-Spain). As white-gloved waiters passed by with silver trays of Sherry, I struck out alone for a walk in the vineyards. Except for the stars, the night was deeply black. The vineyards of Jerez, with their soil that's as soft and fluffy as cake mix, were not exactly high-heel territory. It didn't matter. I was a fugitive on the run. After half a mile, I was surprised to hear voices, then laughter. I soon came upon a small campfire right there in the vineyards in God knows what part of Sherry. There were people sitting around, playing music, and drinking wine. I looked closer. It was white wine! In my bad Spanish and by pantomiming, I asked them if I might taste the wine they were drinking.

You don't want this, *señorita*, they assured me. Yes I do, I insisted. After going back and forth a few times, they reluctantly relented. Sherry starts out as a basic white wine made from a grape called

Palomino. I figured this must be straight Palomino, and I was dying to try it for none of the bodegas had allowed us a taste of their most basic raw material.

The people around the fire handed me a bottle (no niceties like glasses here), and I took a sip. It was ghastly. I mean truly horrible. I could feel every cell from my tongue to my stomach as the liquid made its way down. I thanked my hosts and walked back through the blackness to the bodega, reconsidering my goal of becoming a wine writer.

Days four and five passed. There were dozens more glasses of Sherry and no escape. Grimly, dutifully, I tasted them. And then on day six something happened I could never have anticipated. I picked up a glass of Sherry, tasted it, and it was as though someone had thrown a light switch. I liked it. This turned out to be another wine lesson. I came to see that not all wines are immediately love-able, no more than certain foods are. Some foods and wines require you to work at them—like the willing suspension of disbelief that enables us to enjoy plays and movies. Raw oysters can be like that: Do most people really love their first squishy wet mouthful of raw mollusk? What's amazing is that there seems to be an inverse corre-lation between how hard you must work at understanding a flavor and your subsequent love of it. Sherry went on to become one of my favorite wines in the world.

Since that time in Jerez, I have been drawn all over the world in pursuit of wine and over the last twenty years, have been able to study it in every major wine-producing country. Spending time in the wineries and vineyards of so many countries has taught me that wine is inextricably part of a wine country's culture. Wine is a look into the heart of a place in the same way that food is. Which is why, by the way, I don't believe that wine can be thought about apart from the consideration of the place where it was made. If you listen long enough to German winemakers talk about Riesling you see that what they are after—purity, clarity, and what is sometimes called transparency—is 180 degrees different from what California Cabernet producers are after: power, density, structure.

And so in every country I've spent time in, I've tried to understand the wine in the context of the culture, and of those people who live and breathe the wine every day. This has caused me to have more than a few memorable experiences. I've drunk Amarone while eating horsemeat, a tradition in Italy's Veneto; sipped just-fermented wine from goatskin bags in northern Greece, much as the ancients did; been strapped into a contraption that lowers pickers down the impossibly steep slopes of German vineyards (an experience that momentarily convinced me my life was over); shared wine and cigars with bullfighters in Rioja, Spain; roared through Australian vineyards atop gargantuan mechanized picking machines; ridden through the vineyards of Texas on horseback; eaten octopus and drunk Assyrtiko with fishermen in Santorini (considered by some to be the legendary, lost Atlantis); picked tiny oyster shells from among the remnants of fossilized sea creatures that make up the chalky, moon-crater-like soil of Chablis; waltzed among wine barrels with winemakers in Vienna; and worked for two weeks with a Mexican harvest crew in California, one of the hardest and most rewarding experiences I've ever had.

After all of this, I have come to realize that the road to wine knowledge is necessarily idiosyncratic and anything but linear. Like wine, wine knowledge is personal. It begins unpredictably and moves you to unpredictable places. And so after working that memorable harvest, I gave up my Manhattan life and moved to the top of a mountain in the Napa Valley where I now live with two Dalmatians, twelve ducks, a few coyotes, thousands of grapevines— and one man.

Perhaps not surprisingly, he makes wine.

Karen MacNeil is a consultant, teacher, writer, and chairman of the Center for Professional Wine Studies at the Culinary Institute of America in the Napa Valley. Her articles on wine, food, and restaurants have been published in more than fifty national magazines and newspapers including The New York Times, Food & Wine, Sunset, Wine Spectator, USA Today, *and* The Los Angeles Times. *She is the author of the recently published* The Wine Bible, *the most comprehensive book on wines of the world written by an American author.*

STEVE EDMUNDS

The Angle and the Voice

Terroir *is real, if you listen closely enough to hear.*

I OPERATE A SMALL WINERY IN CALIFORNIA CALLED EDMUNDS ST. John. We produce a few thousand cases each year, and through my struggles and experiences as a winemaker I've begun, I think, to understand a little of what wine is, what place it has in our lives, and what it means to us.

I'd been a home winemaker for a number of years before starting Edmunds St. John, but I still felt an uneasy lack of expertise when we made our first commercial wines in 1985. When the wines seemed to turn out quite nicely, I didn't feel that I'd had much to do with it. To be fair, I was following the guidance of another vintner, whose own approach had always been pretty *laissez-faire* (he characterized it as benign neglect). But somehow I felt that if the wines were successful, I should be able to take some credit for that.

Yet when friends and other vintners tasted the wines and complimented me for how enjoyable they were, I was perplexed by how little of the credit I felt I deserved. I had done only the most rudimentary winemaking. I had an assemblage of what I thought of as non-equipment. All our grapes that first year had been crushed by foot! I tried reassuring myself that merely ushering the wine attentively from grape to bottle demonstrated a form of oenological wisdom, and that conscious manipulation of the process was superfluous, possibly even arrogant. Beginner's luck was another possibility. And, of course, some of the grapes I'd managed to find were exceptionally good; maybe I was, unbeknownst to myself, an especially astute judge of grapes. This last explanation was no more convincing than the others; I threw up my hands and began to wonder if what I was doing with my commercial winery was so different from what I did as a home winemaker.

The best of the wines that first year came from some Mourvedre grapes grown in Napa. It had been obvious to me, despite my lack of confidence in my ability to even discern one grape from another in a vineyard, that those grapes had been vastly superior to the others. The bunches were small, the grapes were in beautiful condition when I picked them up at the vineyard, the taste of the fruit had been wonderfully distinctive. Even the way the grapes felt against my skin as I worked with them in the fermenters had seemed special. Shortly after I pressed the wine off into barrels, I told my friend Kermit Lynch, a prominent local wine importer, that I was making wine from Mourvedre grapes. I knew from his love for the wines of Provence that he'd be interested, and we arranged a date to taste.

He liked the wine a good deal, and asked if he might take a sample to the renowned Domaine Tempier in Bandol, to taste with the Peyraud family when he went there in January of 1986. I was glad to oblige, and it turned out that doing so provided me with an entree when I visited the Domaine a couple of months later, at which time Francois Peyraud hosted a tasting for me.

Finding those Mourvedre grapes in our first year had been a bigger challenge than I'd expected. From the contacts I'd made during my retail wine selling days, I was confident that I'd be able to track down some old plantings of Mataro (as Mourvedre was known in those days to most of the growers in California). Yet again and again I seemed to be just a little too late. Each grower seemed to have one of two responses when asked if he was growing any Mataro he might want to sell. Either he would say "What do you want with Mataro?" or he would say "Gee, it's too bad you didn't call sooner;

we just tore it out…" This latter response usually ended with a time frame: last year, last month, last week, a few days ago; there was one "yesterday."

After making the same inquiries and receiving the same responses for two or three months, I began to wonder if I was on a fool's errand. I'd chosen to pursue grape varieties from the South of France—Grenache, Mourvedre, Syrah—that were not in fashion, that didn't go into the wines for which the market seemed to clamor. I chose them because I'd drunk them over the previous thirteen years. They never failed to bring forth some happy response in me, always made me feel glad for the chance to taste them. So I persisted, and one afternoon while I was looking at equipment in a Berkeley store that sold supplies to home winemakers, I noticed a sign written on brown paper that had once been part of a shopping bag. It read, "SAUVIGNON VERT, an old Napa Valley favorite. $400 a ton. Other varieties available." It also included a phone number.

Because of the nonprofessional look of the sign, I almost ignored it. But something made me read it again, some little hunch, some insistent little inner voice. When I did I began to think of it differently. They led with Sauvignon Vert, which, in current wine circles, has an abysmal reputation. They probably thought the Sauvignon in the name gave it some kinship with Sauvignon Blanc, a popular variety, that might make it more attractive. Since I couldn't think of a less attractive grape than Sauvignon Vert at that moment, I thought there might be a good chance that the "other varieties" might include something of interest. I wrote the number down and called that evening.

An older man's voice answered, slightly musical and dreamy-sounding. I said I'd seen his notice, and wanted to know what he might have to offer, besides, of course, Sauvignon Vert.

"You don't want any Sauvignon Vert, huh?" In the sound of his voice I could feel myself being sized up.

"No," I said, trying to sound polite.

"Well, how about some Palomino? We've got some nice Palomino." I began to be more interested; Palomino produces one of southern Spain's most famous wines.

"No, I'm more interested in reds," I said. "You got any reds?"

"Well," he said, "we've got a little Charbono. Are you interested in some Charbono?"

This was getting good. "Gee, that sounds neat," I said, "but actually—"

He cut me off. "We had some Zinfandel, but I'm afraid it's all sold."

I interrupted him this time, beginning to feel just a tiny bit hopeful in spite of myself. "Let me tell you what I'm looking for: I'm trying to find some Mataro."

"Aw, hell," he said, with a vague hint of disappointment in his voice, "I've got some of that."

A short silence, stunned on my part. "You do?"

"Yeah."

"How much do you have?"

"Oh," he said, sounding like a cat beginning to stretch, "probably a ton, ton and a half.... Maybe two tons."

"Can I buy it?" I said, ready to burst, trying not to let on.

He said, "Well, yeah. But, say—what do you want with Mataro?"

I told him I thought it might make pretty good wine, and that I'd like to come look at his vines, and I asked him where the vineyard was. He said, "Did you ever hear of Mt. Veeder?"

If I had to choose the one place in California where I thought I could produce the finest red wine, Mt. Veeder would probably be my first choice. From the wines I'd drunk that had been grown there, it occupied a near-mythic position in the geography of my imagination. I'd heard of the men whose vineyard I was going to visit, too, though I didn't realize it just yet.

I drove to their property the next afternoon. When I arrived, I was greeted by two men in their sixties who seemed to have the energy and strength of four or five normal men. The brothers Richard and Chester Brandlin had been farming wine grapes on Mt. Veeder their whole lives. Their father, Henry Brandlin, had been born on Mt. Veeder in 1888, and had bought the property known as Mayacamas during the Prohibition era. I'd known about the Brandlins' grapes, as I recalled some months later, from gathering information for an article back in 1976. The Brandlins were practically legends. It seemed to me that they felt I was a curiosity in some way, but it was clear they liked me, and were glad to sell me some grapes. A few weeks later, when their Mourvedre grapes began to ferment in my cellar, there could be no doubt; I was witnessing something quite special here, and I was captivated by it.

One morning the next January, just as the eastern sky began to grow light above the Berkeley hills, Rich Brandlin called me to ask how I'd liked the grapes. "I love 'em," I said. "I want to buy them every year, as long as you'll sell them to me."

"So, you liked them, huh?" He paused. "Gee, Steve, it's too bad you didn't call us a year earlier. We had another four and a half acres, but we tore them out about a year ago."

> *T*erroir has become a buzz-word in English language wine literature. This lighthearted use disregards reverence for the land which is a critical, invisible element of the term. The true concept is not easily grasped but includes physical elements of the vineyard habitat—the vine, sub-soil, siting, drainage, and micro-climate. Beyond the measurable ecosystem, there is an additional dimension—the spiritual aspect that recognizes the joys, the heartbreaks, the pride, the sweat, and the frustrations of its history.
> —James E. Wilson, *Terroir*

Despite that bit of news I felt quite lucky. They were such tremendous grapes, and somehow I'd stumbled onto them. Then, in 1986, they made a wine that was so lovely, so breathtaking, that when Kermit Lynch brought Francois Peyraud to my winery to taste, Francois sniffed this wine, lowered his glass, rolled his eyes back in reverie, and whispered, *"la terre parle."*

The earth speaks.

Even to someone largely unfamiliar with California wines, here was a wine that expressed, clearly and forcefully, the identity of its origin. I've never felt more complimented by a response to any wine I've made than I felt hearing Francois's words. I was reminded, in that moment, of times early in my wine career, tasting wines that had stopped me in my tracks. With a friend who had a job delivering wines, I'd drunk some of the very greatest wines from France, Germany, Italy, and California, through which the earth "spoke" again and again, though each time, to be sure, with a different voice. I found, in tasting them, a kind of recognition, as though, without having encountered them before, I had already known what they would taste like, and, tasting them, found it to be so.

This recognition is similar, I think, to the experience I've had (and probably everyone else has had) of hearing a melody for the first time, some wonderful song, and having a vague sense of having always known the tune, though I cannot, try as I might, recall any other tune that's anything like it. There's some way I respond to it, the way I might respond to a smile, or the touch of a dear friend or family member.

It feels as though there is some part of me "out there" in that melody, some song my soul has always sung to itself, that I've never heard with my ears, and suddenly, there it is, "out there" in the world, and from "in here" I recognize it and respond. Perhaps, too, there is some part of me "out there" in a painting by Cezanne, or in the passing of a dozen Canada geese across the face of Mt. St. Helena on a late October morning, or in a glass of Mourvedre from the old vines on the Brandlin ranch.

Or, to look at it from a slightly different angle, when, as Francois said, "the earth speaks," perhaps when I respond it's because it is I who am "out there," recognizing my place of origin, feeling called by some old, familiar voice, long since forgotten. Could it be that I am some part of this earth that speaks, and when I respond it is because I recognize, at last, my home?

There was also, of course, a less cosmic side to what Francois had said when he tasted the Mourvedre wine from 1986. Each place on the earth is unique, each vineyard has its own singular personality to express. That's why Châteauneuf-du-Pape tastes different at Beaucastel than it does at Vieux Télégraphe. It's why Syrah grown at Cornas is so different from Syrah grown in the Coteaux les Baronnies.

It is possible to manipulate the winemaking process through a variety of means, including technological innovation, and through what has become the increasingly prevalent use of brand new oak barrels, in a way that can all but obliterate those differences. What is currently referred to as the "International Style" has begun to inundate the marketplace in recent years, particularly in California, but increasingly in Europe as well. The wines are sleek, they're oozing with the perfume and vanilla flavors of the most expensive barrels, and they're becoming harder and harder to distinguish, one from another. Why is this happening? Why would anyone want to do this? Marketing speaks. The bottom line speaks.

God knows it can be tough to balance the interests of paying the bills and feeding the soul. I can't imagine what it must be like to run a large winery. But the true gift of wine, I would now suggest, is revealed not on one's palate, but in one's soul. It requires a certain devotion. If the wine makes money, so much the better. If it doesn't make money, an area in which I have some expertise, there is still this gift, and it is measureless.

The technological advances in winemaking in the last thirty years of the twentieth century have made it possible, in the words of one vintner from Châteauneuf-du-Pape, to make wines "in the old way." There are hundreds of examples of wines that are much better, that are much more capable of expressing their origin than they've ever been, because of the improvements in technology. But not just because of those improvements. The winemaker had to make a conscious decision about what he or she wished to accomplish, and how that was best done. If the wines are better, if they are true to their places of origin, the technology made it easier, but the devotion of the winemaker made it *happen*.

So in 1985, when I wondered for the first time how it was that the wines I'd produced turned out so well, what I really wanted to know was this: What was my role? What is the appropriate way for me to influence the development of the wine I'm going to bottle? And my thoughts about grapes, and the wisdom of using good ones, were perhaps not so simple-minded as they may once have seemed.

In fact, I had inadvertently found, in the case of the Brandlin Mourvedre, grapes from a truly great vineyard.

One of the most positive signs I see today in California is the tremendous amount of thought and effort that are going into planting new vineyards, and growing them in ways that make much more sense than the ways so many earlier vineyards had been grown. This trend bodes well for the future, particularly if, after the grapes from these new vineyards are grown and picked, the winemakers can be attentive enough to hear the "earth speak" through those grapes, and to devote themselves to the gift in that voice.

Steve Edmunds founded Edmunds St. John Winery, with his wife Cornelia St. John, in 1985, following a dozen years in the San Francisco Bay Area retail wine trade. The winery was a pioneer in producing wines made from Rhône grape varieties (such as Syrah, Mourvedre, Grenache, and Viognier) grown in California. Also a singer-songwriter, Edmunds recently released a CD of original songs, titled Lonesome On The Ground, *produced by Bluegrass legend Laurie Lewis. Both the wine and the music can be found at www.edmundsstjohn.com.*

MIKE STEINBERGER

★ ★ ★

A Harvest in Alsace

Wine is woven deeply into the tapestry of Europe.

IT WAS THE LAST STOP ON A WHIRLWIND WINE-TASTING TOUR OF
Alsace, and after four long days of sniffing, swilling, and spitting, the
prospect of trying yet another Tokay Pinot Gris *Vendange Tardive*
was, frankly, nauseating. But having been graciously received by
some of Alsace's finest producers, we felt obliged to keep the
appointment, and so just after breakfast on a gorgeous September
morning, my wife and I made the short trip from our hotel to the
village of Sigolsheim and the offices of the Pierre Sparr Winery.

Awaiting us was René Sparr, whose family has been making
wine for nine generations—roots run deep in Alsace, and not just
in the soil. On meeting René, we instantly felt rewarded for having
kept to our schedule, for he was a charming host. A stout but spry
sixty-eight-year-old, he took us on a brisk tour of the estate, ultimately steering us to his tasting room, where a dozen bottles of
wine had been carefully arranged. With grim efficiency, we quickly
sampled the selection. Some light conversation followed. Not wanting to wear out our welcome, we then asked if we could call a taxi
to take us to the city of Colmar, fifteen minutes away, from where
we were to continue on to Strasbourg. René wouldn't hear of it;
he insisted on driving us himself. En route, he said, we would make

a brief inspection of his vineyards. Fine, we thought; we'll nibble a few grapes, snap a few photos, and be on our way. In fact, though, there was something else he wanted us to see.

As driving goes, René was like most Frenchmen—lead-footed— and the ascent up the steep slopes of the Mambourg, one of Alsace's fifty *grand cru* sites, was alarmingly swift. Racing past the endless clusters of Muscat and Gewurztraminer grapes, he commented that the Mambourg was "our Monte Cassino." Before he could elaborate, we reached the crest of the hill, and as the car careened around the final twist in the road, we were unexpectedly confronted not by more vines, but by a war memorial. René parked in front of an American flag planted on a ridge high above the Rhine Valley. While we paused to read the inscription on the marble slab at the base of the flagpole, he explained that Sigolsheim had been caught in the crossfire of one of the deadliest battles of World War II.

In early December 1944, French and American forces had launched a massive campaign to flush the German Nineteenth Army out of the Colmar Pocket, a strategically vital area stretching from the Vosges Mountains to Colmar. Some of the worst combat was waged on the streets of Sigolsheim and in the muddy vineyards above them, notably those on the Mambourg, which came to be known as "Bloodhill." By the time Sigolsheim was liberated on January 21, 1945, nearly all its buildings were charred husks and the Mambourg was draped with corpses.

As René recounted the history, we made our way toward a grassy incline holding the graves of 1,684 soldiers from the French First Army who climbed the hill but never came down. Walking up the steps that slice through the middle of the cemetery, René told us that on December 9, 1944, as the conflict raged around them, he and his parents, together with his ten-year-old brother and toddler sister, had taken refuge in the local Capucins Monastery, the only structure spared during the fighting. There, along with several hundred others, the Sparrs huddled as the war devoured their village, their home, and their business. They remained in the monastery until the wee hours of December 19, when a lull in the fighting permitted them to flee to nearby Ribeauville, a town already in the hands of the Allies.

By now, we had reached the top steps, and as I turned to look at René, I saw something I won't soon forget: tears trickling down his ruddy face. The past hangs heavily over Alsace's hills and valleys, but it threw a particularly large shadow at that moment. We stood in silence for a few minutes, squinting through the haze at the storybook villages beneath us, and then we began to walk down the steps, and as we did, something else caught my eye: the cemetery's long, descending rows of tiny white crosses appeared to merge with the vineyards below.

The last vintage of the century rising up at the feet of the century's noblest casualties; it seemed the most poignant tribute imaginable.

As we said goodbye in a busy parking lot on the outskirts of Colmar, René presented us with a bottle of one of his *grand cru* Rieslings. The wine is now aging in our cellar. I don't know when we will open it, but I do know that when the day comes, we will drink a toast to the Allied soldiers who fought and died on the Mambourg, and to René, who in sharing a memory with us, gave us a memory we will cherish.

"War can wait—the vintage cannot" goes an old French saying. Wine grapes are perfectly ripe for a few days of the year, at most. If inclement weather threatens, that window of opportunity can shrink to a few hours. Thus whole villages have been known, in centuries past, to ignore hostile armies at their gates in order to bring in their grapes. "War can wait" subtly celebrates the agrarian heroism of people keeping faith with nature in the face of bloody conflict. It also reminds us, sadly, how often such heroism has been required.

—TE

Mike Steinberger is a freelance journalist based in Montclair, New Jersey. He is a contributor to the Financial Times *and writes for numerous other publications.*

EMILE PEYNAUD

Exhilarating Virtues
of Wine

Smile and inhale the light.

BRILLAT-SAVARIN CLAIMED THAT COFFEE WAS AN EXHILARATING drink; Larousse says the same thing; but it is a long time since coffee made us smile.

Wine, however, has always been considered enlivening, a drink to raise the spirits. Hundreds of quotations attest to this down the centuries. Is wine really full of good cheer which it spreads through our veins? And is it the alcohol which engenders the sense of optimism? No; alcohol dulls the senses, distorts perception, and makes us lose our sense of identity; I cannot accept that notion of euphoria, dreamy or noisy, being linked to a blood-alcohol level of seventy milligrams per liter. To be merry from too much alcohol is a sad business. What interests me is the effect on the emotions, the happy state of mind that wine causes even before it is drunk. The prospect of wine is so pleasant that it relaxes the face muscles and makes one's eyes light up. Even before the cork is drawn, a good bottle induces a festive atmosphere of good humor and relaxation. The liveliness of flowing wine is infectious. It inspires wine writers to describe wines imaginatively as frivolous, funny, amusing, roguish, chic, jokey, laughing, naughty. In contrast, some wines are said to be serious; I wonder which these are? Wines that are simply dull, or those few rare and expensive bottles whose prestigious image makes even the lighthearted serious?

The most exhilarating of wines is without doubt sparkling wine. The very way of serving it has a promise of fun: the ice bucket, the napkin draped like a scarf around the bottle, the popping of the cork, and the burst of streaming bubbles which make pouring awkward as they spill over the rim of the flute. As an aperitif, Champagne immediately sets the tone and breaks the ice, something which no other drink can do. If Champagne has a happy image, the image of a wine that can be drunk even when one is no longer thirsty, then this is because it is the wine par excellence for happy events.

Wine does indeed have an aura of conviviality. It is enough for a wine professional to identify himself as such for the person he is talking to, to say "So, you're a winetaster are you!" along with a knowing wink, implying an appreciation of the supposed delight of the job as he thinks to himself: "Work is obviously no problem for you!" He is clearly unaware of the pressure on a taster during tasting, of how tiring repeated tests can be, of the discipline required, of the constant availability and good health that the job demands. Even if he is a teetotaler all he can think of is the jovial aspect of wine.

The journalist Jean Ferniot experienced this when interviewing French people, so he knew what he was talking about when he said: "Stop someone in the street, it does not matter who, and ask what the name Burgundy means to them. They will reply wine. And generally their faces will break into a big smile."

One morning I was walking along a crowded pavement in Mexico City. The previous evening I had appeared on Mexican television. My interview with Jacobo Zabludovsky, the Mexican Léon Zitrone, had covered the civilization and the humanity of wine, the preferred drink of Latin races, and the possibilities of wine production in Mexico. The average annual per capita consumption of the Mexicans is barely more than a quarter of a liter of wine (they make up for this with other alcoholic drinks: beer, brandy, cocktails, and tequila). Afterwards, still in front of the cameras, I had managed an improvised tasting of the wines of five different countries fairly well. So, that morning I was recognized among the crowd and addressed in a familiar way accompanied by a broad smile: "Hey! Are you the Frenchman who was tasting wines on the television yesterday?" I had spoken about the pleasures of tasting to people who had perhaps never drunk a drop of wine, and wine had already created a sense of complicity between us. Wine's happy image had shone from their screens and lit up their faces....

I thought to myself one day, wine is still the best utilization of solar energy that we have found. Millions of vine leaves per hectare absorb the sun's rays, turned first toward the morning sun, then heated by the midday sun, and

> Soup should be served at a formal meal, and must at least be tasted: it is rude to leave it untouched. By this means we delicately ensure that everyone present is fortified before wine is served; we also enforce the highly civilized impression that nobody present is anxious to get started on the wine.
> — Margaret Visser,
> *The Rituals of Dinner*

finally following the setting sun in the evening. The vine stores this energy in the tastiest form, in its ripening grapes, and not only as sugars. In fact, it is the formation of substances other than sugars which is of more interest to us: the anthocyanins of coloring matter, the tannins with their savory astringency, and the aromatic essences concentrated in the cells of the skins.

Later on, in the vat, fermentations will liberate this unstable energy. Then one day, several months or several decades later, the product obtained, purified, refined, and settled, will reconstitute those beautiful rays of summer sunshine in your glass in an explosion of smells and flavors. Old wines are always a reminder of fine days, the past regained. Popular wisdom is right: Wine really is bottled sunshine; that is why it is a cheerful drink, warmth to the heart and soul.

Emile Peynaud has trained over 1,500 winemakers in his role as a professor at the Bordeaux Institute of Enology. He has also consulted with such elite châteaux as Margaux, Cheval-Blanc, and Lafite, and is the author of numerous books, including Knowing and Making Wine, Understanding Wine, *and* The Taste of Wine, *from which this story was excerpted. Michael Schuster, the translator of this excerpt, is the proprietor of Winewise, a professional wine consulting firm in London.*

The Passing of Butterflies

To everything there is a season.

RETURNING FROM A YEAR LIVING IN FRANCE, MY DAUGHTER wailed from the back seat of the car on our way home from the airport, "What will I have for lunch if I can't get chevre?"

While I sympathized, because I too had become addicted to the creamy, fresh, sliceable aged goat cheeses we ate daily, I lamented another expected scarcity I would miss after all our time in the Luberon between Aix and Avignon. I had developed a passion for Provençal rosés. These were only two of the tangible losses we were beginning to feel as we headed back to our northern California home.

Even harder to bear would be the curtailing of the freedom we had during our sojourn. Shannon and her brother Brendan had independent study programs that allowed a lot of flexibility for school time. My husband and I wrote, went to markets, and made meals together *a la mode française*, to which we found ourselves naturally predispositioned.

On my last day in Provence I had gone for a walk and been struck by the dead butterflies that dotted the roadside on my way up the hill to Bonnieux. I was considering all the things I would miss, and the sight of the butterflies made me sad to think that they, too, had finished their time in Provence.

The final month of our French stay was during the cherry harvest in Bonnieux in the Luberon where our year began and ended. We had rented Le Petit Moulin, a funky *gite* with a cement sink that drained into the garden. It was owned by Madame Chabert, an elegant grand widow of the region, who put little into décor or embellishment but was quite astute about the worth of her rental. In addition to the *gite*, she leased out the land to a local farmer who raised a couple of acres of leeks, squash, tomatoes, basil, and artichokes for the local *marché*. Madame was quite sociable so we invited her for aperitifs soon after arriving.

"*Ah bien,*" she sighed as she stepped onto the tiny patio that looked out over the garden and noticed the little table of hors d'oeuvres and a bottle of a local rosé wine. "*Rosé est ma favorite!*" she said rather more graciously than I thought she meant.

But she seemed to know the producer, so we felt like we had done the right thing. When she saw that I had put a creamy duck liver pâté from Gascony among the crudités, cheese, and olives, she was quite surprised "I love pâté, don't you?" asked my chevre-loving seven-year-old.

"*Mais oui,*" she replied, "*avec vin doux, pas sec.*" Yes, but with sweet wine, not dry.

Since I hadn't tasted the wine, I didn't know this pale pink wine of the region wouldn't be sweet like the white Zinfandel that passed for rosé back home. My only prior reference to Provençal rosés was from reading M.F.K. Fisher's description of these wines as "nervous" and "thin." I had just assumed they would be sweet, too.

I tasted the wine. A perception of strawberries and cherries filled my mouth and nose, while the crisp, tart wash cooled and refreshed. This wine wasn't one bit nervous. The body was thin but the mouthfeel was sure and focused.

I've since learned that Grenache is the main grape for rosé along the Rhône River and in other parts of Provence. The grapes are a dusty red. When they are pressed, the skins are left with the clear juice just long enough to infuse it with a tinge of pink or salmon or pale rose. The grapes are not overripe and no sugar is added to make it sweet. Most of the rosé in Provence is pale, and some, such as the wine from Domaine Tempier in Bandol, have just a blush.

Before leaving France, we tried many more rosés, from the local *cave cooperative*, from wineries owned by relatives of our neighbors, and from wine shops. One night came an experience that was pure serendipity but which I will forever associate with sunsets. We were dining at a restaurant in Roussillon, a ruddy-colored village perched upon a mound of rouge bauxite rock from which most of the buildings had been made. Sitting on a west-facing terrace, we ordered a bottle of Tavel rosé, a wine we were told was exported to the U.S.

In my experience, descriptions of the light in Provence are never under-reported. There is an opaque brilliance on scenes and vistas that dazzles while it defies clarity and inspires creativity. Here on this warm night, the cold bottle of Tavel rosé became a flame in the increasingly pink sky; the sunset illuminated the now-red stone, our skin—the very air. Our world was rose-colored. We didn't need glasses. We could barely talk. We all sat in awe of this moment. The silence was broken when our little goat-cheese lover bellowed in her best French, *"Tout le monde est rosé!"* Diners around us applauded. We giggled.

Visiting wineries in the Rhône region is not like it is in California, where wineries have PR agencies, tour directors, and tasting rooms. At the most welcoming wineries in the Rhône, it's often a family member who puts down whatever he or she is doing, polishes a few glasses, and gives you a taste. Always call ahead, even if you speak no French at all, and make an appointment. Also try to taste a few Rhône wines before you leave home, such as Côtes du Rhône or Chateauneuf-du-Pape. You will be better able to appreciate the local wine, and local winemakers will be better able to appreciate you.

—TE

Then one sip of the cold wine was enough to allow me to return to the menu. As the wine warmed in my mouth, however, I couldn't help but think how pink we are inside as well. I shared that insight with my family, who thought it was pretty funny. We talked about all the pink things we could think of as the sun slipped into a golden finale followed by a bluish darkness. Soon we would be heading home.

Little did we know what changes were waiting for us. My daughter's wail turned out to be in vain. Back in northern California, Laurel Chenel was making goat cheese just like the French ones we were addicted to. Kermit Lynch was importing many of the rosés we had tried—and more besides. Within a few years, wineries in Sonoma and Mendocino counties were making rosé from a slew of varietals including Provence's Grenache. Equally interesting were those made from Sangiovese, Zinfandel, Mourvedre, Pinot Noir, Pinot Meunier, and Cinsault. I still miss some of the things we loved living in France, but the food and wine are not among them.

A wine tasting I hosted recently brought me back to that last day in Provence. Filled with rosé wine, which colored them from pale salmon to bright strawberry, the balloon-shaped tumblers resembled Easter eggs in a semicircle around the appetizer plates. The assembled company was about to taste rosé varietals with pâté de foie gras. As everyone took bites of the pâté and sampled the rosés, a butterfly landed on one of the glasses. It had already tucked its eggs into the oak tree leaves above us. Now it fluttered wanly, as if to signal that life changes and goes on.

And then it died.

Heidi Haughy Cusick is Mendocino County's wine country correspondent. Her latest books are Sonoma: The Ultimate Winery Guide *and* Mendocino: The Ultimate Wine & Food Lovers Guide. *She lives and writes in a cabin above Ukiah Valley surrounded by the Petite Sirah and Zinfandel vineyards at Eaglepoint Ranch.*

JAN MORRIS

✷ ✷ ✷

Etymology of a Wine Lover

It was such a simple little thing.

I CAN RECALL THE EXACT MOMENT, IN THE AUSTRALIAN SUMMER OF 1962, when I became a gastronome. It was a moment less of metamorphosis than of revelation—as though a veil had been lifted from my eyes, a muffle from my tongue, releasing my responses for pleasures I knew not of. I was in my thirties then, and had never taken eating and drinking very seriously. For the most part I simply wanted to get them over with. There may have been something in my family background (we have a Quaker strain to us) which forbade me to enjoy them too much, and anyway I always had more interesting things to do. It had never much worried me when food was bad, and I was never greatly excited when it seemed better than usual.

Everything changed, however, on that Australian summer day. I was being entertained to lunch by an Australian of Hungarian origin, on his garden terrace overlooking Sydney Harbor, looking inland to the bridge. The day was fresh, warm and bright as only an Australian day can be. The harbor glittered. Ships sailed by, the green of the garden was almost unnaturally green and in my memory the flying wings of the opera house seem to have been soaring with an especially buoyant air of elation.

Into this setting, seductive and half-hallucinatory (for the green was probably no greener than any other, and the opera house had not yet been built), the Australian brought our lunch. It was nothing elaborate—fresh rolls, pâté of some sort, cheese, I think, apples and a bottle of local white wine. In substance it was not so different from the family meal I once shared with American evangelists in Afghanistan, which consisted of peanuts and water. Its spirit, though, was not the same. It seemed to me that my friend laid out the plates in the garden purringly, unguently, and when he came to eat the food he did so with a seductive crackling of bread, a voluptuous spreading of pâté, the coolest possible drafting of white wine in the sun. It reminded me of Andrew Marvell—

> What wondrous life is this I lead!
> Ripe Apples drop about my head;
> The Luscious Clusters of the Vine
> Upon my mouth do crush their Wine…

As it happens nobody could be much less pretentious about food and wine than my Epicurean host that day, and he would have been astonished to know, as he ate his usual simple lunch before going back to the office, that beside him I was enjoying a moment of new vision; yet so it was, and since then I have approached my victuals with a far less Quakerly dispassion.

Drinking for me means only wine, and I did not need my Australian to persuade me of its pleasures. I like to brag that I have drunk a glass of wine every day since the second world war, and though this is not true in the fact, since I have spent much time in places where there is no wine, it is true in the principle—the chance of war introduced me to wine, and I never turned away. I believe in wine as I believe in Nature. I cherish its sacramental and legendary meanings, not to mention its power to intoxicate, and just as Nature can be both kind and hostile, so I believe that if bad wine is bad for you, good wine in moderation does nothing but good. If I am ever challenged, I refer people to that seminal work *Wine Is the Best Medicine*, in which the great Dr. E. A. Maury, pictured on its jacket looking terrifically healthy with a glass of Champagne in his hand, prescribes a suitable wine for almost every ailment—Entre-Deux-Mers for rickets, young Beaujolais for diarrhea, two glasses of Sancerre daily to lower the blood pressure...

When I was very young I drank, like most of us, with a lack of discrimination and an unvarying enjoyment that I now envy. Thinking of myself then, I am reminded of the great Sherpa mountaineer Tenzing Norgay, who I witnessed drinking, I rather think, his very first glass of wine of any kind. It was at an official banquet in London. I sat next to the very old-school and gentlemanly functionary who had arranged the occasion, and early in the evening he remarked to me that he hoped I would enjoy the claret, not just the last of its vintage in the official cellars, but perhaps the last in London. I was much impressed, and looked across at Tenzing, who was most certainly enjoying it very much indeed, having as a standard of comparison only the species of alcoholic porridge the Sherpas call *tsang*. His was a princely figure, and as the lackeys filled and refilled his glass his face shone with pride and pleasure. It was a delight to see him. After a while the old boy on my left turned to me again. "Oh, how good it is to see," he said with the true warmth of approval, "that Mr. Tenzing *knows a decent claret when he has one!*"

My own first wines were all Italian, and nearly all red. The fact that un-Italian wines existed at all was first brought home to me in Port Said, when, on disembarking from a troop ship from Trieste in 1946, I went to a restaurant for dinner with the young commanding officer of my regiment. "Rhine wine!" exclaimed the colonel in delight—"after all these years, Rhine wine!"—and though it has since occurred to me that he must have been hardly more than a schoolboy when he had last tasted it, still his savoir faire made it clear to me that there was more to wine than plonk Chianti.

Since then I have drunk wine of more varieties than my colonel could have conceived. I have drunk Egyptian wines made by Greeks, and Chinese wines made by Frenchmen, and Zimbabwean wines, and Canadian wines, and Peloponnesian draught retsina served in tin bowls, and Scottish wines made from the sap of silver birches, and two wines at least that I swear I will never taste again—the

Indian-made wine called Golconda and the kosher Cabernet that is bottled in downtown Manhattan. Believing as I do too in the mythic meaning of wine, its role as a messenger from the *genii locorum*, I have also followed it to some lovely places. In the days when we could still afford to be addicted to the Burgundy called Échézeaux, I once set out to trail the wine from bottle to source, from my wine rack in Wales to the exact patch of vineyard it came from. I hoped that I would find there some more explicit declaration from the earth gods—and so I did, for when I drove up the stony track to the half acre of hill-slope from which every single bottle of Échézeaux has been derived, the solitary Frenchman working there looked up, saw the Welsh plate on my car and started talking about rugby football.

But I must admit that the best of all my vinous moments have been with the old Italian red after all. We drank lots of it when we were living in Venice, and sometimes after dinner, if friends were with us, we would take a bottle or two and sail the boat out into the darkness of the lagoon. This was magic. It was not that we were drunk, only that the wine's benevolence had made us better, happier people for the evening, had opened our hearts more receptively to beauty and emotion: so that out there in the purple night, watching the lights of the ships, passing the looming tripods of the sandbank stakes, and seeing unfolded before us the grand luminosity of Venice itself, its towers and palaces radiant above the viscous water—absorbing all this in wonder and merriment, we really were touched by the gods of the place.

Perhaps they sound gross, these pleasures of drink, but believe me, even as I indulge myself I relish in memory the loaf of bread, the simple pâté, the cheese, the apple, and the white wine that changed my life so generously beside the sea in Sydney.

Welsh journalist, historian, biographer, and novelist Jan Morris is the author of more than forty books. She is considered one of Britain's foremost travel essayists and historians. What she has called her final book, Trieste and the Meaning of Nowhere, *was published in 2001, and her first book,* Coast to Coast: A Journey Across 1950s America, *was recently reissued by Travelers' Tales.*

GERALD ASHER

Remembrance
of Wines Past

The history of sunlight is written into these bottles.

"WHAT WAS THE BEST WINE YOU EVER TASTED, THE ONE YOU WILL always remember?" It's a question I'm often asked when someone newly introduced first realizes how I spend much of my waking time. How to answer? I think I'm expected to château-drop, to say something glamorous about a Margaux '53, a Cheval-Blanc '47, or a Mouton-Rothschild '45—a monumental wine, by the way, still flamboyantly vigorous when poured for me at a dinner at Mouton itself a couple of years ago. (There's a real château-drop for you.)

But how does anyone compare that Mouton-Rothschild with a Cheval-Blanc '47, last tasted in the 1970s, to decide which was "better"? And what would be the point anyway? Such wines are almost always impressive, and usually memorable. But that isn't the same thing as "always remembered," is it? In any case, one's memory of a wine is rarely a mere abstraction of aroma and flavor. Often it seems to reflect so well a particular context that later we are never quite sure whether we remember the circumstances because of the wine or the wine because of the circumstances. At times the two can even be ludicrously at odds.

Not long ago, while helping a friend clean up an apartment from which the removal men had taken his furniture just hours before, I

47

came across a bottle of Barossa Valley Cabernet Sauvignon, a 1981 from the Hill-Smith estate, overlooked by the packers. We were tired and more than ready to stop. Fortunately, one of us had a corkscrew and there were paper cups in a kitchen cupboard. We sat on the floor, our backs to the wall. The wine was more than remarkable: it was sleek and patrician and elegant beyond anything I'd expected. At that moment, it was the most delicious wine in the world.

When mountains labor to bring forth a mouse, that can be memorable, too. In the 1960s, when my company in London imported and distributed the wines of Henri Maire—an important but highly promotion-driven wine producer in the Jura, in eastern France—I was asked, at short notice, to arrange a small dinner at a distinguished restaurant (my choice) for a few distinguished guests (my choice). The principle dish (Henri Maire's choice), prepared by none other than Raymond Oliver, at the time still reigning at Le Grand Véfour, was to be flown over from Paris hours before the event.

The object was to show—in London and Paris simultaneously, and with precisely the same dish—a wine that Henri Maire had shipped in barrels around the world. In the eighteenth century it had been a custom to send certain sherries to and from the tropics in the hold of sailing ships; the journey was thought to age fortified wines advantageously. Names of certain blends—Fine Old East India, for example—still allude to the practice. The wine Henri Maire had chosen to be dispatched for two years before the mast, so to speak, was an Arbois rosé. He called it Vin Retour des Iles and proposed to offer it to his numerous guests at the Grand Véfour (and to my much smaller group in London) to demonstrate—I think—that Arbois rosé was serious wine and not to be confused with the pretty tipples in designer bottles then increasingly popular at restaurant lunch tables.

I chose to hold my dinner in a private dining room at Prunier's on St. James's Street. Simone Prunier, a consummate restaurateur, was a resourceful woman of limitless discretion, and I knew I could rely on her to pull together what seemed to me to be an adventure fraught with risk. We knew nothing of the dish to be sent from Paris except that it was to be *marcassin* (young wild boar) accompanied by a sauce. It would need only to be reheated.

We composed a menu around this dish: Champagne and canapés to greet the arriving guests; a plain poached turbot with hollandaise (Prunier's, after all, was renowned for its fish but we didn't want to upstage Raymond Oliver); cheeses from the Jura area—the Franche-Comté—to follow the *marcassin*; and a sumptuous pineapple ice, to be brought to the table packed inside the original fruit, enveloped in a veil of finely spun sugar. I selected Henri Maire wines for the fish and the cheese that would allow the special bottling of rosé every chance to be the star.

The dish, transported expeditiously by Air France from restaurant door to restaurant door, was something of an anticlimax: I can describe it only as minced wild boar patties in a brown sauce. Unfortunately, the wine offered neither compensation nor distraction. Henri Maire had decided, at the last minute, that there was barely enough Vin Retour des Iles for the swelling numbers of his guests at the Grand Véfour and therefore none—not a single bottle—was sent to London. I was asked to serve the standard Arbois rosé instead. I have to say, it was a perfectly satisfactory wine. But it was not, as Dr. Johnson once said of a perfectly satisfactory dinner, what you would ask a man to. Least of all at Prunier's.

Who knows what vinous perspectives the actual Vin Retour des Iles might have opened up for us? In a brief but charming book, *La Légende du Vin*, subtitled (in French, of course) *A Short Essay of Sentimental Enophilia*, Jean-Baptiste Baronian, French novelist, essayist, critic, and editor, says that those who appreciate wine find in every glass a trace of a history, of a civilization, and of a gesture that bind together a time and a place.

A few years ago I tasted, on an exceptional occasion in California, the 1771 and 1791 vintages of Château Margaux. Both wines were a vibrant strawberry color and astonishingly fresh; their bouquet was extravagantly scented. In the eighteenth century, wine, like fruit, was bottled for preservation, not aging, and it was common practice to perk the aroma of red Bordeaux with powdered orrisroot, the rhizome of iris. It was used then, as it still is (but in perfume, not in wine) to contribute a scent of violets. In any case, both wines were made before Cabernet Sauvignon, with its distinctive pungency and dense garnet color, had replaced Malbec as the principal grape of the Médoc.

With Fragonard, Couperin, and Beaumarchais as touchstones, anyone speculating on how an eighteenth-century French wine tasted back then would imagine something with very much the delicacy, the luminosity, and the perfumed intensity of those wines. I confess, though, that foremost in my own mind as they slipped down my throat was the thought that I was drinking—in Los Angeles, the quintessential twentieth-century city—wines made by men alive in Bordeaux at the time of the American and French Revolutions. Just to look at Chardin's painting of a bowl of raspberries can be an eighteenth-century experience. But in absorbing alcohol converted from fruit sugar two centuries earlier, I was actually sharing calories transmitted in solar energy that had also warmed the faces of Thomas Jefferson and Marie Antoinette.

But *most* memorable of my life? Were it not that people casually

---

In the late afternoon of a spring day in 1977, I chanced to meet Cary Gott unloading his pickup truck in the parking lot at Corti Brothers, a fine wine and food shop in Sacramento. Cary was the winemaker, general manager, and founder of Monteviña, a winery funded by his father-in-law, an investment banker. In those days, wineries were popping up across the state like mushrooms after some vinous rain, but unlike most vintners, Cary had chosen Amador County in the Sierra foothills, rather than the more popular Napa County to the west. I asked Cary what had brought him down the hill to the flatlands. He grinned and his arm described an arc as he pointed to the cases of wine in the bed of his truck: "Delivering bottled poetry," he replied.

—James T. Lapsley,
Bottled Poetry

met might assume I was making fun of them, I would in fact explain that it was, and still remains, unidentified. I drank it at a mountain inn near the Simplon Pass in the early summer of either 1962 or 1963. From 1955 until 1970 I spent weeks on end visiting suppliers all over Europe to taste and select the wines my firm brought to London. For much of that time there were neither *autoroutes* nor *autostrade*, and I drove a Triumph TR4 (which I'd had refinished in deep Burgundy red instead of its original British racing green) to get myself quickly from place to place. Well, that was the rational explanation at any rate.

I'd spent the night at Sion, in the Swiss Valais, after an evening of *raclette*—molten slivers of the local cheese draped over hot potatoes—and the cooperative's Fendant, a flowery white wine with which we were having a modest success in England. I was on my way to Verona, and had set off early to be sure of reaching Milan by evening.

There was little traffic on the road—the Simplon is more often used as a rail route—and by noon I was high in the Alps with the Swiss-Italian border behind me. It was early June, and for most of the way wildflowers were scattered along the roadside. At the higher altitudes, drifts of snow still lay dazzlingly white in the midday sun. The exhilaration of the climb—the TR4 would respond with its distinctive soft roar as I changed through the gears on those endless, steep turns—the crisp air, the brilliant light, and the grandeur of the mountains, made me feel I was on top of the world. And I almost was, literally. But I was also hungry and had many curving miles ahead of me to Domodossola, where I planned to stop for a late lunch.

Then an inn appeared. It was small, but comfortably appealing. The deliciously simple set lunch of sautéed veal scallops and buttered noodles with a salad of green beans was typical of what one finds in the mountains. My glass was filled with a light red wine poured from a pitcher, left on the table. I was relaxed, carefree, and happy. Oh, how ruby bright that wine was; it gleamed in the sunlight. I remember clearly its enticing aroma—youthful, but with a refinement that surprised me. The wine was sweetly exotic: lively on my tongue, perfectly balanced, and with a long, glossy finish. It was the sort of wine that Omar Khayyam might have had in mind for his desert tryst. The young woman who had poured it for me was amused when I asked what it was. It was, she said, *vino rosso*.

I sat there trying, without success, to put my finger on the grape. It was probably one of those sub-Alpine varieties already then disappearing into odd pockets of vineyard in remote valleys—Bonarda, perhaps, or Ruchè. Or perhaps it was, more conventionally, a Brachetto, a Freisa, or a Grignolino, any one of which was likely to show more than its usual appeal if grown near that altitude. Whatever it was, the wine had been made with uncommon care. It was exquisitely graceful.

I shall always remember that wine, though I have never learned what it might have been. Italian friends have suggested Vercelli, from the Novara hills, just a way farther south; and others, Valtellina, farther east. No wine I've tasted since from either has come close.

But the pleasure in any wine is subjective: we each bring something to what is there in the glass and interpret the result differently. Perhaps, on that June day more than thirty years ago, I had contributed an extra-large dose of well-being. Who can say?

Gerald Asher has been wine editor at Gourmet *magazine for more than twenty-five years. Born in the United Kingdom, he began four decades as a wine merchant there before taking up residence in Paris and San Francisco, where he now divides his time. This story was excerpted from his book,* Vineyard Tales: Reflections on Wine.

PART TWO

SOME THINGS TO DO

CHRISTOPHER WEIR

Cellar Man

Before wine's glamour and romance
come sweat and blood.

A 12-GAUGE SHOTGUN IN HAND, I SKULK THROUGH THE VINEYARD, reluctantly at war with Mother Nature. A ten-acre, dry-farmed estate loaded with 100-year-old Zinfandel vines may produce ethereal fruit, but it will do so only in the smallest rations. Every grape cluster counts. Like some freakish invasion out of a Hitchcock flick, a swarm of ravenous starlings suddenly descends from the infinite blue.

They've already decimated two rows of vines, and they're back for more, sneering at our more civilized attempts to spook them: propane noise cannons, reflective tinsel, recorded sounds of natural predators, and pyrotechnic screamers. I raise the barrel of last resort, pull the trigger, reload, and fire another round. Not into the heart of the swarm, but close enough to scatter their attack to the four winds.

I've just bought another half-hour break from that mild-mannered winegrower's task called bird control.

Two weeks earlier, Bill Greenough, owner and winemaker of Saucelito Canyon Vineyard, had asked if I'd like to pull up stakes, move to his winery thirty miles from nowhere in California's San Luis Obispo County, and serve as his harvest foreman. After a few seconds' reflection, I'd replied, "Sure," then stuck my cat in the truck and headed south.

I was curious. Ever since it sold its soul to the yuppie revolution, the wine industry has subordinated itself to vacuous prattle and nouveau riche adornments. Viticultural spin doctors would have you believe that all wineries are lorded over by *bons vivants* in V-neck sweaters who perpetually tilt a glass of Chardonnay toward the sun. And even producers of low-end schlock favor imagery suggesting that they're protagonists in a noble agricultural soap opera.

But down in the trenches of small wineries and estate vineyards, talk is cheap and affectation even cheaper. Start jabbering about rose petals laced with toasty oak and you'll be condemned to pitchforking grape stems for hours. Here, wine is crafted by hand, not by machines or trends. A cellar isn't an excuse for catered parties, but rather a concrete jungle where weak men die like dogs. And the harvest is nothing less than an extended experiment in sleep deprivation.

Soap opera it isn't.

For the first few weeks, my role as harvest foreman (glorified cellar rat) consisted of watering the dirt roads around the vineyard to subdue rampant dust, controlling winged varmints, running tests on the rising level of sugar in the grapes, and building a bin-dumping contraption.

Meandering back to the winery after my morning bout with the starlings, I noticed a dead coyote near the deer fence, its soulless gaze searching a nearby oak tree. Why, I wondered, would a coyote just drop dead in the vineyard?

When I arrived in the lab—basically a large closet with a sink, gun rack, essential chemicals, and assorted beakers—Bill was there flipping through the day planner where I'd inscribed the morning's vineyard readings. He raised his eyes in resigned disbelief. I just shrugged my shoulders. Here it was, mid-September, the autumn sun blazing on the heels of a fairly warm growing season, and yet all of the fruit was still weeks away from full ripening. Bizarre.

But Bill wasn't overly alarmed. He'd seen everything. He'd built the place with his bare hands, had resurrected the vines from seventy years of weedy anonymity, had nursed six-month-long fermentations that would have sent other winemakers over the edge. He was intimate with the powers of faith and the futility of panic.

Of course, the later the harvest, the more chaos lurked on the horizon, the more chance an autumn storm could ruin the crop, the more we'd have to squeeze an insane amount of work into an ever-shrinking amount of time. I suspected that Bill, like myself, took a certain perverse pleasure in that notion.

A few weeks later, I joined him and his family for dinner at their home in Edna Valley. "Anyone who says winemaking is an art is full of shit," Bill said as we enjoyed the postmortem to a satisfying meal, sipping martinis and discussing life. He leaned over and continued at a near whisper: "That," he said, pointing to a handsome landscape painting on the opposite wall, "is art. Winemaking is a craft. You take what the vineyard gives you, then you go with it."

The following morning, standing on the winery cottage porch drinking coffee in the twilight, I heard the advancing din of salsa tunes. Vineyard chief Luis Mendoza and his crew were rambling through the canyon. Harvest would finally commence. We would go with it.

Saucelito Canyon is not some high-tech, cutting-edge winery with computerized temperature controls, rotating fermenters, and ten-ton presses. Then again, if you make wine in a vacuum, it tastes like wine made in a vacuum. But if you dump the bins onto some jerry-rigged plywood monstrosity, separate the grape clusters with a common garden rake, hand-sort them on a conveyer, and pray that your little crusher will have enough *cojones* to make it through the day, then you will have wine with a sense of time, place, and personality. Wine that cannot be made elsewhere, or by others. In short, wine with a heart.

And so hours passed, days passed, a white noise of winemaking separated by end-of-the-shift Lone Star beer bouts (ancient aphorism: "It takes a lot of beer to make good wine."), pathetic pasta dinners, and precious little sleep. The Saucelito winery crew—Bill, Richard, Peter, Clarence, Adam, and myself—barely evaded zombification. In theory, our first two weeks were as such: we'd de-stem and slightly crush the grapes, run sugar and pH tests (which usually indicated that the vineyard tests were inaccurate in the face of the Zinfandel's notoriously elusive ripening pattern), bump the crushed mass with a little potassium metabisulfide to disarm any little biological nasties, then add yeast to kick-start the process of fermentation, in which yeast cells eat grape sugars and produce alcohol.

But in reality, it was a freak show of equipment rigging, forklift maneuvering, pressure washing, endless pumping, technical failures, perpetual cleaning, potential accidents, bee stings, immature pranks, and bad country music, with the Yodeling Cowboy's *Rolling Stone from Texas* as a sort of harvest theme song. Twelve hours, fourteen hours, sixteen hours.... Days off were about as likely as a Martian invasion.

I observed that wine is, in a strange way, like Chicken McNuggets. Because there's a vigilantly enforced disconnect between the image and the reality, an antiseptic distance that allows us to enjoy these slickly marketed treats without ever confronting the uglier side: the source. In the case of McDonald's, it's the mass neck-breaking of chickens. In our case, it's the winery cellar.

Of course, when it comes to Chicken McNuggets, the disconnect serves an obvious purpose. But what's with wine? The unseen side of wine is really quite beautiful. Yet here comes another dreamy commercial, with two linen-clad lovers blissfully blind to the upwardly mobile butterfly that just perched itself upon their sexy bottle of white Zinfandel.... Okay, whatever, it works. But how about some ads or commercials celebrating the tooth-and-nail aspects of winemaking, the romantic spirit of the immigrant pickers, *the aura of agriculture*. That kind of honesty would sell.

Wouldn't it?

In a normal year, the separate vineyard blocks would have ripened on varying schedules, and the picking would have been spread out over a month. But this time, the entire estate had conspired to ripen in rapid succession. By the end of the second week, both fermentation tanks were full, as were the dozen open-top bins (and an old milk tank, as well as some loaners from another winery) in which various lots were segregated so the grape juice could have extended contact with the grape skins, which give color and other chemical marvels to the wine. Cellar space—or lack thereof—was a big issue, and we were starting to press the first lots in order to free up our fermentation tanks.

Ten acres of low-yielding Zinfandel vines would have been child's play for a large, modern winery. They'd have picked the whole place in a day or two, pumped it into three mammoth fermenters, and pressed it in a matter of hours. They'd have possessed neither the time nor the financial inclination to dissect every acre.

For a small estate, however, the vineyard is not a mass, but rather a mosaic of quirks and nuances, each to be nurtured, even encouraged. And the cellar is not an exercise in efficiency, but a logistical nightmare that leads every cluster of grapes past watchful eyes, and every gallon through capable hands.

The soul of a vintage is like a wanted man: you don't capture it without a lot of footwork.

"I'm telling you, there's a *chupacabra* hanging around this place. I hear it in the middle of the night, sort of between a scream and a growl." I was

Wine in California is still in the experimental stage; and when you taste a vintage, grave economical questions are involved. The beginning of vine-planting is like the beginning of mining for precious metals: the winegrower also "prospects." One corner of land after another is tried with one kind of grape after another. This is a failure; that is better; a third best. So, bit by bit, they grope about for their Clos Vougeot and Lafite. Those lodes and pockets of earth, more precious than the precious ores, that yield inimitable fragrance and soft fire; those virtuous Bonanzas, where the soil has sublimated under sun and stars to something finer, and the wine is bottled poetry: these still lie undiscovered; chaparral conceals, thicket embowers them; the miner chips the rock and wander farther, and the grizzly muses undisturbed. But there they bide their hour, awaiting their Columbus; and nature nurses and prepares them. The smack of California earth shall linger on the palate of your grandson.

—Robert Louis Stevenson, *The Silverado Squatters* (1880)

trying to convince Luis that *el chupacabra,* the legendary Latin American "goatsucker," half vampire, half alien, was terrorizing Saucelito Canyon. And why not? Newspapers were saying it had been spotted as far north as Pasadena. What else could hurl such terrible death rattles into the vacant night?

"Just a big coyote, *amigo,*" Luis grinned as he navigated his tractor back into the vineyard with an empty bin in tow. He wasn't going to let me get away with any of that *chupacabra* crap.

For once, the cellar had actually caught up with the pickers. Richard, the winery's technical guru, set about drawing some diagrams to get the winery's convoluted electrical supply in order. Adam, who was a drummer by night, swapped out the Yodeling Cowboy for one of his demo tapes. Meanwhile, Clarence, the winery's assassin for hire, went to look after the pumpovers, and I started some punchdowns.

As red wine ferments, the skins rise and form a cap. To keep the mass from getting dry, and to encourage texture, flavor, and color extraction, the cap needs to be regularly broken and submerged. For small fermentation bins, this means a punchdown: perching yourself atop a board straddling the open tank, cramming your head between the cellar rafters, then thrusting a paddle into the cap with all of your might, only to yank it out and repeat the maneuver over and over with a sort of Sisyphean resignation.

For large, open-top fermenters, punchdowns are physically impossible (well, on second thought, nothing's impossible in a winery cellar). Thus, the pumpover: sucking wine from the lower part of the tank and then pumping it up and over the cap of dry grape skins at the top of the tank. So there was Clarence, negotiating a one-by-eight board, grappling with a hose that was spitting Zinfandel with all the decorum of a rattlesnake.

"You know," Bill said as he walked past, "I had a friend whose family owned a winery in Santa Barbara, and one of their cellar rats was doing a pumpover one night and he slipped. The next morning they fished him out." He drew his forefinger across his neck. "Dead as a doornail."

It was for such infrequent admonitions that Bill had earned his status as the "Great Communicator." If he was worried about your health or life, he wouldn't insult you by breathing down your neck and telling you to be careful. He'd just level some horror story in your general direction.

But not all of his stories were of the morbid class. Sometimes he would rally the troops and regale us with tales about the glory days of winemaking, a time when innocent aspirations and general saturnalia kept the bottom line in check. He would talk of communal vinification (to the cries of "stomp naked!") in the mountains above Santa Barbara, and of ensuing Age of Aquarius festivities. He would spin the obscure legend of Wild Bill Neely, prolific diarist and patron saint of the Pagan Brothers' Golden Goat Winery. He would evoke that not-so-distant era when the vultures of multinational corporations had yet to perch themselves so arrogantly upon the shoulders of Bacchus.

Toward the shift's bitter end, with the moon glowering overhead, I was standing amid a dysfunction of pumps, hoses, buckets, valve fittings, and flashlights. It's at such moments that a cellar rat—wet, exhausted, and cross-eyed—might be inclined to indulge in the ever-present temptation of sleep-deprived winemaking: to skip that last punchdown, to leave some fittings on the ground, to do a half-assed job rinsing the pumps. And, thus, to make a half-assed wine. No, it's best never to take a bite from that apple. Because a wine made by wimps will turn out accordingly.

Peter, who was last seen ten minutes earlier towing pressed grape skins into the vineyard, returned and brought the tractor to a halting skid. "Listen," he said, his bloodshot eyes flickering with excitement, "there's a coyote in the vineyard, dead, blood everywhere. Something nasty's prowling around out there!"

Maybe a *chupacabra* was, indeed, haunting Saucelito Canyon. We hopped in the winery ATV, picked up Peter's dog, grabbed the 12-gauge from the cottage, and headed for the murder scene. "You bastard," I muttered upon our arrival. "That thing's been here for a month." It was the dead coyote I'd noticed on my bird control rounds.

Peter just let out an embarrassed laugh. But I could see how he'd been fooled. Much of the coyote was still perfectly intact. And spreading outward were spilled grape skins that, in the imperfect light of the moon, appeared suggestively gruesome.

We returned to the winery, deconstructed the pumps, hosed down the cellar, drank a few Lone Stars, and called it a night.

Luis and his crew had now liberated the vineyard of all its precious Zinfandel. The workdays were growing shorter, and a November breeze whispered the season's first chill as wild turkeys roamed the slopes. There was nothing for us to do but drain the fermenters, jump into their oxygen-deprived atmospheres, then stand waist deep in skins and shovel them into the press.

Usually, the skins formed a "cake" around the inside of the press, forcing the wine downward and into a retainer. Sometimes, however, the cake would burst in spots, and high-pressure Zinfandel would splatter everything in its path, including instantly demoralized cellar rats.

Thus, the "intergalactic prophylactic method," dreamed up by the ever-innovative Great Communicator: entomb the press in layers of shrink wrap for containment. When it worked, it worked beautifully. When it failed, it was a sort of slow eruption with a scatological soundtrack.

The free-run and pressed wines were pumped into separate tanks, where the yeast and grape solids would settle out. After a day or two, we'd rack the wine off the solids and into freshly soaked and washed American oak barrels, most of them used in previous years and therefore devoid of any aggressive flavor influence on the wine.

From there, Bill would continue to direct the wine toward a style he'd cultivated over fifteen years, a style that didn't rely on such winemaking stunts as micromanaged blending and obsessive flavor manipulations, but rather on the essence of the vineyard itself. In other words, he would foster the natural flavors and allow them to speak for themselves. It would be a true estate wine, an expression not of the marketplace, but simply of a *place*, its soil and its people.

Walking through the vineyard one last time, I noticed that Bill had picked up the dead coyote and mounted it on a fencepost, suspended in a perpetual, silent howl. A sort of scarecrow for boat-shoed, blow-dried wine snobs.

The fact is that wine is no longer considered a way of life, but rather a lifestyle choice. And thus a great European tradition has been subordinated to yuppie hallucinations and assorted affectations. The result is an entirely unnecessary dividing line between the initiated and the intimidated.

But down in the cellar, anyone's welcome as long as they're good with a shovel and willing to work long hours. Six-packs and country music cassettes are optional. Dedication isn't.

Christopher Weir is a writer specializing in wine, travel, and the environment. He is an avid supporter of the Second Amendment, dry rosé, and wine as a way of life. He lives with his wife, Malei, and two cats in Los Alamos, California.

* * *

How to Conquer
a Wine List

Don't know the lingo? Invent your own.

THERE'S A MOMENT AT THE BEGINNING OF THE MEAL IN A WHITE-tablecloth restaurant that's a nightmare. It's the wide-awake equivalent of those bad dreams we've all had of walking into an exam totally unprepared. I'm talking about ordering the wine. Whenever I get stuck with that job, I always feel as though I'm on trial and anything I say may be used against me.

The anxiety begins right after menus and water when everyone is settled at the table and hungry. The waiter or a smooth-talking sommelier materializes with a leather-bound wine list. He or she expects someone at this table to select the wine for dinner. Everyone goes shifty-eyed. Everyone is too busy studying the silver or staring into space to reach for that list and get stuck with picking out a wine. Me too.

Even if I knew the difference between a Pinot Noir and a *bete noir*, I couldn't tell a Merlot from a wombat. As for vintages, vineyards, or varieties, all I know is they all begin with "v." What's worse, I am sure the sommelier knows I'm a rookie. He's waiting for me to break down and ask for help so he can make an expensive and patronizing suggestion.

I want to order Blue Nun, because I think it's safe, but I know that's like asking for chop suey in a classy Chinese restaurant. Instead I pick the wine the way I would a horse at Hollywood Park. I look for a name I like and then weigh the price. Think of me as a $2 bettor to show, and you'll know what kind of wine I order.

Of course I'm hoping for a winner, one of those Interesting Little Finds that wine writers are always coming up with, but I have as much luck picking wine as I do horses. The few times I've accidentally ordered something drinkable, I wrote down the name and never saw it on another wine list.

I should know by now not to count on wine writers, either. They don't tell me what to drink with anything I usually find on menus: Chinese Chicken Salad, Pork Chops, a Combination Plate. I clip their columns and carry them around in my purse for months against the moment when I will open a restaurant menu and see the simple little *Brandade de Morue* or clever *Oeufs en Gelee* they've matched with a splendid local vintage.

After a losing streak on both fronts, I decided to cut my losses. There wasn't much I could do to improve my track record, but I realized there were solutions to the wine problem. Instant clarification is what I wanted, which ruled out getting help from the usual places: my therapist, the church, or a course from the nearest adult education institution.

Instead I went to the source. I took this problem to the experts in California's wine country.

They didn't make me feel like Forrest Gump. All I needed, the experts said, was a wine tasting. At one of the big wineries I sat down in front of a daunting number of wine glasses called a flight.

The idea was to taste the wine with a bite of cheese (which smoothes out the tannin in red wine), nuts (which don't do anything), apples (Granny Smith), or artichokes, which kill every taste but sweet for a couple of minutes after each bite, no matter what it is.

While I sipped and spat, the experts bombarded me with bewildering wine talk: "character," "robust," "complex," "sweet," "malolactic fermentation," "tannin." (I knew about the last one. It's what makes your mouth feel the way kiwi fruit looks.)

What do you mean, *"sweet,"* I protested. You can't order sweet wine in a restaurant or the waiter looks at you as though you just shuffled in from Skid Row. About the only thing I do know is that I have to order dry wine—and I have no idea what that means, either.

Never mind what they told me "dry" means. "Not sweet" is just half the answer and I didn't understand the rest. Head spinning with "bouquet," "nose," "oaky," "corky," I put my hands over my ears and begged off.

"Just tell me," I asked, "what a wine would be like if it were something else, something I know. Then I'll decide whether I want to drink it or not."

The cellarmaster understood. He looked at me for a long moment and said, "If this Sauvignon Blanc were an apple, it would be a Granny Smith."

Uh-huh, I nodded with relief.

"If this Chardonnay were music it would be the first movement of Beethoven's Violin Concerto."

That was clear.

"A Merlot is hearth bread, a Cabernet, sourdough. A wombat is an Australian marsupial. Your *bete noir* is wine and a Pinot Noir is Brahms's Fourth. A Gewurztraminer is Baryshnikov in midair and white Zinfandel is a Strauss waltz."

> There's a vast amount of history, technology, and geography associated with wine, and everyone falls somewhere on the spectrum between completely ignorant and completely knowledgeable. Those at the far end, toward full knowledge, can be intimidating to the millions of us toward the near end. This has been going on a long time, it turns out. The ancient Greeks liked to poke fun at the Scythians for not watering their wine, and they positively derided cultures that made wine from fruit other than grapes. The good news is, you don't have to know a thing to like wine in general, or a chosen wine in particular. That's one of the best reasons to try new wines when you're far from home. You're more likely to be free of wine prejudices—and wine snobs—that could limit your enjoyment.
>
> —TE

That night at dinner the cellarmaster handed me a wine list that read:

Costello Vineyards Chardonnay, Napa. Rich and mouth-filling with perceptible oak. *Rolling Stones, Beggars Banquet.*

Jacquart Brut Champagne, France. Very fine head; toasty, creamy flavors, long finish. *Vivaldi Mandolin Concerto.*

Chateau St. Jean Semillon D'Or, Select Late Harvest, Sonoma. Apricot and honeysuckle flavors, very long finish. *Flight of the Bumblebee.*

I would take issue only with that last one. "Very long finish" is more like Ravel's *Bolero* to me. But maybe that's the heady arrogance of a former novice talking.

I won't say it changed my life, but this new, easy way of picking a wine knocked the stuffing out of intimidating wine lists. I still don't ask for the wine list or even reach for it in a big restaurant, but if I get stuck with it, I can hold my own.

"Tell me," I ask the sommelier, "which of these Chardonnays would you say is most like the Los Angeles Lakers? How do these Pinot Noirs stack up against a cashmere sweater? I want a Riesling as solid and comforting as a golden retriever."

All I can tell you is that I've been drinking some Interesting Little Finds lately.

Freelance writer Kit Snedaker is still looking for a wine with the panache of a little black dress.

* * *

Among Flying Corks

*Proper etiquette involves more than
manners in Burgundy.*

"WHATEVER ELSE YOU DO," I SAID TO SADLER, "REMEMBER TO SPIT.
Otherwise, we'll never get through the weekend."

"I'll watch you," he said. "We'll spit together, like they do in
synchronized swimming."

We were in Burgundy, with our wives to keep an eye on us, to
attend the greatest wine auction in the world, held each year in
Beaune. I had been once before, with another friend who was a *cheva-
lier du taste vin*, a knight of the grape, and the experience had taught
me what had to be done if you wanted to survive: spit. Spattered
trousers and purple shoes are a small price to pay for the continued
health of your internal organs, your ability to focus and to speak,
and your reputation as a civilized man able to hold his alcohol.

The sadness is, as I told Sadler, that you will often be spitting
when every taste bud in your palate is begging you to swallow,
because in Beaune, during this one long weekend, you will be
offered dozens, if not hundreds, of some of the finest wines in
France. Those names that you gaze wistfully on restaurant wine
lists—those three-hundred-dollar bottles of Burgundian nectar—
are uncorked and passed around with the generous abandon normally associated with lemonade on a hot day. But spit you must.
There are three days of this to get through, and you'll never be there

at the finish if you swallow everything that's waved under your nose.

The tradition started, oddly enough, with a hospital. In 1443, Nicolas Rolin, chancellor to Duke Philip the Good of Burgundy, founded the Hospices de Beaune and endowed the foundation with vineyards to provide it with income. Other charitable Burgundians followed his example, and today, more than five hundred years later, the hospital costs are still covered by revenue from the wine. Every year, traditionally on the third Sunday in November, the wine is sold at auction. And every year, on the days before and after the auction, the local winegrowers arrange a few diversions of their own.

We were invited to one of them on our first night in Burgundy, a *diner dégustation* at the home of René Jacqueson, a grower in Gevrey-Chambertin. It was to be a gentle introduction to the bottles that lay ahead, and it began in Monsieur Jacqueson's private *cave*.

Down a steep flight of steps we went, inhaling the subterranean bouquet, a wonderful musty mixture of oak, wine, ancient cobwebs, and chilled stone. The *cave* wasn't large—by Burgundian standards at least—but it had been beautifully furnished with several thousand gallons of Gevrey-Chambertin, stored in barrels that lined walls furred and blackened with cellar mold. On top of another barrel in the middle of the room were glasses and half a dozen bottles, each identified by the wine maker's shorthand of chalk squiggles. But I saw nothing in the way of spitter's comforts.

"There's no bucket," I whispered to Sadler. "I think it world be rude to spit on the floor. We'll have to swallow."

He took the news bravely. "Just this once," he said.

There were two other couples with us, and we gathered around Jacqueson as he uncorked the first bottle and started to take us through the vintages. At most other tastings I've attended, this is as close to a religious ceremony as you can get without actually going to church. The wine's age and pedigree are announced in the manner of a bishop murmuring a benediction. The assembled congregation sniffs and gargles with furrowed brow. Then it's time for prayers in the form of solemn, muted comments about the wine's quality: "Exceptionally self-assured…Marvelous finish…Classically structured…Amen."

Jacqueson, however, was not at all of the reverent school of wine-makers. He was a man with a twinkle in his eye and a great sense of humor, particularly when he started talking about the overblown language often used on these occasions.

"This one, for instance," he said, holding his glass up to the light, "is what you and I might simply call 'a promising young wine.'"

We all sipped and gurgled. At this early stage in its development, there was enough tannin in it to pucker the liver, although it would probably be wonderful when it grew up.

Jacqueson grinned. "An expert has described it as 'having the impatience of youth,' whatever that means."

This led to another old classic: "Isn't this wine a little young to be up so late?" And as more bottles were uncorked and poured, we compared winetasting phrases that were unusual or grotesque enough to stick in the mind. Some, like *le goût de la planche*, were logical and accurate. New wine in oak barrels will often have the woody taste of a plank. Other terms were nothing more than desperately far-fetched and unappetizing comparisons: *wet leather, wet dogs, weasels*—and, my favorite candidate from the animal kingdom, a *hare's belly*. I have never come across anybody who has admitted to being on tasting terms with a hare's belly—or a weasel or a wet dog, for that matter—and quite how these creatures have crept into the winetaster's vocabulary is something of a mystery. I suppose the problem is that normal descriptions, those words like fruity, powerful, well made, or complex, are too general. They apply to too many wines. And so the weasels and the hare's bellies are brought out in an attempt to express the differences between one wine and another.

This brought the conversation around to professional wine critics, those poor souls who have to strain their imagination and syntax every day in the course of their work, trying to describe what is often indescribable. The prize for the most outlandish description of the evening went to this exchange, reportedly true, between a critic and a grower.

Critic (having swilled, sluiced, and spat): "Hmm. A distinct *goût de tapis*."

Grower (outraged): "What do you mean, 'a taste of carpet'? How dare you!"

Critic (trying to make amends): "But no ordinary carpet, my friend; a very old, very *distinguished* carpet."

Our host was far too discreet to name the critic. All he would say was, "We would prefer him to do his drinking in Bordeaux."

And with that, we went upstairs to dinner.

It was a marvelous marathon of a meal, five courses prepared by Madame Jacqueson, with a selection of Gevrey-Chambertins prepared by her husband. And in the intermission between the duck and the cheese, there was a music lesson.

It was absolutely necessary, Jacqueson informed us, that we learn the ritual gestures and lyrics of the "Ban de Bourgogne." This was the Burgundian battle cry, a chant accompanied by rhythmic clapping and arcane signals, a kind of drinker's hand jive. We were told it would be performed many times over the weekend, and if we wanted to be part of the festivities, we had to know how to join in.

The lyrics of the chant were no problem: "La la la la" just about covered them, sung or shouted, according to choice, from beginning to end. The hand movements were slightly more complicated. Starting position was with arms bent and the hands, with fingers cupped, held up on either side of the head. With the first chorus, the hands should swivel back and forth from the wrist, as if rotating some circular object, such as the base of a wine bottle. For the middle chorus, the hands should stop swiveling to clap nine times before returning to their original positions for the third chorus. This was to be repeated a second time, at top speed, before participants were allowed to recover with the help of a glass of Gevrey-Chambertin.

We tried it. Sadler showed himself to be a natural, with a wonderfully fluid wrist action and a fine *profundo* bawl. The rest of us did as best we could, making the house sound as though it had been invaded by a bunch of well-oiled soccer fans. More rehearsals had us bellowing and swiveling our hands like native-born Burgundians, and by the time we left the Jacquesons' around one o'clock in the morning, we were judged to be competent enough to perform in public.

As we walked back through the narrow streets, Sadler and I compared spitting notes, and we had to agree that the evening had been a pathetic failure. Number of wines tasted: approximately twelve. Number of times wine ejected from mouth before swallowing: nil.

"We have to do better tomorrow," I said. "Expectorate or perish."

"The problem is," he said, "that we need something to do it in. A *crachoir*. Maybe we should buy a bucket."

The next morning found us window-shopping for portable spittoons in Beaune, a handsome, dignified town that has clearly enjoyed hundreds of years of prosperity. The buildings are stone-built, thick-walled, often with steeply pitched roofs decorated with polychrome tiles. There are cobbled streets and courtyards, ramparts, and Gothic architectural flourishes, and, wherever you look, evidence of what makes the whole place tick: wine. Bottles of it, barrels of it, *caves* to taste it in, thermometers to check its temperature, glasses of every shape and size, corkscrews ranging from the standard waiter's friend to elaborately engineered gadgets for the mechanically minded, silver tasting cups, key rings disguised as bunches of grapes, decanters, pipettes, and enough alcoholic literature to start a boozer's library. I imagine you could buy a box of Kleenex somewhere in town, but the chances are it would have a vintage chart printed on it. Local industry is keenly supported, with one notable exception: An official Burgundian *crachoir* doesn't seem to exist. I had been hoping to equip myself with something functional yet elegant, perhaps engraved with the Beaune coat of arms, or an encouraging motto, or the mayor's autograph, but all we could find were inducements to swallow rather than spit. To his credit, Sadler bore this disappointment well.

Even the medical community in Beuane encourages something a little stronger than aspirin and Alka-Seltzer to relieve what ails you. We stopped at a pharmacy near the main square and looked in disbelief at the contents of the window. Normally, French pharmacies go in for tasteful displays of truncated plastic torsos wearing trusses, or photographs of perfectly formed young women toying with anti-cellulite devices, but not here.

In the center of the window was a life-size human skeleton, made from cardboard. A sign beside the grinning mouth of the skull read *With Moderation*, but this was emphatically contradicted (for medical reasons, I assumed) by the rest of the display, which consisted entirely of bottles of wine captioned with their amazing restorative properties. If the pharmacist—a man after my own heart—was to be trusted, almost every common ailment could be cured by the appropriate wine.

A twinge of arthritis? Drink rosé. Gallstones? Wash them away with a bottle or two of Sancerre. Moulin-à-Vent would take care of your bronchitis, Krug Champagne would ward off the flu, and anyone with tuberculosis would benefit enormously from a bottle of Mercurey. Tension would vanish with Pouilly-Fuissé and, for weight watchers, daily doses of Côte de Beaune would make "daily slimming certain." Other afflictions were mentioned, some of an intensely personal nature, and for everything there was an alcoholic remedy. With one exception: Due either to oversight or tact, there was no mention of cirrhosis of the liver.

There was just enough time before the first tasting of the day to see what was going on in the stands and bars around the place Carnot. It was barely 10:30 A.M., but enthusiasts were already taking a prelunch snack of oysters and chilled Aligoté. A group of Japanese, who obviously never left home without their personal chopsticks, were having some difficulties extracting their oysters, watched with interest by a young man wearing a helium balloon attached to the zipper on his fly. And then, with thunderous drum rolls and piercing whistles, a procession of stilt-walkers took over the square. The sound was enough to cause a sharp pain in the temples, and we were happy to escape to the peace and quiet of a tasting in the *caves* of Bouchard Aîné & Fils.

The Bouchard people have been growing and selling wine since 1750, and as you tour their cellars, you cannot help thinking that this may be the perfect spot to sit out a nuclear war or a presidential election. A million bottles, stored in racks, and endless avenues of barrels stretched out and disappeared into the gloom. Famous vineyards, great vintages, the scent of wine dozing toward maturity—the hand felt incomplete, indeed naked, without a glass.

Our host took pity on us and led us upstairs to the tasting room, where bottles and glasses were laid out next to plates of *gougères*. These are small, light, delicious nuggets of cheese-flavored puff pastry that have the effect of softening and thus improving the taste of young wine in the mouth. They are also salty enough to encourage a healthy thirst. But this was to be an exercise in connoisseurship, not an occasion for guzzling. We were shown the stone sinks against the wall and reminded that spitting was recommended for anyone who, like us, had plans to attend the auction that afternoon.

It was interesting to see how a minor sartorial touch separated the practiced connoisseurs from the rest of us. Veteran tasters wore bow ties, or tucked their ties inside their shirts. The wisdom of this became apparent as the first salvo of spitting took place over the sink and the dangling end of the silk tie belonging to a natty gentleman spitting next to me received a direct hit from a shower of Pinot Noir.

"Young wines to begin with," our host had said. "Fish before caviar." And so we started in 1998 and worked our way backward, fortified by *gougères* and, as far as I was concerned, finding it increasingly unreasonable to spit. Young wines were no problem. The test came when age had smoothed out the rough edges and the wine filled the mouth with a soft glow. Others may have found it possible to consign a big, round, luscious 1988 Fixin to the sink without a sense of loss, but not me. To distract myself, I studied the techniques of other tasters, and they put my simple sniffing and swilling to shame.

In contrast to the informal tasting of the night before, this was a serious ritual, conducted with immense deliberation. First, the wine is held up to the light—in this case one of the candles in the tasting room—to assess its color. It is then swirled around the glass to open it up to the air and bring out the bouquet. The nose is applied to the top of the glass for several rapt moments, with the obligatory furrowed brow. A mouthful is taken, the eyes are raised to heaven, and the sound effects begin. Air is sucked into the mouth to join the wine, making much the same noise as a child eating soup. The wine is distributed throughout the mouth, assisted by flexing of the cheeks and exaggerated chewing motions. More gurgling. Finally, when a thorough oral investigation has taken place—the teeth having been rinsed, and the palate imbued with taste sensations—out comes the mouthful to splatter against the stone sink, your shoes, and your trousers. You can imagine how this routine, repeated twenty or thirty times with breaks for learned discussion about the character of the wines, can easily take up an entire morning.

We left the *cave*, and had to dodge a second squad of stilt-walkers who were tottering down the street. Cars had been banned from the center of town for the weekend, but there was still a risk of being run over by some of the pedestrians. Many of them were carrying silver *taste vins* and weaving erratically through the crowd with the preoccupied air of people determined not to miss a single tasting. There were several to choose from—a full day's work if you were up to it and didn't have a busy afternoon ahead.

Over lunch, we were given a briefing by a young and

There's a simple reason that European wine seems complicated compared to American wine. In the States, wines are identified first by the grapes they're made from. You can count the world-class wine grapes on your fingers, and the big five (Cabernet Sauvignon, Chardonnay, Merlot, Pinot Noir, and Sauvignon Blanc) will get you through 90 percent of most wine lists. On the Continent, however, wines are identified first by where they're made, and there are hundreds of wine-growing villages throughout France, Italy, and Spain. Place is so strongly associated with wine naming in Europe that even wineries that stand for their region, such as Mouton Rothschild in Bordeaux, don't name their grapes (mostly Cabernet Sauvignon) on their bottles. If you taste something you like while traveling, ask which grapes are in the bottle so you can turn that knowledge into drinking pleasure back home.

—TE

impressively well-informed lady from the Beaune tourist office. This, she told us, was the oldest charity auction in the world, now in its 140th year. The prices paid for the Hospices' wines, would be a guide to the prices of the Burgundy generally, and historically they went up. And up. And up. In 1990, the average price of a *pièce*, or lot, was 350,000 francs. By 1999, it had risen to 456,000 francs ($65,000). Total sales in the same period had gone from 21 million francs to 31 million (more than $4 million). Add to that the cost to the buyer of keeping the wine for several years, bottling, shipping, and a reasonable profit, and it is easy to see why those three-digit prices appear with such horrifying regularity on restaurant lists.

Even so, there was no shortage of buyers, as we saw when we arrived at the auction. The long, high room was filled with them— mostly professional *négoçiants* from America, Britain, France, Germany, Hong Kong, Japan, and Switzerland—all bent diligently over their catalogs. There was also a scattering of black-clad refugees from show business, one or two glamorous women of a certain age who would not have looked out of place at a fashion show as they crossed their legs and adjusted their sunglasses against the glare of publicity, and an assortment of gentlemen from the media, festooned with electronic appendages.

Bidding began just after 2:30 P.M., with bids being picked up by *rabatteurs*, the auctioneer's assistants who were stationed at various points around the floor. Their task wasn't easy. I looked in vain for any exuberant or even obvious signals from the buyers—a hand upraised, a wave of the catalog, a recurring cough—but there was nothing that demonstrative. It was clear that some very low-key sign language was being used, perhaps no more than the twitch of a pencil or the tap of a nose. It was equally clear that this was not the place to make expansive gestures. One false twitch could cost you dearly, and I noticed that even the French were keeping their hands uncharacteristically still while they muttered among themselves.

As the bidding continued, the smile grew on the auctioneer's face. Once again, prices were up. We learned later that the average increase had been 11 percent. A good day for charity, a good day for Burgundy, and, of course, a good day for Beaune. Walking back through town after the auction, we passed the pharmacy with the skeleton, and the skull's grin seemed to be even wider, as if reflecting the general mood of satisfaction with another record year.

Our day was far from over. Dinner that night—a gala dinner at the Hôtel Dieu—promised to be the most formal event of the weekend. *Tenue de soirée*, or evening dress, was to be worn. We were advised to take a large spoonful of olive oil, neat, to line the stomach in preparation for the downpour of wine. This was not to be an evening of spitting. Another essential, so we were told, was a pair of thick socks to ward off the chill from the flagstone floor—a tip that was wasted on our wives, who felt that socks and evening dresses were somehow not what they wanted to be seen in.

We arrived, as requested on the invitation, at nine o'clock, making our way through a double-line of white-coated waiters into a magnificent barrel-vaulted room hung with tapestries. Candlelight flickered on the bottles and glasses and silverware that had been laid out on thirty-one long, immaculately arranged, and surprisingly empty tables. Where was everybody? There was not a sign of our three hundred fellow revelers, and it was then I remembered that punctuality on formal occasions in France is seldom rewarded by a welcoming glass. Politeness dictates that you wait until the other guests have arrived. They, naturally, would prefer to avoid having to endure a long, dry waiting period, and therefore they make a point of always being fashionably late. So there we were, surrounded by glorious but untouchable bottles. "Meursault, Meursault everywhere," as Sadler said, "and not a drop to drink."

This would pass, we told each other, and picked up the menus in search of a little encouragement. There was a long and heartfelt sigh from Sadler as he reached the page listing the wines that were on offer that evening: thirty-eight of them, the great whites and reds of Burgundy, donated by growers and *négoçiants*, the Hospices de Beaune, and the mayor. Such a list you would find nowhere else, filled with *grand cru* Chablis, Puligny-Montrachet, Échézeaux, Clos Vougeot—the kind of wine Alexandre Dumas said should be drunk kneeling, with the head bared.

It was half an hour before the last empty seats and the first empty glasses were filled. The great room was a picture of elegance: the bejeweled ladies in long dresses (some of them so long I suspected them of concealing thick socks), the gentlemen in their black and white, hair and mustaches sleek with pomade, cuff links and shirt studs twinkling. It was a scene of refined formality. It was destined not to last.

The crack in the social ice came with the appearance, early on in the dinner, of the cabaret, a male vocal group introduced as Les Joyeux Bourguignons. They were dressed in their best long aprons, red and green pompons at their necks in place of ties, glasses and bottles in their hands instead of musical instruments. They set the tone for the rest of the evening with their first song, a perennial local hit entitled "Boire un Petit Coup C'est Agréable" (rough translation: "It's Great to Drink"). This was followed by an audience-participation session as we were led into the first of many renditions of the Burgundy supporters' club battle cry. *La La's* were bellowed and hands were waggled. Almost at once, formality disappeared, never to return.

The food came and went, the bottles came and came, and inhibitions began to be cast aside like corks. A group at a nearby table stood up to perform a series of Mexican waves with their napkins, while one of the men—intent on striptease, by the look of him—climbed up on his chair and ripped off his jacket and tie before being distracted and ultimately subdued with the help of a bottle of Aloxe-Corton. Toasts were proposed: to the greater glory of the grape, to the continuing success of the Channel Tunnel, to the entente cordiale, to heroes of the Swiss Navy, to anything else that might provide an excuse for glasses to be refilled. Not that excuses seemed to be necessary.

I looked down the table at Sadler, who was investigating a bottle of 1993 Échézeaux. We had often talked about the enormous difference between popular foreign perceptions of the French and our own experience of living among them, and an evening like this emphasized the difference. Where was he, the so-called typical Frenchman, with his humorless reserve and his arrogance and his infuriating superiority complex? He was certainly not here, not in this warm, friendly, relaxed, and, it must be said, increasingly tipsy gathering. It seemed to me, as the Échézeaux took hold and I looked around, that they were all wonderful people, drinking a wonderful wine, and living in a wonderful country.

Fixing Sadler with a moist and sentimental eye, I was about to propose a toast to *La Belle France*. How lucky we were to live here, to be surrounded by such delightful people, such splendid architecture, such rich culture, such stirring history, such ravishing countryside. In my wine-sodden French, it would probably have been a disastrously embarrassing moment. Fortunately, Sadler beat me to it.

He raised his glass. I waited for some graceful and appropriate line from Molière or Voltaire or Proust, delivered in perfect, accentless Sadler French. But it was not to be.

"To those who spit," he said. "Poor sods."

Former British ad man Peter Mayle has made a career out of living in the South of France and writing books about it, including the best-seller A Year in Provence. *His eighth book, from which this story was excerpted, is* French Lessons: Adventures with Knife, Fork, and Corkscrew. *Mayle lives with his wife and their two dogs. His hobbies include walking, reading, writing, and lunch.*

Wine and Blood in Puligny–Montrachet

One patron saint, 150,000 wine-soaked revelers.

AN EMPTY HANGAR IN AN ABANDONED QUARRY, BEFORE DAWN ON one of the coldest mornings of the winter, seemed an unlikely place and time to throw a party. As I trudged the last few yards up the hill a figure at my elbow announced in a gruff voice that it was minus nine degrees and the clouds of his breath added to the dank enveloping fog, through which the lights of cars and torches appeared as pale haloes in the dark. Further down the hill a huge and faintly glowing shape—the marquee—was already illumined in preparation for the great banquet of Saint Vincent (scheduled for that afternoon) but here, in the lee of Bernard Clerc's house just below the hamlet of Blagny, the crowds of converging Burgundians met in the shadows and the mist, like the ghosts of Hades.

But these were very substantial ghosts and they had brought their saints. There were dozens of them, patrons, of the village *confréries*, crowded on to the long, frost-rimmed trestles which had been set up outside the hangar, and more were arriving every minute. A man would appear out of the darkness with a carved wooden figure unceremoniously bundled under one arm and a folding carrier under the other. The carrier would be spread across the trestles, the figure placed carefully on top and perhaps decorated with elaborate garlands of foliage and artificial flowers before its guardian hurried inside the doorway ahead of us, to the party. Ranged in haphazard order, side by side, these wooden saints formed a strange and agreeable throng, brought here from as far north as Chablis and as far south as the extremities of the Côte Chalonnaise. Some were finely carved and had the baroque flamboyance of the Saint Vincent from Morey St.-Denis, three or four feet tall; others were simple, rough-hewn and unadorned, like the tiny figure (no more than nine inches high) which had made the journey from the diminutive village of Orches, up in the hills of the Hautes Côtes de Beaune.

Most were representations of Saint Vincent, an obscure Spaniard martyred at Valence in 304 who has come to be the patron of wine-growers because of the symbolic echoes of his name (vin, sang: the sacrament of the Last Supper) rather than for any particular affinities with the story of his life or death. But some village *confréries* have chosen other saints, for reasons which range from the obvious (Saint Aubin, name of both village and patron) to the patriotic (Monthélie's choice of Saint Louis) to the obscure: Volnay is curiously represented by a gay, gilded cherub in a perspex case, labeled Saint Cyr. Puligny's *confrérie*, one of the earliest to be founded (in 1826), is dedicated to the great Cistercian, Saint Bernard—a native Burgundian whose monks did more than anyone else to establish viticulture on the slopes of the Côte d'Or and who gave their name to the road, Chemin des Moines, by which we had ascended the hill to Blagny.

For well over a century it has been customary in each of the wine villages of Burgundy to celebrate the Feast of Saint Vincent on January 22 by taking the *confrérie's* saint on a tour of the village. He is carried in procession to the church for mass and thence to the house of a family of *vignerons* who will have the honor of looking after him for the succeeding year. The new hosts naturally welcome the other villagers to their cellars for a glass of wine, after which everyone sits down for a splendid feast. Thus the saint "turns" from house to house every year, as the honored guest of each confrère in succession.

In 1938 the Chevaliers du Tastevin organized the Saint Vincent

Tournante as an event on a much grander scale, hosted in turn by a different wine village on the first Saturday after January 22. This celebration has grown bigger year by year and it has become customary for each village to try to outdo its predecessor in the scale and splendor of the decorations, the magnificence of the feasts, and the size of the crowds. In 1991 it was Puligny's turn. For over two years this tiny community of 500 inhabitants had been preparing to welcome 150,000 visitors within the space of two days. But the real celebration, more important than all the razzmatazz for the tourists, began with this party at dawn for the *confrères*, the saint-bearers from all over Burgundy.

Inside the hangar (which normally houses the tractors and mechanical harvesters of Bernard Clerc) approximately fifty wooden barrels stood on end, one for every *confrérie*, each identified by a card bearing the village name. On top of every barrel was a magnum of the Cuvée St. Vincent (a blend of Puligny-Montrachet made with wine contributed by the growers of the village), a ring of glasses, and a pile of bread; and around these essential supplies were clustered the representatives of each village, cheerful red-faced men and women, well wrapped against the cold. Some wore *tastevins* on silver chains, some sported curious caps or sashes or badges of office. Various bands were warming up in the corners of this cavernous hangar, with squeaks of pipes, clatter of drums, and the deep burp of enormous tubas, whose fat serpentine coils wound their way around stout bandsmen, wearing uniforms which ranged from the full-dress absurdity of potentates from the land of Babar (complete with white spats) to a simple blue peaked cap, tilted casually over one ear. Louis Carillon, president of Puligny's *confrérie* and therefore host for this occasion, stood with an air of cheerful self-importance, surrounded by his *confrères*, as new arrivals pushed through the throng to shake him by the hand, greeting him grandly as "Monsieur le Président." A film crew conducted interviews, under the blaze of portable arc lights, and local pressmen pointed flashguns at all the pretty girls. Towards the edges of this heterogeneous crowd were several knots of people who seemed to have found their way to this gathering from the bleak fastnesses of a more primitive age. My attention was caught by a particularly wild-eyed bunch from St-Romain: gleeful, angular men (all elbows and knees) and big, voracious women, wearing clothes so roughly cut, from such thick material, that they might have been chopped with an axe from felt wadding and elephant hide.

Each village is expected to send two representatives (rewarded for their presence by a dinner at Clos Vougeot as guests of the Chevaliers du Tastevin), but most had come in parties of six or eight. Several hundred people were crowded into the quarry and the first arrivals had been drinking since before seven; a cloud of cigarette smoke hung in the air and the noise was deafening.

As the darkness faded into a gray dawn there were calls on the loudspeaker for everyone to form up outside in the designated order of procession. Two men from each village shouldered the little wooden stretchers on which the saints were carried, another took charge of each *confrérie's* banner (richly embroidered with a pair of clasped hands or similar device, symbol of the mutual assistance which the *confrères* are sworn to provide one another in times of sickness or misfortune) and everyone else fell into place along the route. It was all remarkably well organized, with stakes at regular intervals along the first couple of hundred yards, adorned with the name and coat of arms of each village, and with several stewards armed with walkie-talkies coordinating the formation and departure of this great procession and ensuring that the four or five bands were stationed at sufficient distance from one another to minimize the clash of different tunes. A black squirrel raced up the pine tree beside me and suddenly we were off.

It was a cold morning; misty air, frost on every branch and vine, a chill smokiness that muted color and softened every sound. A quiet murmuring of cheerful conversation ran along the lengthening line, a droning continuos beneath the music of the bands, but many remained silent and self-absorbed. Imperceptibly I became aware that whatever the promotional trappings of the rest of the weekend's festivities, there had survived in this procession an unexpected devotional camaraderie, a sense of pilgrimage and penance, celebration and thanksgiving. As the banners and the bands, the people and their saints flowed down the hill and through the vineyards, time flickered. This was a Journey of the Magi, illuminated in the winter landscape of the medieval Book of Hours, or a nineteenth-century Mission of the Cross, painted by Courbet; and every face had been viewed through the lens of Marcel Carnet or Cartier Bresson. Whether mobile, melancholy, and down at heel or jaunty and sharp, alluring or dowdy, stiffly gaunt or bonhomously well-fed, each was unmistakable, indefinably and timelessly French.

Ahead of me the band fell silent, save for the rattle of the drums. The white-gloved hands of the uniformed bandsmen dropped by their sides, swinging loosely as they marched, but the right hand of one brushed the left hand of another, then caught and twined together across the narrow gap that separated a spotty, lovelorn boy from his mischievous girlfriend. She turned to him and smiled, then their hands parted and they raised their cornets with the rest, for an exuberant fanfare that blared through the morning mists like the risen sun.

But the sun itself stayed hidden as the procession curled down the lane above Clos de la Garenne and turned right across the hillside

---

One moment Burgundy's wines are praised as marvelous, in the next breath, they may be faulted for maddening inconsistency. The two principal grapes, the Pinot Noir and Chardonnay, have found a genuine compatibility with the soils of the Côte d'Or with the potential for producing exceptional wines. The inconsistency arises with a number of growers in a single *terroir* making their own wine in their own way, so there is no one Chambertin, no one Le Montrachet. Neither the praise nor blame lies altogether with nature or man. Important but obscure variations in the geology and soil occur in very short distances. One *terroir* may produce superb wines while an adjacent one, which on the surface appears quite similar, yields wines of lesser quality. This is one of the confounding fascinations of wine.

—James E. Wilson, *Terroir*

between the low walls of the ancient track which leads to the Cross of Montrachet. Here, at the junction that separates the Premier Cru vineyards of Le Cailleret and Les Pucelles from the Grands Crus of Montrachet and Bâtard, the marchers turned left, to the east, towards the village. The entire route, like all those leading to Puligny, was lined with scraggy Christmas trees which were embellished with colorful paper flowers and bows of blue and silver foil, and as we approached the first houses the decorations grew more lavish. Green arches spanned the road, there were flags above our heads and every bush and branch sprouted flowers, hundreds and thousands of them, a startling paper counterfeit of spring.

Crowds awaited our coming at the entrance to the village and the procession slowed almost to a standstill. Many of the throng were already clutching glasses of wine and the noise was of bubbling excitement. The frozen fingers of the bandsmen seemed to find life again, the drummers beat a rhythm that echoed from wall to wall across the narrow streets, and we pressed on in triumph into Puligny, with the saints swaying above our shoulders, the banners of the *confréries* raised to meet those that sagged across the road, and the urge to dance lifting the heels of the lighthearted as they linked arms in anticipation of the evening.

The procession pushed through a dense hubbub of onlookers down the Rue de Poiseul and erupted into Place Johannisberg where more crowds were awaiting us, clustered around an absurd but spectacular set piece: two vast prancing horses, twenty or thirty feet high, mounted by knights in cardboard armor whose stuffing was packed in lumpy legs like drooping sausages and whose shields bore the arms of Puligny. Other figures were propped on balconies and grouped in courtyards around old wine presses or siting astride ancient tractors: figures of monks and knights and maidens in medieval dress, and *vignerons* in smocks and berets, with straw poking out from underneath their hats or behind their masks or with the stiff elongated fingers on rigid limbs which betrayed their transformation from shop window dummies. At intervals across every street hung blue banners emblazoned in gold letters with the names of Puligny's vineyards, from the glory of Montrachet to the humblest *lieux-dits* of the village. And everywhere the flowers.

A line of cherry trees had burst into vivid pink blossom along a pavement in Place des Marronniers and the window boxes of the Hôtel Le Montrachet dripped with pink and purple sweet peas, so real you could almost smell them. Yellow roses climbed in profusion up the wall of their neighbor's house, above a bed planted with giant irises in every possible and improbable color. Pale purple wisteria dripped from one balcony, cascades of laburnum from another. There were pots of pink geraniums, tubs of hydrangeas, baskets of azaleas and dahlias; tulips sprouted from the pavement and a magnificent *Magnolia soulangiana* spread its white flowers over the angle of a wall. As we processed down La Grande Rue, turned left down a narrow alley, and wound our way slowly around the edge of the village to return to the Place du Monument, we passed hedges bright with paper petals and huge opulent bushes of gaudy roses, pushing their improbable blossoms through the bars of an old railing. In a small walled kitchen garden the leafless branches of a dozen willow bushes sprang from the bare red earth, apparently covered in tiny white catkins. Above a nearby fence erupted the long stems of winter-flowering jasmine, streams of yellow against the gray sky.

With the bands blaring and the marchers stamping their feet and slapping their hands against the penetrating cold, with breath rising like the steam from Monsieur Champion's still, the sheer surreal splendor of it all made the head spin. Halted momentarily in a side street as the procession squeezed its way towards the square, I noticed a bush of yellow forsythia, no more than four feet tall, and it occurred to me to count the tiny flowers. A rough calculation showed that this single bush was covered in at least three hundred yellow paper flowers, each individually made, each individually wired to its slender shoot or branch. Multiply that figure by the hundreds of bushes and trees, the hedgerows and the gardens, the tubs and pots and baskets and bouquets and garlands of flowers which decorated midwinter Puligny and you begin to get some idea of the extraordinary scale of the preparations which had occupied the villagers for the previous two years.

And so, finally, we arrived at the Place du Monument, already seething with people. The stewards with their walkie-talkies struggled to maneuver the bands and the saints into their allotted positions near the center of the square, where a gaggle of small children dressed in traditional Burgundian costume chatted and nudged one another at the feet of the red-robed dignitaries clustered near the war memorial, the officers of the Chevaliers du Tastevin. Their standard bearer was a benevolent old duffer who beamed through his spectacles at the children, while his colleagues stood around in their quasi-historical splendor, mimicking the characterful profiles of early Renaissance portraits. They were attended by half a dozen lean, booted men in red coats, white stocks, and riding caps, with hunting horns curled around their shoulders and faces like foxes, sniffing the crisp morning air. There, too, was the mayor of Puligny, Monsieur Lafond, with a tricolor sash slung slantwise across his overcoat, and the Sub-prefect of Burgundy, and the gendarmes, and of course the pressmen who obligingly snapped their shutters as the Sub-pereect, an experienced politician, made agreeable small talk with the mayor.

The band struck up a drum-roll, the mayor laid a wreath on the war memorial, and there was one of those brief unexpected silences, perfectly timed (like a ripple of wind across a field of standing barley) before it was hats off for the Marseillaise. As this hymn of the revolution lifted over the crowd, lifting our hearts with it irresistibly, I thought of that fevered night of brandy and inspiration in Strasbourg, when Rouget de Lisle scribbled music and words in a frenzy of patriotic exhilaration, with the sure, show-stopping instinct of Rodgers and Hammerstein.

Then everyone was smiling and chatting again and the guardians of the saints from all the other villages of the Côte d'Or packed up their charges and furled their banners and raced home for their own celebration of the feast day, while the bands began to play and the men of Puligny lifted the little figure of Saint Bernard and started on another circuit of the streets, and we all headed for the church.

Simon Loftus is a wine merchant, hotelier, restaurateur, and writer of wine catalogs as well as books. His books include Anatomy of the Wine Trade, A Pike in the Basement, *and* Puligny Montrachet: Journal from a Village in Burgundy, *from which this piece was excerpted.*

DEANNE MUSOLF CROUCH

Catching Dinner

Wine country can inspire rare
culinary creativity.

CULINARY ADVENTURES SEEMED TO BIND CATHY AND ME. AND food brought out the best in us. Mischievous by nature, Cathy was always 100 percent authentic when it came to her ingredients. Normally impatient and glib, I would go to the most tedious ends for a good meal. As a culinary team we were unstoppable.

While students in England, we trudged up sodden grassy hillsides behind a curious man we'd met caving who claimed fungi expertise, and we plunked various wild mushrooms into our bucket at his dubious nod.

We conjured up Mexican food in an English town devoid of poblano chiles, cilantro, cumin, and pinto beans—even covering our clothes in flour while making homemade tortillas—to surprise Cathy's German roommate.

In a college dorm kitchen we played baseball with a doomed batch of chocolate chip cookies (for neither of us would ever deign to eat bad food, no matter how broke or hungry). Later, we dared take an advanced cooking lesson from the chefs at the Los Angeles Biltmore and relished even the most useless of techniques, happily filing away details such as how to bone and deep-fry a turkey.

Our postcards to one another over the years detailed not scenes but culinary solace: the ceviche I ate in a tiny Ecuadorian coastal town, or the delicate flavor of the sushi she made sailing the Pacific from Mexico to New Zealand. And whenever we got back together we seemed drawn into food; shopping we'd end up not trying on clothes but squeezing lemons or fantasizing over smoked salmon. In our homes we'd invariably end up in the kitchen, chopping and simmering, sampling and sharing bites, and talking about other meals we'd had since we'd been together last. In conversations with Cathy, heady aromas would invariably arise.

So when I moved to Brion-sur-Ource, near France's Burgundy-Champagne border, briefly, to write *á roman* as doomed as the chocolate chip cookies (but, alas, not salvageable in makeshift baseball), it was no surprise that my first stroll with Cathy when she came to visit was along the Ource River. It ran silkily through the disused *manoir* I called home, I pointed out, past the picture-perfect French *jardin* with tiny lettuces lined up like so many three-dimensional *fleurs de lis*, past the *orangeraie*, and on to the fish canals.

"Fish canals?" Cathy stopped abruptly. "You mean there are fish in this river?"

Before I could reply we were dragging the rowboat out of the ice house down to the river and paddling out into the stream. Sure enough, there were fish in the river, their undersides flashing flirtatiously in the sun. "Trout," Cathy proclaimed. Then she looked at me pointedly and added, "Flash-fried, with a little caper-lemon butter." The gauntlet had been thrown down.

Seeing is not searing, however. For the first time, we had met a food that was our match.

For the rest of Cathy's visit we dedicated ourselves to stalking a meal of French trout. We were totally new to the fishing game; we had held nary a pole between us. We had to invent trout fishing from the ground up. First, we borrowed the net belonging to the concierge's son, Aurelian, and tried netting one from the boat. I had netted *le coquillage* at Aurelian's bidding many times before, but we discovered that nonshelled creatures could be a bit more wily.

Next, we fashioned poles out of broomsticks then willow branches. Using those, we experimented with a variety of bait from worms to dragonflies and spiders. We even tried macaroni. Alas, not a nibble. The trout were earning our respect—they seemed as picky about their food as we were.

Meanwhile, as a back-up, we gathered a herd of enormous escargot (much easier to catch than trout, we discovered) and each night as we analyzed the day's fishing failings, we fed bits of tender lettuce to our snails corralled safely in a fruit crate.

"The boat's movement is frightening off the fish!" we decided one evening. The next day we crept into the boat and fished from where it was moored. No luck. "They can see us in the boat!" we exclaimed that evening, and then tried slinking into the boat below the gunnel and fished by feel. We fished under trees and in bright sun; we cast our die in early morning and dead of night. Still, we rowed home each time with our bucket empty.

The night before Cathy's last full day in Brion-sur-Ource, we gave up on *la truite*, and instead prepared and savored our escargot in the Frenchest style we could muster.

With only one full day together remaining, we decided to abandon the Ource altogether and hitchhike to Chablis for a sure-fire culinary adventure: wine tasting.

> When traveling, you can match food and drink relatively easily with two questions. In humbler places, simply ask for the local wine. *Vino locale, vin du pays*—use whatever phrase you have, and you will be brought what the people of the area drink with the food you are eating. In swankier eateries, just ask your waiter what he would have with the same dish at home (the idea is to get a good match at a reasonable price). There is a third alternative, which works a surprisingly high percentage of the time: order a beer.
>
> —TE

After we had a bit of a run-in with the French police (it is not illegal to hitchhike, but it is illegal to leave home without your passport we were informed), an old woman with a station wagon full of yapping, licking, frolicking Corgies picked us up. She dropped us at the far end of the town of Chablis. She pointed out the best *caves* and wished us a *"Bon journée."*

Like Dorothy and her friends entering the Emerald City, we slowly, savoringly, virtually tiptoed up the road toward Chablis and over its old stone bridge. Ahead lay rolling hills of vineyards combed with vines, disappearing into the distance. I couldn't wait to stop at our first *cave*. As we topped the bridge, I could almost taste the wine on my tongue.

Then Cathy caught my arm. Silently she pointed over the side of the bridge into the wide, translucent Seine. There, huge trout hung in the current, the size of Toyotas. Cathy and I looked at each other. Our desire wouldn't be slain; wine would have to wait. The next thing I knew we were standing at the counter in a sporting goods store, trying to buy a net—without the word and with precious little to describe it in hand gestures.

Once we had procured a net, I tossed it jauntily over my shoulder and we made our way back to the Seine. *Truite almondine*, trout in wine sauce, trout sushi, I didn't care. One of these bad boys would clearly make several meals. We suddenly felt very at home in France; we could fish anywhere, anytime!

We cemented our plan even as we descended the steep long bank: I would go upstream and "frighten" the fish by slapping the water with a branch. Meanwhile, Cathy, stationed downstream, would lie in wait for one of these big dudes to cruise by in flight. In the rarefied wine country sunshine, amid the fantasyland of vineyards and *caves*, it seemed almost logical. We took up our positions.

Thigh deep in the Seine, Cathy gave me the nod, and I started slapping. I watched the water intensely, but, from where I stood, the sun hit the water just so. The river wound away into the darkness under the bridge like a rippled sheet of foil. I never saw a fin flicker, never saw a trout flinch, never saw a trout, in fact. But Cathy must be able to see them, I decided.

Nimble, ever-ready Cathy, too, watched and waited. And waited. And, chagrined, waited some more. She motioned for me to hit the water again. She crouched, holding the net like a tennis player holds her racket: at the ready, poised for action. I hit the water with my branch again. Nothing.

Then, from up on the bridge, we heard someone clear his throat. We looked up. A couple had stopped to watch our little show. In a very American accent, the man laughingly called out, "You're American, aren't you?"

Cathy's shoulders dropped. The spell was broken. I suddenly saw this through their eyes: Our food quest had been reduced to nothing more than the foolish antics of vacationing Yanks. Embarrassed, we quickly splashed to the bank, then back up the muddy slope to the bridge. There the couple (dentists from Los Angeles) said no more about the fishing; instead they invited us to join them on a winetasting tour in their plush, air-conditioned sedan. We soon forgot our quest. Instead we sipped and laughed and enjoyed. Afterward, they offered to treat us to dinner.

Once seated at an outdoor wrought-iron table set with crystal and white linen, the man leaned forward on his elbows and asked, finally, "So what *were* you doing down there in that river?"

Oh, no, I thought, a knot growing in my stomach. Here it comes: the ribbing, the jokes.

But Cathy looked at me and flashed her mischievous grin. "We were trying to catch dinner," she said. "And," she added, raising her glass to them in a toast, "it looks like we did."

DeAnne Musolf Crouch writes a travel column and a food column for the Santa Barbara News-Press. *She has also written for numerous magazines including* Life, The Economist, The Washington Post, Fortune, Shape *and* Longevity, *and was editor-in-chief of* Rock & Ice, *a climbing magazine. One of her outdoor adventure stories, on shark diving in Tahiti, won a national magazine award in 1999.*

DAVID DARLINGTON

✦ ✦ ✦

Wine Fiascos

In Italy, a "fiasco" might be a bottle
of Chianti—or it might not.

FOR THE SEMI-KNOWLEDGEABLE WINE BUFF, TRAVEL IN EUROPE CAN be a dream—or it can be an adult version of pin-the-tail-on-the donkey. Success depends, as in most areas of travel, on how adventurous you are, how well you know the language, and how much guff you're willing to give (and take from) people who can hardly understand you to start with.

On a recent trip to Italy, my experience bore a decided resemblance to the parlor embarrassments of youth: don a blindfold, spin around, and stick your companions with something that only a mule would accept.

The game wasn't made any easier by the local rules. Italy produces and sells more wine than almost any other country on earth—a circumstance heralding good news and bad. On the up side, wine is everywhere; however, as the venerable Hugh Johnson writes in *The World Atlas of Wine*, "Italy has a serious drawback: an impossible confusion of names. Because wine is omnipresent, so much a part of everyday life, made by so many proud and independent people, every conceivable sort of name is pressed into use to mark originality." Factor in the national characteristic of go-with-the-flow insouciance (not to say passivity or indifference) and you can find yourself groping for an oenological donkey as big as a brontosaurus.

My first fiasco occurred near the town of Voghera, on the border between Lombardy and Piedmont, southwest of Milan—excellent wine country, as it happens. By way of a disclaimer, let me note that I was traveling with a group of American bicyclists—people not especially noted for their gourmet tastes. (A wine buff doesn't know the meaning of depression until he asks a table of a dozen people, "Who wants wine?" and nobody raises a hand.)

On this particular evening, four of us had gotten separated from the main group, so an opportunity suddenly loomed to eat something other than pizza for dinner. We made our way to the nearest town and found the central square, where a clutch of nattily attired students informed us that it was a holiday and everything was closed. Except, that is, for a pizzeria.

The joint was jumping when we arrived, which we took to bode well (even if it *was* the only open place in town). There were lots of wine bottles on the walls, but Italian Wine Problem #2 is that relatively few restaurants offer anything other than general categories on their wine lists. The most important things to know are years and producers, but a typical list will say only: *"Barbera—Dolcetto—Valpolicella,"* etc.

In this simple small-town eatery, most of the names were so obscure that even my pocket wine encyclopedia failed to include them. I did recognize a word in one of the names, however: Sangiovese, the principal grape of Chianti. I pointed it out to the waiter and sat back, anticipating a satisfying encounter with an unknown—but undoubtedly delicious—local wine.

American yuppies abroad might be surprised to learn how finicky Italians aren't about wine. For example, seldom is seen such foolishness as displaying a label before pulling a cork or offering a taste to the person who ordered. Our waiter had uncorked the bottle before it reached our table, where he banged it down and vanished without so much as a *"Va bene?"*

Unfortunately, I could already see through the backlit glass that *bene* it wasn't. There was another word in the name that I'd over-

looked: *"Rosato."* As I could now clearly see, in this stronghold of
solid red wine, I'd ordered a rosé.

Oh well—live and learn.
On to the Alps and the town
of Aosta. In the morning I
climbed a mountain on my
bicycle, then spent the late
afternoon strolling around the
city, an ancient Roman
colony. On a side street near
the glacier-fed Dora Baltea
River, I watched a car full of
correspondents from *La
Gazzetta dello Sport* pull up
and pile into a trattoria.
Needless to say, these veteran
cycling journalists didn't share
my companions' aversion to
the grape.

On the way back to my
hotel, I stumbled on a beguil-
ing little restaurant in an alley.
Decorated with a colorful
painting of a funny-looking
bird, it was called Pam Pam—
"Trattoria degli Artiste." I
asked a lady in the store next
door if the place was good,
and she said that it was. So I
returned that evening with
three friends: one American,
one French, one Italian.

In the entryway were sev-
eral photographs of the
tanned, mustachioed, curly-
haired proprietor with

One of the surest signs that
an American has been to
Europe is a willingness to drink
pink wine in public. *Rosé* is the
French word for blush wine,
which falls halfway between reds
and whites not just in color, but
in weight, texture, alcohol, and
other respects. Italians call it
rosato. Spaniards drink enough of
the stuff to have categories for
it: *rosado* for the more intensely
colored wines, and *clarete* for the
lighter ones. Rosé is the most
versatile of wines with food. In
the Mediterranean basin, it's
often the lunch wine of choice:
hearty enough to stand up to
flavorful, rustic cooking but not
so heavy as to knock you over.
If they can, champagne makers
almost always make a rosé version of their bubbly, because it
too is a fantastic accompaniment
to food. There are dozens of
rosés made in the U.S., although
you have to move fast when you
find a good one—those in the
know scoop them up.

—TE

tanned, mustachioed, curly-haired Italian pop stars. A cornucopia of glistening antipasti graced a side table; another inviting collection of wine bottles adorned the wall. Nevertheless, the list still showed nothing but types.

Determined to get a good wine this time, I decided to ask the owner for help. In his stead, a sommelier appeared: lean, narrow-eyed, and unsmiling, the man seemed to regard me with suspicion. I asked the vintage of the Chianti Classico; he answered 1995, which at the time seemed a bit young. The other choices— Barbera, Bardolino, et al.—though undoubtedly decent, didn't pique my interest. There was, however, an Amarone, a red wine from the Veneto that I'd heard described as big and rich. The steward said it was a '91.

This time he poured me a taste, though in retrospect I'm not sure why. I took a sniff and wrinkled my face. The wine smelled old or oxidized or something, the way it would if it had been stored over a stove. I offered the glass to my Italian companion, who simply said: "So strong!" The sommelier himself took a whiff, glanced at me from the corner of his eye, and muttered, *"Particolare."*

Reluctant to cause a ruckus, I shrugged and accepted the wine. Then, true to emerging form, I found out what I'd ordered by examining the label in closer detail. The wine was 16 percent alcohol— a late-harvest level of strength, arrived at by drying grapes in the sun after harvest. According to a hangtag on the bottle, this technique had resulted in an "excellent dessert wine." *Particolare,* indeed.

By the last night of the trip, I was ready to quit being creative. Chastened by my own spirit of enterprise, I suggested that we eat at a pizzeria and ordered a trusty Barbera as soon as we sat down; I didn't even ask the year.

It turned out to be a 1994 Barbera del Monferrato. I fondled the brown-tinted bottle warmly, sanguine in my abandonment of initiative, ready to relax with a regular wine, laid-back as the Italians themselves who simply order *"Rosso."* Until, that is, I poured it into my glass and it started fizzing.

As a home winemaker, I've seen that fizz before. To me it indicated instability: excess yeast, the dreaded *Brettanomyces*, incomplete

malolactic fermentation—bacteria continuing to do something in
the bottle that they're supposed to have quit doing. Fizz is inten-
tional in sparkling wine, where yeast and sugar are added to induce
it, but red wine is supposed to keep still.

I poured more of it into my glass, hoping that the bubbles would
disappear as they sometimes will when exposed to air. No luck.
Perhaps influenced by the visual effect, I was now sure that the wine
tasted yeasty. Trying to play things safe and conservative, I'd gotten
a defective bottle. If only to appease myself for the disappointments
of the trip, I called the young waitress over.

"*Una problema,*" I said as pleasantly as possible. Then, pointing to
the bottle, "*Frizzante.*" The girl's smile disappeared, as did she. In
her place appeared a swarthy sergeant-at-arms, a man who obviously
wasn't inclined to take any crap from tourists. I noticed over my
shoulder that several other waiters had assembled, and every diner
in the room was looking at my table.

The martinet frowned at the glass, then at me. He said, in effect:
"It's normal. Shut up and eat." Then he walked away.

At that point I determined not to pay. But then, as if from on
high, another waiter appeared. He asked what was the matter, and
when I repeated the F word, he studied the glass for a moment.
Then he too departed, but he returned a moment later with another
bottle, identical to the first except for two things: The new one was
a '95, not a '94; and the label on the fizzy one contained an extra
word that I, er, hadn't noticed. The word was *vivace,* meaning "lively."

In any case, the angelic peacemaker gave us the '95, which
turned out to be utterly delicious. My companions were more
impressed that I'd identified "liveliness" than annoyed that I'd missed
it on the label (not that it would have mattered, I rush to reiterate,
since they open it as soon as you order it anyway). The room's other
patrons returned to their meals, and for the first time on the trip the
wine finally did its proper job, imbuing the table with a great good
glow and a buoyant, jocular sense of well-being. Celebrating our
averting of an international incident, we left the waitress a tip so
huge that she came running after us, trying to return it. As we were
leaving, the Good Waiter made a point of shaking my hand.

When I got back to the hotel, I found my pocket guide and looked up Barbera del Monferrato. It was described as "pleasant and slightly fizzy."

For wine buffs, it seems, a *little* knowledge is a dangerous thing.

David Darlington is the author of Area 51: The Dreamland Chronicles, The Mojave: A Portrait of the Definitive American Desert, Angels' Visits: An Inquiry into the Mystery of Zinfandel, *and* Zin: The History and Mystery of Zinfandel.

TONY ASPLER

The Wine Label

How can you recognize a crack vintage?

WHILE THE FRENCH AND THE ITALIANS MAY AGREE ON SOME things, their attitudes to wine and wine shows are quite different. Just visit Vinexpo in Bordeaux, and Vinitaly in Verona and you can see the differing national attitudes.

Vinexpo happens every other year, in odd years, in June at around the time of flowering if the vintage is good. Vinitaly occurs every year in April.

Vinexpo, while showing off the best that France can provide, also welcomes the world. It is the most international of wine shows; even Ontario and British Columbia wineries feel compelled to have a presence there. Vinitaly invites other wine regions to exhibit but basically it's an Italian event and in Vinexpo years tends to be overshadowed.

Vinexpo is located just outside Bordeaux, the undisputed wine capital of the world (after all, when you think of vintages, your first thought is red Bordeaux). The exhibition hall is a kilometer long, set by the side of an artificial lake. There are ancillary tents along the lakeside for regional and national restaurants (which are uniformly very good and difficult to get into) and other tents and hospitality areas on the other side rented by the large companies.

Invariably it is hot in Bordeaux in June. Blazing hot. And those who were there in 1989 will never forget just how hot. The hall had no air conditioning and the build-up of heat made the place feel like a furnace. Corks rose like magic from the bottles as the alcohol expanded but no one wanted to taste the tepid wines anyway. All we wanted was water. The temperature was said to be 47 degrees Celsius (116 degrees Fahrenheit) and even hotter in those stands that had an upper deck. There were stories of oysters boiling on the half shell and winemakers collapsing with heart attacks—apocryphal, no doubt, but certainly it was terribly uncomfortable for those who attended. The stands that had their own air conditioning were much in demand....

That year was my fiftieth birthday and I had been invited to dinner, along with some 200 other guests, to Château Mouton-Rothschild. We lined up on the gravel driveway to be received by Philippine de Rothschild prior to a champagne reception outside and then into the cellars for a candlelit dinner.

I was staying at the Terminus Hotel in Bordeaux which is above the main railway station. It was not air conditioned and I was forced to sleep with the windows open—which was the lesser of two evils since Vinexpo coincides with La Fête de la Musique when itinerant musicians can perform at all hours of the day and night. Mainly night.

I changed into my tuxedo and took a cab to the smaller local station from which the private train to Mouton was to leave. But the cab driver did not understand my French and took me to a station that was boarded up and abandoned. It did not take me long to realize that I was not going to join the party from there. The train was due to leave in fifteen minutes from a station I had ascertained from a passerby was *"pas loin d'ici."*

It was still blisteringly hot and I looked around for a passing taxi but the streets in this part of Bordeaux were deserted.

I began to run.

Sweat was pouring off me in buckets. I felt like Niagara Falls. I had five minutes to make the train and I was a good half mile away from the station. I ran faster. My dinner shirt was drenched.

I arrived just as the train was about to pull out of the platform and jumped on board. I might as well have been in a Turkish bath....

Two glasses of champagne helped to cool me down and by the time the train arrived in Pauillac I was merely as hot as the rest of the gathering. In the reception line, I ran into a fellow Canadian who worked for the Alberta Liquor Board. He had been a wrestler in his youth and when he had taken more wine than a liquor board executive should he was prone to putting head locks on people in bars.

We had drinks on Mouton's terrace and then moved into the cellar for dinner.

The menu read as follows:

> *Mosaïque légumes au foie gras*
> *Cuisse de canard en civet à l'ancienne*
> *Pâtes au basilic*
> *Fromages*
> *Gourmandise à la vanille au coulis de framboise*

The accompanying wines were:

> Opus One 1982
> Mouton Baron Philippe 1970
> Mouton-Rothschild 1939
> Sauternes Baronnie 1987

The centerpiece wine, served with the cheese, was the Mouton-Rothschild 1939 in magnums. Since this was my birth year I was over the moon—even though the vintage received no stars at all from Michael Broadbent, who described it in print, having tasted it in May 1978, as "lightish in color; sound and nice bouquet with an acceptable twist of acidity."

It hadn't improved in eleven years but it was fun to try. I asked Philippine de Rothschild if she would autograph the label for me which she graciously did.

The dinner ended about one o'clock; by then the weather had cooled somewhat. We drank cognac on the terrace and my colleague from Alberta approached me, suggesting that I would be better off coming back to his air-conditioned hotel and sleeping there rather than embarking on the long journey back to Bordeaux and the Terminus Hotel. Recalling my sauna-like room and the street music, I decided to take him up on his offer.

He was staying at the Relais de Margaux, a luxury hotel, in a room with twin beds.

It was around two o'clock by the time we arrived back at the hotel. I have no recollection of how we got there. Someone must have driven; I hope it wasn't the Albertan.

I decided at that point that I had to soak the label off the magnum of Mouton 1939. Now the French have invented the ideal contraption for soaking labels off wine bottles; a bidet. I filled the bidet in the hotel bathroom with hot water and then filled the bottle with hot water so that it would lie immersed.

The whole town has an air of almost depressing opulence, an appearance which culminates in the great *place* which surrounds the Grand-Théâtre—an establishment in the highest style. One feels it to be a monument to the virtue of the well-selected bottle. If I had not forbidden myself to linger, I should venture to insist on this, and, at the risk of being considered fantastic, trace an analogy between good claret and the best qualities of the French mind; pretend that there is a taste of sound Bordeaux in all the happiest manifestations of that fine organ, and that, correspondingly, there is a touch of French reason, French completeness, in a glass of Pontet-Canet. The danger of such an excursion would lie mainly in its being so open to the reader to take the ground from under my feet by saying that good claret doesn't exist. I should be unable to tell him where to find it. I certainly didn't find it at Bordeaux, where I drank a most vulgar fluid.

—Henry James,
A Little Tour in France

The combined heat on both sides of the glass would melt the glue and the label would come away. (This method works for most wine bottles, except those with gold on the label. For some reason gold seems to stick limpet-like to glass.)

Mouton's magnum label came away very easily. It measured six inches by four and three-quarters inches, slightly larger than the label for a 750 ml bottle; and as a 1939 bottling it bore the Rothschild crest surmounted by a crown and held by two rampant rams. It was not yet an art label (for every vintage since 1945 the later Baron Guy de Rothschild, and latterly his daughter Philippine, have commissioned renowned artists to design the top band of the label). Over the years the works of such luminaries of the art world as Picasso, Chagall, Dali, Miro, Henry Moore, Andy Warhol, and Jean-Paul Riopelle have graced the top band.

The design for the 1993 vintage, by Hartung, caused something of a scandal in the States; a pencil drawing of a nude pubescent girl. The Bureau of Alcohol, Tobacco, and Firearms, the federal department that polices wine labels (!) was outraged; so Mouton had a special label printed for the U.S.: one with a blank white space in place of the buff colored image. This bottling has already become something of a collector's item.

I placed the 1939 Mouton label lovingly on the flat surface next to the sink and patted it dry with a towel. It would make a fine memento of Vinexpo 1989. The wine of my birth year. By the time I had finished, my roommate was already in bed, sitting bolt upright.

"Hurry up," he said. "I'm turning out the light."

I undressed quickly and slid into the single bed next to his. The light snapped out and he said, "Good night."

Almost immediately there was the sound of a match being struck and a flame illuminated the room.

"What are you doing?" I demanded.

"Having a smoke," he said. "I always have a smoke before I go to sleep."

"In the dark?"

"Yes."

"I'd rather you didn't."

"Okay," he said, obligingly.

There was the sound of a cigarette being stubbed out in an ashtray and the rustle of sheets as his head hit the pillow. Within seconds he began to snore. Great window-rattling inhalations that pierced through the pillow I used to cover my ears.

After twenty minutes I decided there was no way that I was going to fall asleep with the rolling thunder from the neighboring bed.

I picked up the pillow and a blanket and walked to the bathroom. The bath itself was too short to sleep in so I made up a bed on the marble floor. Then it occurred to me that the sleeping volcano in the bedroom might want to get up in the night to use the bathroom. I would be in his direct path to the toilet. So I moved sideways until I was positioned under the wash basin and vanity unit. My ear was next to the pipes and when anybody else in the hotel that night flushed a toilet or turned on a tap I was jolted into consciousness by the noise even more devastating than my neighbor's snoring.

"How did you sleep?" he asked me the next morning over breakfast.

"As well as might be expected," I replied. "And you?"

"Great," he said, " but this morning when I went to the can I couldn't find any toilet paper so I had to use a god-damned wine label."

Tony Aspler is wine columnist for the Toronto Star, *a wine consultant and educator for hotels and restaurants, and co-founder of the charitable foundation Grapes for Humanity (www.grapesforhumanity.com). He is also creator of the annual Air Ontario Wine Awards competition and the author of nine novels. His latest series is a collection of wine murder mysteries featuring itinerant wine writer Ezra Brant. This story was excerpted from his book,* Travels With My Corkscrew: Memoirs of a Wine Lover.

A Tale of Two Meals

*In which an American merchant turns
the tables on a French chef.*

ONE NIGHT, OWING ANDRÉ ROUX AND HIS WIFE COLETTE A FAVOR,
I invited them to dinner.

It had to be somewhere special because during one of my trips
they lent me a four-hundred-year-old townhouse in downtown
Sablet, a rustic little village near Gigondas. It was paradise, a house
instead of yet another hotel, a kitchen in which to dabble rather
than the hit-or-miss risk of yet another restaurant. During the
daylight hours I worked the wine villages of the southern Rhône,
tasting in dark moldy cellars and bright stainless-steel-furnished
installations, tasting hundreds of wines—mostly powerful, tannic
wines—until my mouth felt like the inside of a barrel. Returning
home evenings, I would search across the flat, vine-covered plain for
Sablet's Romanesque bell tower in order to gauge the distance I still
had to cover before I could kick off my shoes, pour myself a glass of
André's refreshing white wine, and begin concocting some simple
dinner based on olive oil, garlic, and usually one of the small-leafed
basil plants that are available in the markets during the spring and
summer months. I would read myself to sleep to the sound of the
gurgling stone fountain outside my window.

I invited André and Colette to a nearby restaurant of some

repute. The cuisine was fine enough; I ate it, then forgot it because of everything else that occurred. The wine list was dazzling. One page listed *domaine*-bottled reds and whites from nearby Châteauneuf-du-Pape. The right-hand page listed rare old Bordeaux and Burgundies. The great growths. The great vintages. At irresistible prices! I fell for the 1929 Château d'Yquem. I had never tasted the 1929; I knew I would never see it again at such a low price, and I thought it would make a rather memorable thank-you gift to André and Colette, whose eyes widened in disbelief when I ordered it.

Even though I had invited André, we had to fight over who would pick up the bill. It is an unceasing battle to "outgenerous" André. With one hand I held him back by the throat, with my other I tossed out my American Express card.

"We don't accept credit cards," the waiter announced. My high good humor turned to shock and silence. I felt as defenseless as when I first noticed my thick head of hair turning thin. No credit card? The '29 Yquem was cheap, but not so cheap that I had enough cash on me. Of course André reached for his checkbook, but I stopped him firmly with a glance that let him know that I was not playing. He was my guest; he would *never* have ordered that '29 for himself.

There had to be a way out (apart from the back door). This is a serious restaurant, I told myself, and upon arrival I had introduced myself to the chef/proprietor and transmitted to him the best regards of some mutual friends. I would simply explain my dilemma to him and he would offer a solution.

I left my guests and asked at the cashier's desk for the owner. He came out of the kitchen in his white chef's suit, toqueless, unsmiling, and I explained that I had expected to pay with a credit card. The man exploded into a tirade against credit cards. He had never accepted them and never would! He made me feel like a credit-card salesman.

"I understand," I said carefully, even if I did not, "but I am in a delicate situation. Normally, I carry enough…"

"Your friend can pay," he said.

"He is my guest. Believe me, that is not the solution."

I was coldly informed that *none* of the great restaurants take credit cards.

What was his problem? I told him to check his *Guide Michelin* and show me a three-star restaurant that refuses credit cards. A three-star meal is so horridly expensive, only drug dealers would carry enough cash to pay cash. The French have checkbooks, of course, but the gastronomic palaces rely on foreigners for survival these days, so they accept cards as a matter of course.

I was imagining walking out without paying. Instead, I proposed that I go to a bank the next day and send him a cashier's check. He accepted this solution, this obvious solution, which any gracious restaurateur would have proposed at the outset.

The taste of that fabulous 1929 Yquem stayed with me. One of my favorite wine-drinking companions is Jean-Marie Peyraud, the winemaker at Domaine Tempier. We both love wine, we are long-time friends, and we never agree about anything we taste. If a wine seems tannic to me, Jean-Marie is just as likely to say it lacks tannin. If it is tart for me, it is flat for him. We discuss, dispute, define. One night I was rhapsodizing the qualities of the 1929 Yquem. We decided to return to the scene of the crime together to celebrate something and try another bottle of the '29.

When I arrived alone, the chef was at the door, but neither of us acted as if we had ever met. I gave the name Peyraud because the reservation was in Jean-Marie's name.

At table, Jean-Marie and I spent half an hour going over the wine list. There was an old La Tâche, Latours and Lafites from the '30s and '40s...not exactly cheap, but, relative to the going price, irresistible. One red could not be ignored, the legendary 1947 Cheval Blanc. Some have called it the finest Bordeaux of the century. From our waiter, who seemed to be strangely breathless throughout the meal, we ordered a 1947 Cheval-Blanc and a 1929 Yquem. The chef arrived a few moments later and apologized; there was no more '29s. "An American took the last bottle last spring," he said. "However, there are some older Sauternes in the cellar which do not figure on the wine list. Climens 1928, Yquem 1921 and 1947, Coutet 1947..."

"Why don't you remove the '29 from your list if it is no longer available?" I asked.

Jean-Marie spoke up quickly. "Fine, we shall discuss it and let the waiter know our decision."

A platter of *amuse-gueule* was placed on the table, then the waiter arrived with our 1947 Cheval Blanc. It lay in one of those straw baskets for decanting. He carefully cut the lead foil, removed it, and then his mouth dropped open. I followed his eyes to the top of the bottle and my mouth fell open, too. There was no cork there.

"Ça, c'est curieux," said Jean-Marie.

I thought to myself, now this is going to be interesting. The waiter could take the bottle away and start all over with another. However, it must be difficult to pour a rare hundred-dollar bottle into the stockpot just like that. He was torn for a moment, then he lifted the basket and poured a taste into my glass. The wine was brown. I sniffed it. It was oxidized. I shook my head no, that it would not do. He left with the bottle. Jean-Marie and I raised our eyebrows at each other. Awaiting the next scene.

"How could it happen?" I asked. "Was there ever a cork? Did it fall into the wine, carrying it up from the cellar? Or has the capsule been the wine's only protection all these years?"

Our waiter reappeared with the news that the chef had tasted the wine in the kitchen and pronounced it drinkable.

"We did not order it to have something merely drinkable," I said, thinking to myself that it was about as drinkable as warm prune juice.

The chef sped from behind the curtain across the dining room to our table, causing other diners to perk up and pay attention. He moved rapidly, without much upper-body movement, as if he were riding a unicycle. He plopped the enormous wine list into my lap and asked, "Maybe you would prefer something else?"

That surprised me. I expected him either to refuse to take back the bad bottle or to offer us another. Was he going to resort to his "last bottle" routine? Given our history, it would have been more politic had I left it to Jean-Marie, but I said, "We ordered the 1947 Cheval Blanc. It was a bad bottle. We would like to stay with the 1947 Cheval Blanc."

His jaw turned to steel; he grabbed his wine list out of my hands, spun away, and pedaled off. I began to think that dining out is not all it is cracked up to be. Then the waiter appeared with the second bottle, pulled its cork, and poured a healthy splash of purplish/black liquid into my glass. I swirled and sniffed, thinking any wine that looked so good must smell good, and it did. There was an impressive aroma, thick and dusty like the door to Ali Baba's cave opened. Jean-Marie started laughing out loud when he sniffed his. It was that good. I looked up at the waiter, who was waiting for a sign of approval, and I nodded yes, good, this is it, all that we hoped for…

Throughout our meal, we argued about which Sauternes to take. The 1921 Yquem seemed a likely substitute for the 1929, but once before I had fallen upon a 1921 Yquem that had not aged gracefully. After the corkless Cheval Blanc, I was in no mood to take chances. As we nibbled our cheese, we agreed, "Let's stick to the year 1947 and follow our Cheval Blanc with Yquem." I signaled to our waiter and ordered the wine.

"*Très bien, monsieur,*" he said and walked back to the curtain. After enough time to pronounce the words "1947 Yquem," the chef came bursting out and accelerated triple time to our table.

He glared at me and spoke through clenched teeth. "*C'est la deuxième fois que je ne suis pas content avec vous, Monsieur Lynch, c'est la deuxième fois que je ne suis pas content avec vous!*" Perhaps he repeated himself for emphasis, or did he think my French lacking? And now, all of a sudden, I was Monsieur Lynch! And what did he mean by "*la deuxième fois*"? Which had been the first time that I displeased him, the credit-card dispute or the corkless Cheval Blanc? I sat waiting. It was all rather delicious.

"For a great bottle like the 1947 Château d'Yquem," he proceeded, "one must order at the beginning of the meal so it can be properly prepared."

Prepared? What is there to do? You pull the cork and pour. "Is it in your cellar here?" I asked.

"Of course, but it must be at the proper temperature."

Proper temperature? What an odd thing to say.

"Why? Is your cellar too hot?" I asked.

At that he turned purple, and of course my question was insulting, but what else might the problem be? For an old Sauternes, especially Yquem, cellar temperature is likely to be the perfect serving temperature. Too cold and its qualities will be deadened; too warm and it is unpleasant. If cellar temperature is not quite right, you simply slip the bottle into an ice bucket for a few moments or minutes as necessary. I told him to serve it at cellar temperature, "and we shall see if it needs further chilling."

The bottle required five minutes in an ice bucket. It was an impressive wine but still young, a bit tight, a bit closed. We enjoyed the perfection it promised, fifteen or twenty more years down the road.

When the bill was presented, Jean-Marie reached for his checkbook, because we had agreed to split it. I stopped him, pulled out my wallet, and laid my American Express card on the dish. When our waiter arrived, I spotted the chef peeking out at us from behind the curtain. I thought the waiter was going to faint away when he saw the credit card. "We don't accept credit cards," he said warily. I winked at Jean-Marie, who knew the whole story, and we pulled out our checkbooks. Between the two meals, I had opened a French checking account.

Kermit Lynch is a wine importer and retailer based in Berkeley, California. This story was excerpted from his book, Adventures on the Wine Route: A Wine Buyer's Tour of France.

BOB BLUMER

AKA THE SURREAL GOURMET

When in Romanée...

A Burgundian vendange becomes
a harvest of memories.

PICTURE YOURSELF CONDEMNED TO A CHAIN GANG, HUNCHED over in the early morning mist, ankles deep in mud, and muscles screaming for mercy. A bell clangs, a tractor roars into view, and you hear corks pop. Around you, sixty-four aching bodies lay down their tools and converge around the tractor. In an instant the world turns from black and white to Technicolor as you are handed a glass of chilled rosé and a Camembert sandwich. This is the constant cycle of agony and ecstasy that defines the life of a grape picker at Domaine de la Romanée-Conti, the legendary winery in Burgundy, France.

Every year, for ten days in September, an elite team of pickers arrives from near and far to harvest the precious fruit from the Domaine's seven small vineyards. One recent year they allowed a novice to join the ranks: me.

During the previous year's harvest, while on a research trip to Burgundy, I had made it my mission to visit the winery. This was no easy feat, because Romanée-Conti, or "DRC" as it is known in the wine industry, is part of that rarified group of wineries that don't need to blow their own horns. Outsiders visit by appointment only. It took a letter of introduction from one of my wine gurus to get me through the fabled gates. During my vineyard tour, the sight of happy pickers filled my head with naive and romantic notions about running away and joining the circus. I asked my host if I could "help out for a day or two." With thinly veiled amusement he told me that the *vendangeurs* (grape pickers) were highly trained workers who came back year after year, and worked the entire harvest. In short, he was all but laughing at my request. In a moment of foolish bravado I tried to salvage my dignity by asking if I could come back the following year for the whole harvest. This only seemed to increase his amusement, but he gamely suggested that I should send a fax detailing why I wanted to be a grape picker.

It wasn't until I returned home that it dawned on me that I had fumbled my way into a rare opportunity that any oenophile would kill for: a glimpse into the inner sanctum of Domaine de la Romanée-Conti. The fact that I had to pick a few grapes while I was there seemed a small price to pay.

The winery is located in the village of Vosne-Romanée (population 350) nestled within the Cotes du Nuits wine-producing region, twenty miles south of Dijon. The Domaine's holdings include six adjacent tiny plots of land and one parcel thirty miles away in the white-wine-producing region of Puligny-Montrachet. Each plot has a different name and yields an eponymous and distinct wine: La Tache, Richebourg, Romanée St. Vivant, Grands-Échézeaux, Échézeaux, Montrachet, and the jewel in the crown, Romanée-Conti. The latter yields on average 6,000 bottles annually which retail for $1,500 when they are released, and escalate exponentially with age. In fact, to purchase a single bottle of Romanée-Conti, retail stores must buy a mixed case of DRC wines. It is so scarce and so expensive that few wine lovers actually get to drink it in their lifetime.

All seven of the Domaine's wines are grand crus—a distinction irrevocably granted in 1939 to the top 2 percent of wine-producing properties in Burgundy. What distinguishes a grand cru property from other less worshipped plots is its *terroir* (an intangible concept best described as the harmonic convergence of soil, subsoil, sun, air, and the passing of wine-making *je ne sais quoi* from generation to generation).

But not all grand crus are created alike. Two things make Domaine de la Romanée-Conti the big Kahuna of Burgundies: the magical combination of skeletal limestone, clay, and marble soil which forces the vines to work harder, thereby generating a lower yield of grapes—but grapes with infinitely more concentrated fruit. DRC is also known for a total lack of compromise in transforming its natural bounty into wine.

The Domaine is not known to compromise on its grape pickers either, but I seemed to be an exception—perhaps in the name of international diplomacy. In early July I received a fax. "We are pleased to confirm that you will be part of our grape-picking team. Be prepared to arrive in Vosne-Romanée on September 10. P.S., The date may change without notice, depending on the status of the ripening grapes." Like the winemakers themselves, I was now at the mercy of the grape.

On September 14th, after an eighteen-hour journey, I arrive in Vosne-Romanée. It's the kind of picture-perfect French village that you see on posters in travel shops. Stone houses, narrow streets, geraniums in the window baskets, and only one shop, which in truth is the front vestibule of someone's house.

My accommodation is a small, unfurnished stone house owned by the Domaine and located twenty feet from its front gates. My tiny room has a bare light bulb and a narrow bed with a sagging mattress—a scary thought considering the back-breaking work ahead, not to mention the delicate condition of my two recently herniated discs. Upstairs in an equally bare room is an oeneology student with whom I share a kitchen table and a bathroom with no door. I am feeling positively monklike in these Spartan surroundings until I discover that they are downright luxurious in comparison to the accommodations of the other twenty boarders who are housed three to a room on folding cots. And even that is lavish in comparison to what awaits many pickers at the surrounding châteaux, who, after a grueling day in the fields, come home to a tent. Grape picking, camping, and pissing in the woods: the French equivalent of an iron man triathlon.

The first night I fall into slumber at 11:00 P.M., then awake completely disoriented to the loud clanging of a bell. It's 2:00 A.M. From my open window I discover the source: a large church steeple, just fifty meters away. For the rest of the night on the half hour the bell reverberates loudly. Between my jet lag and the noise, sleep is not an option. With nothing to do but read, I fully digest *Romanée-Conti: The World's Most Fabled Wine* by Richard Olney—a fascinating study of the Domaine's properties, beginning with its ownership by the Saint-Vivant de Vergy monastery in the seventh century.

At 7:00 A.M. I finally get up, barely refreshed by my three hours sleep, but extremely well informed about my surroundings. I wander to the dining hall where coffee, cocoa, bread, and jam are set out. Then I am invited into the office of Gerard, the field manager. With a toothy smile he equips me with a pair of tall rubber work boots, a hand clipper, a green rubber rain suit, and a pannier (a plastic basket). The pickers congregate outside of the garage that houses the tractors. I feel like the new kid arriving at summer camp. The returning pickers greet each other warmly while the new ones stand alone or huddle amongst those they came with. At 7:45 we are led up a short gravel road, just past the famous stone cross that marks the Romanée-Conti plot. We turn right and row upon row of the neatly groomed vines of the Richebourg plot spread out before us. Gerard divides us into three teams. Each team is comprised of a specially designed tractor that straddles the rows of vines, a driver, two foremen, and twenty-one pickers. I am intentionally placed between four veteran pickers, all women.

Just then, the tall, willowy, gentle-mannered Aubert de Villaine, the third-generation co-owner and patriarch of the winery, comes out to greet the pickers. He says hello to the familiar faces and welcomes new ones, shaking hands with the men and kissing the woman on both cheeks.

Gerard positions each of us in front of our own row of vines, like sprinters in their lanes. The clock strikes 8:00, Aubert shouts, "*Allez, courage!*" and we start picking. After a crash course by Gerard on how and what to pick, I am left to my own devices.

Unlike Napa and other warmer wine-producing regions of the

world where the vines are trained high, in Burgundy the grapes hang six to eighteen inches above the ground. This allows them to absorb the warmth of the soil at night and avoid frost during the colder part of the growing season. Consequently, contrary to popular belief (and the dire warnings of my friends), grape picking is not about the back as much as the thighs, which bear all the weight as we squat down in front of the vines.

The routine is as follows: One hand acts as a weed whacker, ripping the lower leaves off the vines and exposing the hanging grape bunches. Then the other hand swoops in with the clippers. Sometimes, the deep purple grapes dangle in multiple tiny clusters, requiring the dexterity and finesse of a precision hairdresser. Other times they hang in large bunches, and with three or four snips the vine is bared.

Before each bunch is placed in the pannier, the picker must eyeball it and, if necessary, trim off any sections of the bunch that are rotted or dried out. Depending on the microclimate and the year, this can be a cursory task or a time-consuming process. It is compounded by clippers piercing the swollen grapes, causing them to squirt you in the eye.

Not every grape cluster is picked. On some vines, a second, latent growth appears. These grapes are similar in color, but they are younger and the acids have not converted to sugar. Sometimes they are easy to differentiate, but other times the only way to know for sure is to bite into a grape and do a quick sugar analysis on the fly before moving like a crab to the next vine.

About every fifteen minutes, the first person on the team to have filled their basket shouts "Pannier!" and all of the other pickers immediately stand up in their lane and fall into line with military precision. Then the panniers and their twenty-five pounds of fruit loot are hoisted up and passed over the vines like water buckets at a fire, until they reach the tractor. The two foremen on the tractor gently empty the grapes into shallow plastic cartons that are designed to stack up on each other without squishing any of the precious cargo. As the empty panniers are passed back and the pickers return to work, the grapes are ferried to a flatbed truck that transports them to the *couverée* (vinification room). There they are placed on a conveyor belt. As they roll by, a team of ten men weeds out the undesirable grapes that the *vendangeurs* have overlooked. The remaining grapes continue along the conveyor belt through a machine that partially de-stems them, then pass into another one that lightly crushes them. Finally, they are dropped into a giant wooden cask where they soak in their own juices and begin to ferment.

The *vendange* is executed like a military exercise. Vines are counted off, and pickers assigned to rows in the same order every time. Sometimes without warning, we are marched to other parts of the vineyard. Later, I learn that the winemakers gather before dinner in a war-room to taste vineyard samples, study analysis, and decide which parcels of grapes are ready to be picked the next day, and which ones require more "hang time."

At the clang of 9:00 A.M., work in the field comes to an abrupt halt. I have only been on the job for one hour, but I am sensing what I am in for—and I'm pathetically grateful for the break. We leave our panniers in our respective rows and congregate by an old stone wall at the end of the vines. Paper-wrapped packets are distributed. Each one contains a hunk of bread with a thick slab of sausage (on alternating days the bread contains a wedge of Camembert cheese). It is always accompanied by two sticks of dark chocolate, which I eat on the first day but eventually learn to squirrel away for a much needed late-afternoon pick-me-up. Bottles are uncorked and rosé is poured freely (I rarely drink before noon, but when in Romanée...). It's an energy-boosting breakfast that could have been designed only by a French nutritionist. We lean against the wall, literally and figuratively chewing the fat. After a post-meal Gitane, it is time to return to work. *"Allez courage."*

We continue picking until 10:00 A.M. when it's time for a quick cigarette break. Never has a non-smoker supported the habit with such enthusiasm. During this brief respite, everyone stays in their respective alleys leaning over the vines to converse like neighbors gossiping over a fence.

At 11:25, the first grape picker goes down for the count, having severed his thumb with an errant snip of his clippers and subsequently fainted. A crowd gathers around him for a minute as he is revived and bandaged up, then it's back to picking. The distractions of the morning begin to fade. My quadricep muscles are cramping and my back is twitching in pain. I have run marathons and cycled 100 miles in a day, but neither compares to the physical demands of grape picking. They told me to bring lots of sunscreen, but Ben Gay would have been more appropriate. The next thirty minutes feel like hours, then mercifully the clock clangs twelve times, and with a collective sigh of relief we head in for lunch.

> Give strong drink unto him that is ready to perish, and wine unto those that be of heavy hearts. Let him drink, and forget his poverty, and remember his misery no more.
>
> —Proverbs 31:6-7

After hosing the mud off our boots, the sixty-five of us, along with the rest of the workers from the *couverée*, seat ourselves at four long vinyl-covered tables. Each place is set with a plate, a Duralex glass tumbler, a knife, and a fork. The plate is used for all four courses and the glass for water, wine, and coffee.

I am about to discover the paradox of the *vendange*: hours of physical punishment are juxta-posed with pure hedonistic pleasure. Along the center of each table are four unlabeled wine bottles and four pitchers of water. I gulp down some much-needed water, then pour myself a glass of wine. It is a soft wine with oodles of flavor, primarily raspberry, and a long lingering finish that transcends its humble destiny as *vin de table*. Most châteaux bottle their best juice for their signature wines, then package the rest under another label which is sold as their second wine. At DRC, most of what is not used for the seven legendary labels is blended into a wine that is served in-house. For the entire duration of the *vendange*, this wine flows freely at lunch and dinner.

Lunch begins with tomato salad topped with crumbled egg, shallots, and a pungent Dijon vinaigrette. The room hums as every-one unwinds and the conversation builds. The rudimentary French of my Canadian upbringing saves me from being left in the cold and

I am swept up in the warmth of the atmosphere. Each new course arrives looking like a magazine cover photo. The entrée is a meaty peasant stew served over couscous. It's followed by the traditional cheese course, and the meal ends with an apple *tarte tatin* with a flaky buttery crust. The food is prepared by a husband-and-wife catering team from nearby Nuits St. George. They come every year to cook for the *vendangeurs*. Three women, including the indefatigable Charlotte, a tiny wiry woman who has been working at the Domaine for twenty-three years, ferry the family style platters to the table, and, more importantly, replenish them.

After lunch we lounge on the grass outside. The omnipresent cigarettes are lit. The morning haze has burned off and the warm sun massages my pained legs. Just as I doze off, the clock tower clangs 1:30, and sends us back to the fields. *"Allez courage."*

In the glow of the wine-filled meal, the first hour of squatting, clipping, and lifting passes rather easily. But the buzz wears off and the pain returns — and then intensifies. The golden sunshine of the morning has turned into a punishing midday heat. Layers of clothes are peeled off and reconfigured as makeshift sun hats. Two hours later, my quads have permanent charley horses, and the strength in my upper body is so drained that I can barely hoist the panniers to hip level in order to pass them over the vines. It dawns on me that I have another seven days of this. I contemplate throwing myself in front of the tractor.

I begin to hallucinate. I see the gorgeous deep red wine being poured into a crystal glass from a bottle of Romanée-Conti. I realize that I'm in Las Vegas. In the din of the casino I see a fat cat Texan who has just rolled big at the craps table and has ordered a bottle of DRC to impress his date. The good ol' boy's entire focus is on her amply displayed cleavage as he thoughtlessly knocks back a wine that most connoisseurs can only dream about. The vision does nothing to improve my mood.

The church bell clangs, bringing me back to reality. My nighttime nemesis has become my new best friend as it slowly counts off the hours of the day. I am obviously not doing a good job of masking my pain since the women around me motheringly ask *"c'est pas trop dure?"* ("it's not too difficult, is it?"), and motion to the foreman to get me some rosé. I lamely drag my sorry ass up the seemingly endless row of vines until the single bell at 5:30 P.M. mercifully puts an end to my misery.

I limp back to my house. I am dying for a long hot bath with Epsom salts. Well, this may be a culinary paradise, but it ain't no spa. My shower is a two-by-two-foot stall with a hand nozzle that has no place to hang it. I drizzle the mud and dried sticky grape juice from my punished body, then dry myself with a washcloth-sized towel. I collapse onto my cot for an hour before dinner.

Dinners are a more intimate affair than lunch, attended only by the twenty pickers who are being housed at the Domaine (those who live within driving range have all returned home). We gather at one table where the wine and water sit in their familiar places. With my first sip of wine, the pleasure-pain pendulum swings back into the pleasure zone. We start with onion soup served with crème fraîche followed by Beef Stroganoff. Over the course of the ten days, we are treated to salads of carrots, beans, beets, greens, and tomatoes, almost always with the now-familiar Dijon mustard vinaigrette. The entrées are all classic French dishes such as Boeuf Bourguignon, roasted chicken halves *au jus*, and *Tartiflette* (a crowd favorite made from boiled potatoes, French pancetta, and caramelized onions, topped with an entire Réblochon cheese and baked into a hearty gooey mess).

Sleep comes easy on my tiny mattress. The next time I hear the church bells, they ring seven times and the cycle starts all over again.

By day three my fingernails are gnarled and thick with dirt. My cuticles are stained purple and my hands, especially my weed whacking hand, is scratched from the vines and full of gashes where my clippers have cut through the vines and continued into my flesh. My ability to wield a chef's knife is in jeopardy, not to mention any potential career as a hand model.

But after another day, the pain starts to become manageable and I begin to find my groove in the fields. Over time, one develops an economy of movement and a sixth sense about which leaves the wayward bunches of grapes are lurking behind. Individual grapes become less precious as I begin to see the bigger picture. All sixty-three acres must be picked quickly in order to avoid the threat of rain, which will further exacerbate the *pourriture* (rot) that already existed on many of the clusters. A bit of triage is required to decide how much time is worth spending to save one-eighth of a bunch of grapes.

I am beginning to be able to take my eyes off the grapes and appreciate the splendor of my surroundings. The blue skies, rolling hills, and endless vines are hypnotic. The serenity of the countryside is interrupted only by the distant purr of passing trains and the occasional French fighter planes from the Dijon base as they fly their maneuvers overhead.

I am also moving beyond pleasantries and getting to know my fellow pickers. In the less coveted Appellation Controlée vineyards, the pickers are comprised of gypsies, North Africans, Poles, and French migrant workers. Here at DRC, they are college students and adults who work in banks, real estate offices, lingerie stores, and shipyards. Some are even grandfathers and grandmothers (including one who has picked here for twenty-two years). Most are French; a few come from neighboring countries. The majority are on vacation time, and many tell me that picking grapes helps them participate in, and connect with, this vibrant element of French culture. Everybody says they come for the camaraderie. Consequently, there are no walkmans or mirrored wrap-around sunglasses. During the entire *vendange*, I hear a cell phone ring in the field only once.

By mid-week everyone is catching a second wind. Those who are boarding even have enough energy to gather after dinner in the nearby St. Vivant monastery where several of the pickers are staying. Jojo, one of the foremen staying there, has a guitar and requires little encouragement to use it. The others sip Pernod, scotch, or beer, and sing along to the traditional Burgundian songs.

In the village of Vosne-Romanée, there are perhaps two dozen châteaux, all of which produce wine from grapes grown in their respective vineyards surrounding the village. The teams of pickers at these Domaines are as distinctive as the wines they produce. I experience this firsthand one night while weaving home from a docile sing-along with the DRC pickers. In the darkness, I hear a U2 song echoing through the stone-lined streets. Starved for some familiar music, I follow the sound to a nearby château. I stick my head in to investigate and engage in a brief conversation with a wobbling red-faced man leaning closest to the door. He tells me that they are celebrating their *Paulée* (the traditional end-of-harvest party), which had begun at noon that day—eleven hours earlier.

My bad French accent immediately gives me away as a foreigner and I am invited in and presented with a glass of the château's '82 vintage. In the glow of my good fortune I wander on to the dance area. No sooner do I start dancing than a French novelty song that was a momentary hit the previous summer is tossed on the CD player. The lyrics demand that all men take off their shirts. Without warning, my sweater is lifted over my head and I am standing half-naked amidst a group of totally schnockered French women and men.

The revelry continues for another two hours. As we drink our way through several of the Domaine's finer vintages I begin to realize that not all groups of *vendangeurs* are cut from the same cloth. We close the party and continue drinking at a nearby house. At three in the morning, I stumble back to my mattress.

After four hours of sleep, my head throbs as I plod from vine to vine in the cold and drizzly vineyard. My newly acquired skills elude me. Without saying a word, the women on either side of me surreptitiously snip away at the grapes in my row, allowing me to keep pace. To compound my misery, the drizzle turns to rain.

Then by the grace of God and the declaration of Aubert de Villaine (almost the same thing), the picking is halted after an hour and a half. When it rains, most vineyards keep picking, but at DRC, de Villaine doesn't want the residual water covering the grapes, and the drops trapped amidst the tightly bunched clusters, to dilute the intensity of the wine. My first instinct is to sleep. However a primal need takes over: laundry. Every single piece of clothing I own is stained and sticky. I hitch a ride to Nuits St. George. As my clothes tumble in the coin-operated machine at a laundromat, I wander off in search of a pair of rubber gloves.

Because each of my tender and scarred hands are performing

completely different tasks, I buy a pair of thick rubber gloves for my weed whacking hand and a thin, more responsive pair to use on my cutting hand. (Note to self: in my next life, return as a rubber glove magnate and create a special package of intentionally mismatched gloves for the grape picking industry.)

After a day off and a full night's sleep, I spring out of bed with renewed energy. A big orange sun rises over the horizon. To add to the pleasure, we are picking Grand Échézeaux. This borders Clos de Vougeot, a walled-in plot next to a postcard-perfect château. Life is sweet.

Through observation and some lessons in broken French, I begin to learn tricks of the trade that ease my transition from dilettante to seasoned picker. For instance, by taking the tiny, unripened grapes from the top of the vine (the ones we don't pick) and rubbing them between my hands, it is possible to produce a juice that's all acid and no sugar—perfect for cleaning sticky hands and sterilizing small cuts. I learn to replenish waning energy with grapes that are so brimming with sugar that they taste like tiny bon-bons.

The tactile experience of being so close to the grapes also helps clarify some of the theories and mysteries of wine. In the fields it is not uncommon to have a sixty-year-old vine with its thick, twisted trunk growing beside a spry young specimen. In theory, older vines produce fewer but more concentrated grapes. Some wineries bottle wines from older vines under the label *"vieille vignes"* and charge a premium. Sampling grapes from both vines produces a subtle, yet distinguishable difference in sweetness and concentration.

And during a walk-around at dusk through the different vineyards, the temperatures and humidity differ noticeably. These micro-micro climates affect everything from whether the grapes will rot to how sweet they will get. It is easy to understand how one wine can be so different from another, though they are produced in adjacent vineyards.

Another three vineyards away, less than 400 meters from the DRC plots, lie the much less distinguished Vosne-Romanée Appellation Controlée vineyards. These vineyards produce wines that are good but not exceptional. This is partly because the *terroir* of the flatland is not as good as the sloped areas, but it is equally due to the pampering the best houses give their grapes at every step in the winemaking process. The next time a wine clerk tries to sell you a wine from a producer who is located "just down the road" from another (usually more prestigious) producer, don't let the leap in logic fool you.

The days fly by and the mood lightens in the fields. On the morning of the seventh day of picking, word spreads that only one more day remains—and more importantly, that the *Paulée* will be held on Sunday at noon. By design, the *Paulées* always begin at noon, in order to give the pickers time to sober up before the drive home.

Sensing that the end is near, the natives begin to grow restless. Where we previously tossed the odd grape at each other, we now toss full bunches. Occasional squirts of water turn into complete Vittel showers. I am given diplomatic immunity from most of the guerilla warfare—that is, until the end of the last day, when no one is spared.

Even at this late point in the harvest, when the legs and back have grown strong, there is a certain level of discomfort and monotony that sets in after a two-hour stretch of picking. Speculation about the wines to be served at the impending *Paulée* provides the perfect distraction. Though everyone knows that the feast includes a selection of older wines from the DRC cellar, the question is which vineyards, and more importantly, which vintages will Aubert choose? The veteran pickers raise the hope that he may dust off some of the precious Romanée-Conti itself, as he is rumored to have done in the past.

On Friday, our last day, several of the older women bring homemade coffeecakes and beignets, which they unwrap and share with us at the 9:00 A.M. break. Spirits are high and I feel I have finally hit my grape-picking stride (although perhaps it's the sugar rush). For the first time since we started, I fill my basket first and am able to utter the word that has eluded me for the whole week. "Pannier!" I cry triumphantly. Applause breaks out amidst the vines.

Later that afternoon, Gerard places us in front of our final row of grapes. There is a buzz in the field and it's easy to tell that something is brewing. An hour later as the last round of panniers is being passed along the line, all hell breaks loose. Suddenly grapes are flying in every direction and being squashed down on every imaginable piece of clothing. It begins with the rejected clusters that the warriors pick off the ground, but quickly progresses to the panniers, and finally to a raid of the grapes that have already been loaded onto the tractors. It's like a food fight in a Sevruga caviar packing plant. I am sorry to report that several cases of precious Échézeaux are sacrificed in the traditional end-of-harvest *bataille*.

After the free-for-all ends and the sugar levels subside, we load our grape-stained bodies onto the tractors and flatbed trucks and ride in a convoy with horns honking for a victory lap around the village. Stray grapes fly at anybody within range. And it ain't over yet. As we reach home, the ringleaders leap off the tractor, commandeer the pressure hose that we use to clean the mud from our boots, and turn it on us. Everybody, including the foreman, is thoroughly drenched. Those foolish enough to try to make a break for it are quickly cor-

I n 1993 I worked the harvest at Château Lynch-Bages. One day, they decided to inaugurate me into the *equipe*—the team. Little by little, throughout that day, they would tease me by perhaps stuffing a bunch of grapes down the back of my boots, or into my turtleneck. They became brasher as the day went on. I was called up to the *table de Tries*, the sorting table. This was considered a promotion, because you got to stand upright, and you got to throw the reject bunches of grapes at the other workers in the field. You were no longer the target, or so I thought. That's when they got me. They hoisted my body up onto the sorting table, bombed me with fruit, and sent me, along with some suitable grapes, of course, into a vat of what was to become Chateau Lynch-Bages 1993. It was official. I was a member of the *equipe*.

— Catherine Fallis, M.S.,
"Taking the Plunge"

nered and doused. Even de Villaine and his wife are caught in the melee, and he gamely returns fire. Only then is everyone prepared to call it quits and head to the showers.

Later that night, I leave a party at the monastery of St. Vivant. Nostalgically savoring my last glass of the table wine I've grown so fond of, I wander up to the cross at the Romanée-Conti plot. In the darkness I see the vague outline of several lone individuals. A familiar voice calls out my name, and I realize that like me, my fellow pickers are paying homage to the grape gods. In the darkness I lie down on the stone wall beneath the cross. Its sharp outline is silhouetted against the magical star-filled sky, adorned with the brightest Big Dipper I have ever seen. This is how the grapes of Romanée-Conti spend their nights.

Had I been told after that first grueling day that I would be sad when the end arrived, I wouldn't have believed it—in fact the mere concept of finishing the week alive seemed unfathomable at the time. But when the *Paulée* finally arrives, it is bittersweet.

Everyone appears at the Domaine Sunday at noon, scrubbed, groomed, and full of anticipation. After an aperitif of *crémant* (local sparkling wine), the dining hall doors open to reveal an amazing transformation. The familiar lunch tables have been dressed up with white tablecloths and bowls of wild flowers. In place of the Duralex tumblers are beautiful tulip-shaped crystal wineglasses. We enter and take our seats. The first course is *Feuilletté d'escargots a l'Oseille* (snails served in a puff pastry with a creamed herb sauce). After welcoming us and applauding us for completing a difficult picking season, Aubert introduces the first wine, a 1987 Puligny-Montrachet. It has a very deep, almost Sauterne-like color. The nose is all honey. It glides down the throat and provides a perfect foil for the escargot. To my surprise, after our table finishes the two bottles, another one magically appears. Not a bad start.

The entrée is filet mignon. Two huge magnums of 1988 La Tache are placed on the table. I am astonished by the generosity— each one of these would fetch $1,000 from collectors in seconds. After spending eight days communing with the red grapes, touching them, nibbling them, and breathing in their aroma, the foreplay is finally over. It's time to consummate the relationship. I bury my nose in the glass and inhale its intense bouquet, then close my eyes and take a sip. Its viscosity is much thinner than I had imagined. The predominant impression is sour cherry, and the finish goes on and on. It is a great, very great wine, but not transporting.

As we finish the entrée, I notice Aubert leave his seat and walk into the kitchen. From my vantage point I see him pull eight dusty bottles from a wooden crate. After carefully opening each bottle, he pauses to taste it, like a sommelier. Could this mean…?

A cheese tray is passed around. Finally Aubert emerges. With obvious pleasure he announces that we are being served 1961 Romanée-Conti. A hush comes over the room. I had dared to dream that I might taste a Romanée-Conti, but never a vintage as rare and priceless as this. The wine is a deep crimson, with shades of burnt umber. A considerable amount of sediment is evident around the punt at the bottom of the bottle. The wine is poured. It has an intense, explosive aroma of such opulence that I am dazzled. I pause for a minute to meditate on the heady perfume, then take my first sip. The wine dances on my tongue. It's an exhilarating sensation: all finesse.

I have had wines that were more instantly gratifying, but never one that was as complex and intellectually stimulating. The pleasure is compounded by my intimate knowledge of its heritage. Minutes later it gets even more sublime as it opens up in the glass. We are all acutely aware of the privilege that Aubert has bestowed upon us. A wine that serious collectors would kill for is being shared with sixty-five glorified field hands. The meal is capped off with a rich *gateau au chocolat* and a round of Domaine's marc (a rough cognac-like liqueur distilled from the pressed grape skins). And suddenly it's all over.

We all say our goodbyes, we exchange addresses, and I head to my room to pack my bags for the flight home to Los Angeles. In another eighteen hours, I will be back in a fast-paced world full of familiar faces, creature comforts, and fleeting moments of glamor. But now, that world seems daunting. How will I survive without the daily triumphs over sheer physical pain, the communing with

nature, the camaraderie without complication, the 9:00 A.M. rosé
with Camembert sandwiches?

Allez courage.

*Culinary adventurist, wine enthusiast, and professional bon vivant Bob
Blumer is best known as the author and illustrator of three cookbooks under
the* nom de plume *"The Surreal Gourmet." Whether he is picking grapes
in Burgundy, poaching salmon in a dishwasher on the Food Network, or
concocting recipes in his own Pee-Wee's Playhouse-like kitchen, his insatiable
appetite for adventure constantly leads him off the eaten path.*

ROBERT DALEY

Drinking an 1806
Château Lafite

In vino veritas, ergo bibatum.

CLIMBING, THE ROAD TWISTS BACK AND FORTH ON ITSELF AND THEN comes up over the escarpment and the village is visible out at the end of its white crag. I get out of the car and gaze across at it for a moment. I haven't been here in a long time. From this distance it looks desolate, jagged-edged. It looks unchanged. The wind is blowing my hair around. The wind always blows in Provence. It is wind that makes the air so clear and the colors as brilliant as they are this afternoon. Les Baux was the site of a singular experience in our lives....

The Michelin guide had awarded the Baumaniére restaurant first one, then two, then its highest accolade, three stars. Nowadays there are usually twenty, sometimes more, three-star restaurants in France, but at that time there were four in Paris, only six in the provinces. The Baumaniére was the only one even reasonably close to Nice.

We went there because we had been to the bullfight. We knew nothing about the Baumaniére's history, had never heard Thuillier's [the owner's] name. And when we had taken our places in his vaulted dining room what impressed us most was his wine list, especially the oldest and most expensive bottle on it, an 1806 Château Lafite. We wondered what such a wine would taste like. We wondered who could possibly afford it, for the price was 30,000 francs [approximately $4,000]. We knew little about wine. Hardly anyone did in those days. But though we closed the menu on the 1806 Lafite, ordering I think a Beaujolais, we talked about it wistfully. Perhaps someday we would be rich enough to come back and drink it. What would a wine that old taste like?...

I made an appointment to see the editor of *Esquire*.

In France a wine is felt to be alive, I told him. It is born, matures, and later dies. I had conceived the notion of getting his magazine to buy me that bottle of wine. In exchange I would write an article about it. If a wine should hold all or even most of its color, bouquet, and taste for upward of a century or more, I told him, then it became more than a great wine. It would be opened with reverence. It would be lifted to the lips with trembling fingers in a room so hushed as to resemble more a bullring than a restaurant, at the moment before the bull was put to the sword. The comparison was apt, I continued, for the result would be to kill this wine, to destroy this object of veneration.

I looked at the editor, who was peering at his hands. For a moment I thought I had oversold him.

His head rose. "Sounds good to me," he said. "Go ahead and do it."

So I wrote to Thuillier, whom I may have seen but had never met or spoken to. "I think," he wrote back, "that this wine is still perfect enough to appreciate it, judge it, and love it, but you mustn't forget that it was born before Waterloo. However, I don't think the drinking of it will be a defeat, much less a disaster."

I began to research the wine as best I could, and also Thuillier. Who knows what Bordeaux weather was like in 1806? But for the wine to last this long, if in fact it had lasted this long, conditions must have been close to ideal: mild weather during the flowering in spring; sufficient rain all through June and July; little or no rain during August and September, lest the maturing grapes swell up with water; and none at all during the two-week harvest, which would have begun about October 1. We know that fine weather existed all across Europe that fall, enabling Napoleon to crush the Prussians at Jena.

The 1806 harvest was allowed to ferment on its husks for two weeks or more. Nowadays it would be drained off into casks after a few days, producing the "modern" wine esteemed by the public for its lightness and by winemakers because it matures quickly, can be bottled quickly, and the money banked; whereas the 1806 Château Laffitte (as it was then spelled) was for a decade or more so austere as to be undrinkable, not to mention unsalable. No wine ever made again would last such a length of time. Of course it was not certain that this one had either.

Because the vintage was possibly going to be a great one, a few bottles were buried in sand in a stone tomb in the château's cellar for future use. The decades turned into scores of years, and the wine remained undisturbed. It was unlikely that any of the men who put it down imagined that the future would extend two-thirds of the way into the next century. The bottle we would open would have had three owners: the château, Thuillier, and me. Thuillier had owned it since 1954 when he got his third Michelin star. I would own it an hour.

We reached France, drove much of the day across Provence, and were trembling a little when we presented ourselves to Thuillier. This was partly fatigue, mostly nervous anticipation. He was seventy years old, thin, energetic, with a quick step and a warm manner. By now I had read much of what he had written about cooking, which he considered an art form: "What is art in general if not the harmonious and subtle expression of all that can be conceived of the grand, the beautiful, the sublime by the human mind for the pleasure of the senses? *La cuisine*, par excellence, addresses itself to one of the most delicate and difficult senses to satisfy: taste."

And again: "Relishing a fine dish requires as much attention and culture as appreciating a sonata or painting. To practice the art of fine cuisine requires broad knowledge, real patience, long hours, and a poet's soul, sensitive to beauty. You have to have a feeling for appropriate harmonies and a sense of nuance in order to create a dish and give it life."

I was a bit awed by him. He was an artist, and in his field a superstar. He was twice as old as I was as well, and I sought to reassure him that I knew something about wines and cared about them. I did not want him to think that his only bottle of 1806 Lafite would be drunk by ignoramuses as a kind of gastronomic joke. But he smiled and patted my hand, and I had the impression he understood what I was trying to say. He suggested an aperitif on his terrace, which was surrounded by masses of geraniums and roses. Then perhaps we would want to see the bottle on its shelf in the darkest and quietest part of his cellar.

The trip to the cellar did little to quiet my nerves. The bottle—our bottle—lay alone on its shelf. Nearby were other old bottles, none this old. We stood in a clean, well-lighted corridor lined with raw pine shelving, some of which sagged from the weight of bottles, the way cheap bookcases are sometimes bowed by books. It was a cool, moldless, unvaulted, beamless, unromantic, entirely businesslike wine cellar.

The, well, enormity of what I proposed to do began to build up in me. It felt presumptuous. To be there at all felt presumptuous. This was one of the problems of magazine writing. Subjects were usually glad to see you; the resulting publicity figured to help their businesses, advance their careers, did it not? You were, in effect, an invited guest. Nonetheless the relationship was an artificial one and, ultimately, you hadn't been invited at all; it was you who had invited yourself, and the result sometimes was this feeling of discomfort.

Emerging into the waning sunlight, I told Thuillier that, if he agreed, we would drink the 1806 Lafite at luncheon tomorrow. We were too tired from the drive to do it justice now. But what I meant was that this whole idea would take a little more getting used to.

Thuillier smiled, and again seemed to understand what I was not saying....

In the morning the maid brought café au lait, together with croissants from Thuillier's kitchen that were as light and flaky as the *tartes* the night before, and a morning paper, and she threw back the shutters to let in the sun.

We had made a date with the sommelier, René Boxberger, to open the 1806 Château Lafite at eleven-thirty, immediately after he would have eaten his own lunch with the staff.

Too nervous to wait, we got up to the main building fifteen minutes early. Boxberger, a friendly, burly man, fifty-six years old, wearing the leather apron of his trade, was pacing back and forth. No, he hadn't eaten yet. He wasn't hungry, he said. He asked when we would open the wine. We noted that he had cut himself three or four times shaving. He was at least as nervous as I was.

He got the bottle up from the cellar. It was hand blown, somewhat lopsided, and the glass was impregnated with air bubbles. Its shape was one no longer used in Bordeaux, being wider at the waist than at the base. Thuillier guessed that in its long life its cork had been changed twice. "I have some other bottles which are almost 100 years old," he said, "and their corks haven't been changed at all yet." He speculated that the cork was changed for the first time about 1900, and a label affixed to the bottle. When the cork was changed again in 1953, a strip bearing this information was affixed below the label and joined to it by the château's stamp.

According to Plutarch, wines were most affected by the west wind; and such as remained unchanged by it, were pronounced likely to keep well. Hence, at Athens, and in other parts of Greece, there was a feast in honor of Bacchus, on the eleventh day of the month Anthesterion [February-March], when the westerly winds had generally set in, at which the produce of the preceding vintage was first tasted. In order to allure customers, various tricks appear to have been practiced by the ancient wine-dealers: some, for instance, put the new vintage into a cask that had been seasoned with an old and high-flavored wine; others placed cheese and nuts in the cellar, that those who entered might be tempted to eat, and thus have their palates blunted, before they tasted the wine. The buyer is recommended by Florentinus to taste the wines he proposed to purchase, during a north wind, when he will have the fairest chance of forming an accurate judgment of their qualities.

—Alexander Henderson, *The History of Ancient and Modern Wines* (1824)

With the bottle in a silver cradle, Boxberger knocked the wax off the cork. Inserting his screw, he yanked nervously at the cork, and half of it came out and the rest stayed in there.

Together with Thuillier, the *maître d'hôtel*, and most of the waiters, we stood over the bottle watching Boxberger work. We were all tense. He worked at the remaining segment of cork but succeeded only in pushing it further into the bottle. He went to fetch instruments resembling tiny forceps. At last, triumphantly, he got it out.

He held it up for all of us to see. He was ebullient now. He sniffed it. He passed it around. We all had a sniff.

The bouquet it gave off was strong, robust, all the things it should have been....

But what would it taste like?

Boxberger decanted the wine, poured a generous dose into a big, crystal glass. He swirled the wine to air it, then filled his mouth. The rest of us waited for the verdict with our jaws hanging slack. All the while staring into the glass, he gargled the wine, then swallowed it, chewing all the while. He masticated that wine drop by drop it seemed, slowly, all the way down. I had always wanted to see this done by an expert. It was an excellent show.

Boxberger stared thoughtfully into the glass. He frowned, he smiled. Still we waited. "It doesn't quite leave to the palate what it promises to the nose," he said finally.

In truth it was the strangest bottle of wine I have ever drunk. It had the bouquet of a mature, confident wine, and its color had gone off only slightly from its original ruby red. Though not vinegary at all, it tasted thin, almost like a new green vintage that wasn't ready yet. And yet in the background at all times was the robust taste of the great wine which had once been there.

"It's like an old man who's still in pretty good shape," said Boxberger, "though of course he can no longer run the one hundred meters in ten seconds."

I thought of it more in terms of an old baritone whose voice was gone, but who nonetheless could still bring out certain notes that were as beautiful as ever. The former great taste was still in there somewhere; one moment it was on your tongue, the next it was gone.

Luncheon started with *foie gras aux truffes* with hot toast, after which came another of Thuillier's creations, a *poularde á l'éstragon*, chicken boiled in a closed *cocotte* so that it comes to the table with the skin still white and the meat inside very tender. It was served with rice, and over this was spooned a cream sauce tasting principally of tarragon. We had not been allowed to see the menu; Thuillier had decided for us in light of the very old wine we were to drink.

It tasted best with the *foie gras*, its voice coming out in one final absolutely strong, perfectly pitched note, and it seemed to me that I could tell exactly what it had tasted like 100 or so years ago when it was such a great wine, so absolutely sure of itself, that it must have thought, if wines can think, that it would live forever.

All this time people stared at us from neighboring tables, the way film stars get stared at in restaurants. Our waiter stared at us too, so that I said to him, "Would it amuse you to taste this?"

"Oui, Monsieur," he said almost fervently. "A wine like that one tastes once in a lifetime."

"Get a glass," said I.

He took it into the kitchen to sip, and after that our table was surrounded by waiters, as happens in certain poor restaurants where they are hoping for tips. Here it was not tips they wanted but a taste of that wine, and we gave some to most of them. At times the floor was nearly empty; they were all in the kitchen tasting.

Towards the end, though its bouquet was still a pleasure to sniff, the wine began to lose its taste altogether. It got thinner and thinner. It made us think of a feeble old man about to breathe his last, and P. said to a final waiter: "Won't you please have some? It is dying fast and soon it will be too late." We wanted them all to taste it because their curiosity was so great and because it amused us to imagine them impressing patrons for decades to come: "That reminds me of the 1806 Lafite I had the pleasure of drinking once…"

But all day our strain and excitement had been intense, and as we drove away from there, rolling through the villages of Provence in the sun, we both were exhausted. I felt as drained as sometimes after a great football game or a great theatrical performance, and presently

I laughed and said to P., "I'm looking forward to the wine we'll drink with dinner tonight. It will be a one-year-old rosé de Provence costing $1.75, and no one will stare at us while we drink it."

And that is what we did.

Robert Daley's work has appeared in numerous magazines, including Esquire, Playboy, Vogue, Reader's Digest, *and* Paris Match. *He has served as a New York City deputy police commissioner and gone hunting for sunken treasure in the Caribbean. This story was excerpted from his book,* Portraits of France.

PART THREE

GOING YOUR OWN WAY

MICHAEL PENHALLOW

A Vineyard of His Own

Planting new vines can dissolve old differences.

OPPOSITES ABOUND EVERYWHERE IN LIFE, BUT CAN THEY POSSIBLY attract? I am a transplanted Englishman, ignorant of the romance and whimsy of a vineyard let alone the planting and design of such a project. No one could be further from the image most people must have of the typical vintner. Who am I to have such flaunting expectations? The rows that I navigate daily are purely urban by design. They run up Broadway to Union Square, New York City, far beneath the shallow, concrete facades of thick urban blight. California, on these hazy city nights, seems so far away.

Yet I have made a deal with fate and, success or failure, it will be a long shot. There are plenty of problems to overcome in creating a vineyard on my small plot of land in California, and I have so much more to learn. All of my learning thus far has come from dusty books in local libraries or has been borrowed from people encountered along the way. There are no living, breathing vintners in my immediate circle of friends. My family history, I am told, has veered towards urban life, certainly not toward toiling on a damp spring morning to plant long rows of noble grapevines.

It is almost eleven A.M. The rays of the sun warm through to the bone and the heat radiates off the damp, loamy soil. From the valley below the thick mist rolls out to the ocean a few miles to the west, its path revealing the faint contours of an ancient redwood forest. High above, the sun breaks through the shrouded trees and casts thin shafts of light onto the heart of a decaying orchard, which in my imagination will soon be rows and rows of newly planted grapevines.

I am lucky to be alive, here in the Russian River appellation of Sonoma County. South of the sunny fields of Healdsburg and west of the dot-com startups, telecom giants, and antique stores of downtown Santa Rosa, perched on a small hill overlooking the apple orchards planted over a century ago—back when Gravenstein apples were proudly sent throughout the country a full month before anything was available back East. But New Zealand apples put an end to all that and the ranchers and farmers of this area have since found salvation in grapes.

This is what wine people call perfect Chardonnay country. The golden grape is supposed to reach deep into these fertile soils and produce a wine rich in honeyed, fruity tones. However, I am under the influence of the ABCs: the "Anything but Chardonnay" club. It is as yet only a minority of renegade wine drinkers, consisting mostly of disgruntled restaurateurs, writers, wine merchants, and wine aficionados who are fed up with the heavy California Chardonnays they encounter every day. The ABCs do have a point to make; rich, luscious California Chardonnays are admittedly dramatic but frequently so heavy in oak that they are hard to enjoy—and they are so high in alcohol (14 or even 15 percent) they have become tiring and overwhelming to drink.

Not too far from me lives an old Frenchman by the name of Monsieur Poisson who is an ardent member of the ABC Club. He was brought over by the winemaking Sebastiani family many years ago, when they made their great push into these parts. This experience instilled in him a fervent anti-Chardonnay ideology. He has offered me advice in the past; perhaps he can steer me in the right direction again.

He welcomes me at the door of his two-room cabin surrounded by tall redwood trees and we sit down to talk. As is his custom even in these early hours, he pours two glasses of red wine from a dusty, unmarked bottle and we raise our glasses in respect.

"So, what is it that's so important?"

"I want your advice on the type of grape. I'd like you to decide on my millennium vineyard."

He smiles briefly to himself, a deep furrow appearing atop his brow and a low snort emanating from his elongated Gallic nose.

"Millennium, what do you know about the millennium? All I know is that an auspicious year for mankind can often mean great years for wines." Instantly, I think he is about to lay into me and accuse me of being a neophyte and certainly not worthy of his great expertise. But he takes several deep breaths and a different voice fills the void.

"Take, for example, the magnificent year of 1945. It was a terrible, terrible time after World War II. There was no food, no work, and the Germans had destroyed everything in their destructive retreat from France. But the wine that year, it was the best vintage I have ever tasted, there's been nothing like it since. It helped us through a difficult time. Man and grape, we all sighed a huge relief at the end of the war. I was there, I can tell you, it was one big party. And what made it all the more memorable is we celebrated life with the finest vintage of the entire century."

Monsieur Poisson's face took on the full weight of his story as he stared out his cabin window into the ancient redwoods. He smiled as he thought about yesterday and the fond memories that our conversation evoked.

"After the war they planted anything that would grow. Anything that would produce bountifully with little labor. But now with resistant rootstock, quantities increase every decade. People are looking for character, something different from the mainstream."

I knew what he meant. Still, I wanted to steer the conversation to the present.

"If I go to the trouble of planting the vineyard, I want to choose vines that are unique. Something really worth the effort."

He looked deeply into the distance and swilled the wine for a while in his mouth.

"You are willing to work with the soil?"

"Yes, of course. That's why I moved up here."

"It's a lot of work. You must prepare the soil well for planting."

"I know. Actually, I am looking forward to that part."

A smile appeared on his rumpled features. "We'll see about that! But if you are willing to work, I would advise a more finicky grape. One of the Burgundy varieties." He swilled the glass around and sniffed the aroma of the wine. "Pinot Noir, very tricky. It's really tough to grow, it's all about climate and *terroir*. The results when perfected can be most rewarding."

I looked at his face and saw it lit up for a change. This man had a true passion for the vineyard, especially a new one.

"Pinot Noir is far different from all other dark-skinned varieties of *vitis vinifera*."

"Venus what?" I asked.

"*Vitis vinifera,*" he repeated. "All the best wines are made from this family. Anyway, Pinot Noir has intense flavors but with fewer tannins than most types and is more prone to oxidation. For these reasons, it is especially sensitive to climate, to its treatment in the vineyard or what we call *terroir*." He poured out another glass. "I think it just might be particularly well-suited to your little orchard."

The mild cherry and plum flavors of Monsieur Poisson's home-made wine began to overpower my senses and it wasn't long before I felt the alcohol rising to my head.

"What are we drinking?" I asked, with a tiny sense of premonition. He gave me a look, a look that the French reserve only for their English neighbors.

"Look out back, young man, beyond the redwoods. I grow what I cannot buy."

The fog had started to lift and I could see the faint image of vines disappearing into the hills.

"I'll admit something that might shock you. Chardonnay and Cabernet bore me. I am sick of hearing about the newest Chardonnay, they are everywhere in Sonoma, just as Napa is full of Cabernet. They are easy to get, too easy. I can purchase them from any grower up here. But Pinot Noir. Let's just say that there aren't enough good Pinot grapes to go around. If you can grow them, the winemakers will beat a path to your door."

There and then my mind was set. As I left the cabin and walked back home, I was full of dreams of ten-year-old vines stretching as far as the eye could see, dark ruby-red bunches hanging down, touching the sun-baked California soil.

So I have found a mentor and the show is about to begin. Monsieur Poisson has arrived for work in a gray, dented '56 Ford tractor and parked it in the field. I can't believe the luck I've had in finding this man, without whom I certainly wouldn't be contemplating this folly. And what could possibly be in it for him? I know I can do with any help I can get but he knows this only too well, a complete stranger does not do this type of work for nothing. I asked him and he was quite straightforward: "I have volunteered for a price." I said nothing, expecting the bad news but he just smiled and contin-

All countries and all separate regions within them have their particular types of vines, which they designate in their own ways. Some vinestocks have also changed their names when they are grown in new places, and some have had their individual personality so changed by transplantation to a new place that they are unrecognizable. And so in our native Italy, not to speak of the whole wide world, people in neighboring districts can disagree about the names and characterization of grapevines. Therefore it is the mark of a wise teacher...to lay down as a precept...that no variety of grape should be planted except one generally approved by local reports, nor should any variety be kept for long if it does not deliver good results.

—Lucius Junius Moderatus Columella, *On Agriculture, Book 3*

ued. "*Metayage*, that's what we call it in France: the owner of the land pays the costs, the farmer does the work, spraying, pruning, and picking. When the vineyard is mature and becomes productive you give me a ton of grapes each year. Everything planted within the posts will be my responsibility, everything else, including the roses, the orchard, and the rest of the garden, will remain yours."

Metayage.

Payment in the weight of my own grapes. I could not have dreamt of a better deal.

So we went to work immediately. I laid out eighteen rows that ran the whole length of the vineyard from north to south and between them the temporary lines that serve as guides for planting. It was a damp, spring morning and we were raring to go when I looked over at Monsieur Poisson to see that besides his customary hoe and clippers, he carried two mysterious pieces of timber.

"All vines will be planted four feet apart, except for one at each end."

He told me that the first vine should be planted close to the end posts and trained in order to utilize the sturdier and larger support. This technique, which produced a stunted, rather homely vine, he had learned in Burgundy. It allowed him to squeeze in one extra vine per row, which, he explained, starts to add up when one is planting many rows.

He began by driving a stake for each end post. I decided I would not question such a wealth of knowledge, but merely observe it at work. He lit up one of those hand-rolled French cigarettes that we all know from the French noir films of the 1950s. I mentioned that I wanted to plant a rose bush at the end of each row.

"Fine, but we finish the vines first. Every bit of space will be used, nothing goes to waste in a vineyard, everything has its place."

He laid down his plank and sprayed a small mark on a length of twine; a green fluorescent stripe that was visible from all angles, no matter how you looked at it. I could smell his cigarette as we passed by each other. At this point he pounded a stake and checked that it was square, so I watched him intently and emulated his technique heading along the western part of the vineyard. One after the other, I sprayed the stripes onto the twine and pounded the stakes, marveling at the developing image we were creating. And it wasn't too long before I began to see a vineyard arising in this labyrinth of noughts and crosses.

The ebb and flow of fog make the Russian River a winemaker's paradise. On this morning, the fog was thick and only gradually rolling back to the Pacific Ocean fifteen miles to the west. I pounded in more stakes, completing several more rows before I was halted by a shout from Poisson's end of the vineyard. Thinking there was something wrong, I took off through the fog toward his voice. As I got closer and could see him clearly, he waved me over excitedly.

"Cèpes!"

"What?" I still could not hear him.

"You have cèpes. *Champignons.* Look!"

I looked down, unable to share in the amusement at his discovery. "Those are mushrooms," I said.

Like many people, I have a certain wariness when it comes to fungi. Fairy tales and goblins aside, I prefer to buy my mushrooms packed in plastic, preferably in the isles of a trusted supermarket. I told Poisson as much without any sense of shame.

"Mushrooms?" He gave me a look of utter disgust. "Only the English could invent such an ugly word for something so delicious. You are all the same. Your love affair with food stops at frying and boiling everything to death. Why don't you do yourselves a favor and leave the cooking to the French."

He pulled out a pen knife and began prodding around the base of the mushrooms.

"Sounds like a good idea to me."

"What does?"

"The French doing the cooking. There's only one problem though."

"What's that?"

"The problem is what would be left for us?" I asked, weary of the never-ending jokes and general lack of respect for English cuisine.

"That's true, I didn't think of that," he said as he cut through the base of a beautiful brown mushroom.

He thought for a moment and puffed on the last piece of his cigarette. "You can do the fighting! Your countrymen seem to be rather good at that. What do you call them, 'hooligans'?"

"Yes, unfortunately." The world had become only too well acquainted with this unfortunate aspect of English society.

"Here, taste this." He cleaned off a golden, round mushroom and offered it to me.

For a second I hesitated, but I didn't want to offend him, especially after all the experience and knowledge I was chalking up for free. I nibbled a small piece of his offering. I was unable to hide my skepticism, which he intuitively sensed.

"You don't have to worry," he said. "I know my way around mushrooms. I learned from my father and he from his." Still, I held the stuff in my hands and sniffed it. "No fear, the Poisson family knowledge goes back generations. Try it."

I held the mushroom between my teeth, the taste somewhere between a smoky truffle mixed with a distinctive earthy finish.

"Bolete, cèpes, maybe you know it as porcini? Anyway, you are lucky, these are the most sought after around here. Very rare. See the dark brown *chapeau*? Notice its bun shape and tubes instead of gills inside the cap."

I inspected the bounty he had dug up. "How do you prepare them?" I asked, careful not to spit out the cud directly in front of him.

"There are so many ways. You can grill them whole or slice them, add them to soups or sauces. But my favorite, above all, is in an omelette. It is the best taste I can imagine."

When his back was turned, I couldn't help it and spat out the contents of my mouth. It did not taste like any mushroom I had known.

"If you have one cèpes, chances are you have many," he uttered with a faint smile on his face. He was transformed. A different man, flush with success. A man on a mission.

The vineyard work was set aside as we hunted for mushrooms the rest of the day. Most of our success came at the foot of a grove of old oak trees that had somehow survived when the orchards had been planted a century ago. Here was a veritable wealth of cèpes. The oaks were thick-trunked, tall and full of Spanish moss. I had always thought them rather ugly. But they had ended up concealing a considerable bounty that until now, I had never considered.

I asked him why we tended to fear mushrooms.

"You don't know enough about them. That's why you're so scared of them. It's much easier in France. If you have a question then you're off to the local pharmacist to ask their opinion."

"The pharmacist?"

"They are all trained to identify the edible species."

I wondered for a brief moment what a curious thing it would be to pull up to the local Rite-Aid pharmacy with a bag of unidentified mushrooms.

Meanwhile, Poisson continued to describe the most deadly of all mushrooms, the "Death Cap" (*amanita phalloides*). He explained, in the way I'm sure his father had before him, how to distinguish it in the field. The strong aroma, lack of gills, the size and shape.

Although I was at first skeptical I soon learned when to pick edible mushrooms and how best to prepare them. It turned out to be a treasure hunt I will never forget. When the day was through, we had gathered over twenty pounds of wild mushrooms which we duly split between us.

Poisson taught me a great deal that day. I had found gold in my own backyard that had revealed itself to me effortlessly. The millennium vineyard could be planted another day, but the mushrooms were to be enjoyed now, while they were fresh and tasty. Mushrooms are seasonal and only come around once a year, if you are lucky.

The next morning I was a little late due to a slight back pain. I had eaten more mushrooms in one evening than in my entire life and I was still standing upright, breathing, and conscious. Given what I had eaten the night before, this in itself was a miracle. No stomach aches, no strange hallucinogenic dreams. Nothing. Monsieur Poisson had passed his first test.

In the corner of my eye I caught sight of a huge delivery that, I swear, had not existed the day before. I realized that Poisson had been here earlier and dropped off this huge haul. Upon closer inspection, I saw the telltale dots of hundreds of small one-gallon pots. Out of every pot stuck a lone, solitary stick; about a foot long, some a chopstick in diameter, others thicker than a finger. I couldn't help but wonder how he had carried this bounty, how an old man could work with such heavy loads. For a moment I wondered if it could be in the water around here. Poisson always talked about the water; maybe there was something to his stories, after all. Before I could reflect much further, he appeared driving his old Ford tractor, pulling a trailer that was stuffed full of similar pots.

I shrugged my shoulders as he pulled the tractor in front of me and turned off the engine.

"I was planning on expanding this year. But with the illness, I don't think I'll have the time. They'll be perfect for your spot."

"But I've already ordered rootstock. Besides, I can't take this from you. How will I repay you?"

"Don't worry about it. We'll work it all out later. As for your order, I've already canceled it."

"You've done what?"

"Oh, I wouldn't get too upset. They're all con artists you know."

"What do you mean, those were certified rootstock!"

"Yes, sure. Look, I used to work at one of those places, I know what goes on there. As for certifying rootstock, that's just a scheme that the universities come up with to line their fat pockets. The place you ordered from sells terrible cuttings. The quality is absolute *merde*! You'll have more success with these."

If the old man felt so strongly against the rootstock companies, maybe there was something to it. I calmed down a little as he went on to explain that with the enormous expansion of vineyards throughout California in the '90s, good plant material has become harder to obtain and certainly a small grower who is ordering only a few hundred plants is virtually guaranteed to get inferior material. It made sense, the local papers had already reported on disgruntled farmers who'd had to plant again after receiving inferior rootstock. They were in the process of suing their suppliers for damages.

Monsieur Poisson had been grafting *vitis vinifera* for over fifty-five years. When World War II came to an end, he applied for the first job he could get and worked taking in the famous harvest of 1945 in France. He stayed on at the vineyard, eventually becoming vineyard manager before emigrating to the States.

Close to his home town of Beaune, in the Burgundy region, the

Nazis had set up a garrison that patrolled the villages and vineyards. Towards the end of the war, when Poisson was in his teens, his village had sheltered one American and an RAF officer for a few months. He had shared in bringing food and medicine for the duration of the war or until the men could find their way back to England. These airmen taught him his first words of English and the words to "White Christmas," which he whistled frequently.

I thought maybe it was some strange French joke at my expense but one day he explained it. The American pilot had won a bet from the RAF officer, which entitled him to choose the song they would teach the locals. The idea was that, after the war was won and when the Allied armies eventually came to liberate the village, the locals would sing this song and hence explain their act of kindness under the merciless German occupation. Sometimes I wondered if this was the only American song he knew, since in the vineyard he whistled it constantly come rain or shine. But why disturb him when he was so obviously contented in his work?

When you start out studying something, you sometimes don't actually realize how complex the process is until much, much later. I was so naive that I jumped right in and after a year when the vines survived and actually began to flourish, I thought, "Now I've finally got it. I know all there is to know about growing grapes." Only now do I realize how little I actually knew in the first place and how enjoyable it will be catching up on the rest.

I also have questions. Will absence really make the heart grow fonder? Separated from the vineyard for extended periods of time, will I miss it too dearly? There are no other alternatives, life has to go on and for me this will mean a bi-coastal existence.

In the meantime, I have made some observations over the past year, or maybe they have been made for me by some outside beneficial force. In the vineyard, there is an equilibrium born between natural processes and introduced phenomena, an observation that seems to parallel life itself. A vineyard is an equation that by its nature must create its own equilibrium.

If we give a vine support, it will naturally grow strong. If we give it none, the wind flails it around, and, bruised, it eventually gives up and dies. Vines should be allowed to grow freely, as they would in nature, but not so freely that they cannot fulfill the purpose we intend when we plant them: production of wine grapes.

Likewise, sugars should be allowed to develop but not so high as to impair fermentation. The optimal weather for grape production is warm days and cool nights; a hot summer to ripen the grapes, a cold winter to set next year's buds.

Such balance of opposites, as in life itself.

Michael Penhallow is an Englishman who spends much of his time in New York City where he works as an editor and screenwriter. He was a finalist in the prestigious Nicholl Fellowship in 2001. What time he has left is split between his vineyard in the Russian River Valley and his two dogs who help rid the vineyard of gophers.

★ ★ ★

Red Wines and Rednecks

*Why bring French wine when you
can bring a Frenchman?*

MEETINGS BETWEEN FUTURE IN-LAWS HAVE ALWAYS BEEN A SCARY
business, but this one promised to be particularly traumatic. The
overwhelming majority of my family was male, Southern, and
hard-core Republican. The rest of it was Southern and extremely
conservative Republican. And my significant other was, well, not
to put too fine a point on it, he was French. Okay, it's worse: He
was Parisian.

Elegant, fastidious about his clothes, Sébastien shyly spoke an
accented English taught by British professors, which I must just
say—and no criticism to those British professors—simply does not
prepare a Frenchman for two weeks of Georgia redneck conversation. To top off these handicaps, he had, with some innate perversity,
despite living in the second most conservative capital in the western hemisphere (after Madrid), two pierced ears and a Polynesian-
inspired design tattooed around his right biceps. If he had a beer can
or an American flag tattooed there, God knows, some common
ground might have been possible. As long as the earrings went. But
no. Those damn French never have known how to compromise.

To be perfectly frank, when I started dating Sébastien, Georgia
seemed so far away I'd forgotten to consider what my family would

think of him (or what he would think of my family). Now I realized we had a slight compatibility problem. My family was going to think he was a high-falutin' Parisian snob. My oldest brother had threatened to shoot anyone my niece dated who sported earrings, and he made a practice of cleaning his shotgun whenever potential dates were around. And Sébastien was going to think my family was a horde of barbarians. My oldest brother was a horde of barbarians in and of himself, and that was before you started counting the next three.

I tried to reassure myself. Sébastien *was* the only French male I'd ever met who knew how to fire a handgun, so he might show *some* promise for getting along in the Southern world. But it was a slim hope. Besides, my brothers had never accepted any male brought home by any of their sisters, ever—and one sister had been married for fifteen years. The idea of Christmas, that whole beautiful, family season, with one fiancé and four brothers arriving at our parents' home one after the other, was starting to stand all my nerves on end.

My parents seemed a little tense about it, too, which was understandable, because they'd seen me and my brothers get into way too many fights already. "He's *French*," my mother said.

"I'm *sorry*," I said defensively. "I didn't mean to. You know. It just happened."

"What should we serve him to *eat*?" my mother said, looking panicky.

No one knows better than I the phobia of exposing anything remotely culinary to a Frenchman's chauvinistic palate. I don't mean to criticize anyone else's manners, but for people who have fits if you can't finish everything they load onto your plate, they sure are quick to express disdain for anything you offer *them*. So I gave my mother a quick dose of therapy: "Don't worry. He's dying to try real Southern food, that's all he's talked about. Biscuits, cornbread, cookies, brownies, some good grilling, fried green tomatoes—I think fried green tomatoes are the real reason he's making the trip over here."

"It *was* a good film," my mom admitted, distracted.

"Food," my dad said. "You think food is a problem?" His eyes held the tense, suppressed look of a man on the brink of desperation. "What *wine* should I get?"

I guess it's a good thing I never became a psychotherapist, because I couldn't think of a single encouraging thing to say in response to that. "Don't even try, you're doomed," seemed just a tad negative. I remembered Sébastien's tendency to compare American beer unfavorably to his cat's little carpet accidents, and smiled a malicious smile. "He said he wants the authentic Southern experience, Dad. I'm sure he'd love a nice, cold beer."

My dad looked at me incredulously, and right then I knew that the one-week conference he had attended in France thirty years ago had scarred him more than I thought. "He's *French*," he said despairingly.

Meanwhile, on the other side of the ocean, Sébastien's best friend (son of a wine bar owner and source of fine wine, reasonably priced) was staring at him incredulously. "You're bringing wine to a party all the way across the ocean? Don't you think that's a little excessive?"

Often we have ridden through villages redolent with vinous aroma, and inundated with the blood of the berry, until the very mud was incarnadined; what a busy scene! Donkeys laden with panniers of the ripe fruit, damsels bending under heavy baskets, men with reddened legs and arms, joyous and jovial as satyrs, hurry jostling on to the rude and dirty vat, into which the fruit is thrown indiscriminately, the black-colored with the white ones, the ripe bunches with the sour, the sound berries with those decayed; no pains are taken, no selection is made; the filth and negligence are commensurate with this carelessness; the husks are either trampled under naked feet or pressed out under a rude beam; in both cases every refining operation is left to the fermentation of nature, for there is a divinity that shapes our ends, rough hew them how we may.

—Richard Ford,
Gatherings from Spain

"They're American," Sébastien said. "Work with me here."

"Oh, come on, don't be mean. You know Americans are trying really hard to learn about wine."

"Listen, Laura told me what kind of beer they drink, and it's not Belgian."

His friend looked horrified. "You mean…?"

"American," Sébastien said grimly. "Now do you want me to get stuck drinking that?"

The friend hauled out his father's wine list. "How about this one?" he suggested.

On the phone I told Sébastien flatly: "Don't go overboard. They're mostly beer drinkers, you know, and you can only bring two bottles through anyway."

"Umm," said my boyfriend.

"I'm warning you, when I bring back wine with me, they don't even drink it all. A few sips, and the bottle gets shoved into some corner, half-full."

"That wine you pick out at the big tasting shows?"

"Yes." Despite the fact that I don't actually drink, going to the frequent winetasting shows in Paris was one of my favorite things to do, and I went to a lot of effort to pick out the very best, most interesting flavors for those in my family who really did want to be wine connoisseurs.

"Umm," said my boyfriend.

They didn't even stop him in customs, the jerks. All those trips when I had stayed up until three trying to figure out how to fit a couple of extra hidden bottles into my luggage in a way that wouldn't get them broken, and he just *told* them how many bottles over his limit he had and strolled on through without being stopped or taxed or anything. Sometimes I could just about kill the French.

Introductions went tentatively. I could tell my brothers were making a real effort, in spite of the earrings, because they didn't shoot him and they even kept speaking to him. I'm sure Sébastien was making an effort, too, because he was being very successful at hiding the fact that he hadn't understood a word spoken in that molasses-and-music drawl. I would have liked to help out and translate for him occasionally, but my oldest and biggest brother, the alpha wolf, stopped that in its tracks. "No French," he barked.

I glared at him. "Don't you think you're being just a tad xenophobic?"

"No." He folded his arms smugly over his enormous chest. "I don't like people saying things around me I can't understand."

Sébastien started out his before-dinner Christmas Eve presentations with the cautious gift of a corkscrew. "Now, I was sure you all had one," he lied, "but this is a style I really like." It was a nice piece of work, too, with the simple elegance of a tool with one purpose in life, no frills, no experimentations, only the best. My father and brothers, who routinely compared their latest Swiss Army knives and Leatherman tools when they got together (some kind of phallic ritual, I guess) passed this corkscrew from hand to hand. In their eyes, I saw a first gleam of appreciation.

And I noticed something else. I didn't know if it was unheard of politeness or what, but in my huge, rambunctious family (nearly twenty of us), everyone had gathered near the table to watch. No one was saying, "Let's eat already," and no one was wandering off to the bathroom or lingering in the living room over a chess game. I hadn't even had to herd them to make a good show. I had just said, "Sébastien brought some wine for dinner," and they came running. The last two bottles of wine I had snuck through customs at great risk had been abandoned on my brothers' wine racks and never commented on again. I scowled.

"First I have an aperitif," Sébastien said, breaking the wax seal and uncorking it with that no-nonsense smoothness Peter Mayle has often celebrated and which my brothers watched with calculating admiration. I could almost see them anticipating exactly how many bottles they would have to open before they reached that smoothness.

Although I have never tasted a before-dinner drink I've liked, I took a glass to be supportive. I needn't have bothered. Everyone of age in my family took a glass, exclaimed over how good it was, some even took seconds, and they stood around talking and sipping and enjoying it *just like French people*. There was food on the table, and they weren't rushing to eat.

I eyed the Frenchman on my left warily, hoping he wasn't secretly seeing himself as some missionary among the savages, leading them to salvation. It would be just like a Frenchman to be entertaining that kind of fantasy among Americans.

The dinner wine he brought was greeted with equal enthusiasm, and Christmas morning over breakfast I found the youngest—and normally most reserved—of my brothers interrogating Sébastien in his most carefully pronounced English on how to choose wines.

"Y'all come up to our place tomorrow," the oldest of my brothers said. He pointed his big, callused finger at me. "But no talking French."

No sooner had we stepped out of the car than he landed on Sébastien. "Say-bas-tee-YON!" he called. We hadn't managed to persuade him to stop martyrizing Sébastien's name and use its English version like the rest of the family. "That's not his name," he had protested. "Say his name again, Laura? There you go, that's what I'm saying."

"Say-bas-tee-YON! Come with me." I watched in alarm as he grabbed his keys and marched toward his truck, custom-made to be the biggest in the Southern states. At least his new shotgun wasn't anywhere in evidence. "Honey," he called to his wife, "we're going to get some wine."

"Umm, shall I come along?" I asked nervously.

"No, you'll only start talking French again. We'll do just fine."

They arrived back in an hour, Sébastien grinning from ear-to-ear, both arms wrapped around a paper bag chock-full of wine bottles. My redneck brother was similarly loaded. "I thought we should stock up while we had an expert around," he said. "And while we're at it, where's that wine from Alabama? And that jug of wine that guy told me was as good as all that fancy stuff? Let's see what Say-bas-tee-YON thinks of it."

Eleven in the morning, the day after Christmas, and the kitchen island was soon sporting half a dozen opened bottles of wine. The appalled look on the poor Parisian's face when he tasted that jug of "as-good-as-the-fancy-stuff" wine was priceless. "It tastes, ah, very similar to glue," he said as politely as he could. "Glue? Isn't that the right word in English, Laura?" he checked as laughter erupted around him.

"Don't worry, we understood 'glue,'" my sister-in-law said.

The Alabama wine was next. After he sipped it, there was a lengthy and puzzled pause. "Is it meant to be wine?"

My big brother David, who had bought the glue and the meant-to-be-wine, was roaring with laughter. "I just got a new shotgun, Say-bas-tee-YON," he said, clapping him on the shoulder. "Why don't you come out and shoot it with us?"

And the emphasis on the "with" is why a Frenchman never leaves civilization without a corkscrew and some wine. But, personally (and not to underestimate the force of nature that is a Frenchman bearing wine) I think his acceptance was sealed— accent, sharp clothes, earrings, and all—when he outshot my biggest brother on his own shotgun the whole afternoon. "I guess I was just made to be a redneck," he grinned. A truly terrifying idea.

After that, I had as much hope of seeing my fiancé during the whole Christmas vacation as seeing snow, and I finally hauled him off to New Orleans for New Year's to get him away from the inseparable fivesome he and my brothers had become.

Only one thing continues to make me nervous. On the long drive down to New Orleans, I apologized, a little embarrassed, for some of my shotgun-toting, tobacco-chewing brothers' more barbaric habits.

"That's what you call barbaric?" Sébastien said, looking worried. "I don't know how you're going to take my father's side of the family, then."

Laura Higgins has lived in French Polynesia, France, and Spain, and despite intense research into fine wine still finds herself an embarrassment to her French future in-laws. She is currently working on a book on the cross-cultural adventures of a Franco-American couple in France and the U.S., and is only disappointed that the title Close Encounters of the Third Kind *has already been taken.*

* * *

Sometimes a Man Just
Needs a Drink

Of all the gin joints in all the world…

A SATURDAY NIGHT POST-THANKSGIVING NOSH AT THE ULTRA-HIP
Black Cat restaurant in San Francisco's Little Italy had spilled me
onto the street full of rib-eye steak and a fine Merlot. And I was
still aglow from Thursday's Chardonnay as well as its abundant
provender and its mayonnaise-laden leftovers on Friday, and all the
cheery and vinous company of kinfolk and friends gathering their
powers for the next few weeks of indulgence. And how the wine
would flow.

Happy holiday crowds, mostly young, clustered and thronged
along the streets as I made my way west on Broadway. A clutch of
gawky Green Tortoisites admired the well-dressed line of would-be
dancers waiting outside Broadway Studios across the street; men
held car doors open for women; a cop politely gave a ticket for
jaywalking to a repentant tourist. All seemed afloat upon the fumes
of wine and no one thought of pains. There were no homeless in
sight. "Enough of this," I thought. "I can only take so much of a
good thing."

Too much of the high life will grow fat on the soul and surfeit
of pleasure unmans me. Regular doses of luxury require the cathar-
sis of hardship and danger. The torpor-inducing certitudes of

American life call for measures of Third-World officialdom to slap me back into reality. Floods of Merlot leave me longing for beer, and I don't mean microbrew or premium stuff from foreign countries. I'm talking suds, plain and simple. With pretzels. And if not that then workaday gin with the humblest tonic. Or maybe a glass of red from a jug, but nothing with a fancy label or a French or Napa pedigree. I want something that a prissy, bent-pinkie sommelier would sniff at, or resolutely ignore with his own professionally bemused disdain.

I grew up in the rural wine country, far from any town. My grandmother's high school boyfriend was a guy by the name of Martini. Maybe you knew him. Wine came to our house in jugs when I was a kid. Fine folk tended to sip Scotch whiskey, but my people guzzled Paisano. And at the age of twelve I began to drink it mixed one-to-one with water. From a shot glass. I learned from that early age to respect wine but not to be awed by it. I learned that wine could be an integral part of a well lived life, if you let it serve you. But not if you became a servant to wine.

I never touched stemware before the age of sixteen. Everything was a blend of different grapes, so if I drank a varietal wine before eighteen I don't know about it. Wine spilled on the table was hailed as a sign of good luck. A bad stain maybe, but good luck. Sniffing the cork? Who knew from corks? Oh, and that tedious ceremony of tasting the wine? There was a time when that had purpose. When corks and packing and shipping were less secure. But nowadays you're more likely to get a flat Coke or a warm beer than a bad wine. Of the countless bottles of wine I've tasted over these decades I've sent back but one. And yet I could have drunk it, one-to-one with water, from a shot glass. And I would have scandalized the sommelier. But of course he must earn his keep and play his role in the pricey world of modern wine culture.

So on this now suddenly stultifying Saturday night, overfed deluxe and my decks awash with the best of California's grape, I knew that only a slide into a dive or two would make me a man again. Because sometimes a man just needs a down-and-dirty drink. I was on the cusp of Chinatown, where Grant Avenue begins its plunge. The garish neon of the Bow Bow Cocktail Lounge at 1155 Grant promised redemption.

A Chinese man in a black leather jacket and an Elvis hairdo stood outside the door yammering into his cell phone and smoking copiously. He never left his station, nor his phone, nor his smoke. Through a cloud of his effluent I stepped into the deep, narrow confines of the bar. Red light suffused throughout and a certain whorehouse feel thereby obtained. A couple of red paper dragons flew above the rows of liquor bottles. A neon-lit clock glowed mouthwash green above the door. Dean Martin sang "Volare" from the ancient jukebox, and two TVs showed the same football game, the volume down to zero. No wine list. No tables. Just a jet-black bar, with wall mirrors fore and aft. So you can look at yourself looking at yourself while you shed your vanities. The Bow Bow begs introspection.

Candy Wong has owned this place for fourteen years. She matches the decor. For this I am thankful. And I am thankful for her chatting me up and flirting just a little bit,

---

P erhaps the nearest I come to gluttony is with wine. As often as possible, when a really beautiful bottle is before me, I drink all I can of it, even when I know that I have had more than I want physically. That is glutinous.

But I think to myself, when again will I have this taste upon my tongue? Where else in the world is there just such wine as this, with just this bouquet, at just this heat, in just this crystal cup? And when again will I be alive to it as I am this very minute, sitting here on a green hillside above the sea, or here in this dim, murmuring, richly odorous restaurant, or here in this fishermen's café on the wharf? More, more, I think—all of it, to the last exquisite drop, for there is no satiety for me, nor ever has been, in such drinking.

Perhaps this keeps it from being gluttony—not according to the dictionary but in my own lexicon of taste. I do not know.
                    —M.F.K. Fisher,
          An Alphabet for Gourmets

something I cannot expect at the posh wine bars I hate to love. Where people pontificate *ad nauseum* about the merits of their Merlot or the subtleties of their Sauvignon; propound about pH and boast of their Baccarat.

Candy brings me gin and tonic in a plain, heavy glass made in Taiwan, with no comment beyond a genuine smile as the music changes to Sam Cook. Down the bar, a twenty-first-century Fred Flintstone is holding forth for the benefit of Barney, Wilma, and Betty. He is discoursing upon the relative merits of nuclear-powered vs. conventionally powered submarines. He confesses that if he had ever seen one, or at least been in the navy, he could enlighten them further. Barney has lost interest and steals glances at the game; Wilma is either attentive or glassy-eyed; Betty is stoned. Candy just wants to know if my drink is satisfactory, not if it has an oaky nose or is displaying itself well in this atmosphere. "You relax," she says. "No worries here."

So I stay a while and let the maddening crowds maddeningly throng, a mere block away, and yet so far. Another G&T, another Dino croon. Italian and Chinese in comfortable incongruity, here in the confines of the bar and out there on the opposing shores of Broadway. As I look into that double mirror at me looking at me I am reminded that legend has it that Marco Polo brought pasta from China to Italy. And in that mirror, as I sip that humble G&T, I see Candy applying new lipstick, and legend tugs at me to say that it was also Marco Polo who brought the kiss from Italy to China. She sees me watching through the red lit mirror. She winks, smiles, and blows me a kiss through time and reflection all the way from Chinatown to Little Italy. You can't get that from even the swankiest sommelier. Not at any price.

Richard Sterling is the author of The Fire Never Dies *and* The Fearless Diner, *four books in the Lonely Planet World Food series, and editor of* Food *and* The Adventure of Food. *Currently he is either tasting a fine wine or is perched on a tattered barstool. But we don't know which.*

THOM ELKJER

Wine Wild West

American wine is still conquering
new frontiers.

A BIG NEW YORK PUBLISHING COMPANY WAS ON THE PHONE, offering me a contract to write a book with "Wine Country" in the title. This got my travel juices flowing, because wine is made all over this good green earth, and wherever there are winemakers there is wine country. I figured I'd be making a series of exotic, vinous voyages for a couple of years at a minimum. When I mentioned this to the editor at the publishing house, he seemed confused.

"This is a wine country book," he said.

Now I was confused. Then it dawned on me that the book was supposed to be about *American* wine country. This cooled my excitement somewhat, but soon I saw the bright side. There's wine made in almost every one of the fifty United States, and I was eager to visit as many of them as possible. Suddenly I had visions of vineyards in Virginia, wineries in Wisconsin, and barrels in Boise.

Again, my new editor was bewildered. "Boise?" he asked. "I thought we were talking about the wine country."

This brought me up short. "Let me understand clearly," I said. "You mean the West Coast, right?"

"That's right," came the reply. "Wine country."

Well, that was still okay. There are some fascinating vineyards and winegrowing regions in Washington and Oregon as well as California, and I started to describe them.

He interrupted me, in that gently pointed way that long-time publishing people use to manage their exuberant authors.

"Thom," he said, "We need to focus the project a little bit. For the marketing people. You understand?"

"Umm, yes," I said. "You want California, right?"

"That's what we want," he said soothingly. "Wine country."

"So let me run a few ideas by you," I said, trying to sound like a really non-exuberant marketing person. "I believe our readers are ready for, in fact they need, quality information about such emerging California viticultural areas as Monterey, the Sierra foothills—"

"This is about *wine country*," came the response, more emphatically now. "Everyone knows what that means."

He meant the Napa Valley. Perhaps I had known it from the beginning of the conversation. But I hung in there, and in the end got permission to put the wine regions of Sonoma County and Mendocino County in the book too.

I don't mean to make this guy out as a provincial New Yorker who never gets out of Manhattan; he's actually a cosmopolitan European who knows there's wine everywhere. We were just having a terminology problem. In fact, I got one of my all-time-favorite, wine-country assignments from another publishing guy in New York, the executive editor of a big wine magazine. He sent me to Tucson, Arizona, to write about the disproportionate number of restaurants with outstanding wine lists there.

It was a surprise to discover that an hour outside Tucson—or about as far as Napa is from San Francisco—there is a wine region capable of producing wonderful wines. It's microscopic compared to Napa, and it's at the far opposite end of the glamour spectrum, but those very qualities make it much more lovable.

My first evening in Tucson, I had planned to have dinner with someone I'd read briefly about during my research. Gordon Dutt is a retired soils science professor at the University of Arizona in Tucson. This enterprising gentleman had, years before, been given the job of identifying agricultural crops that would prevent erosion of the high prairie southeast of Tucson, while generating some income for the state's depressed agricultural economy. In the course of his investigations, he found that the mineral-rich, reddish-colored soil in an area near the town of Sonoita was similar to soils in parts of California, France, and Australia—places people had been making outstanding wine for a long time.

So he planted a vineyard. Never mind that the windswept grass-lands of Sonoita range well above 4,000 feet of elevation, and that Nature herself had put little there besides gnarled trees. Never mind that temperatures can be fierce in both winter and summer, that little rain falls, and that the last winegrowers in Arizona had been Spanish missionaries trying to keep up with their daily need for sacramental wine. Never mind that people laughed at him, some openly. He persevered, and eventually established a winery. I figured he would provide oddball local color for my story about the real Tucson: a hedonistic paradise of golf courses, spa resorts, and deluxe restaurants.

That's not exactly how it turned out.

When my wife and I arrived in Tucson on a January afternoon, we were physically and mentally beat. We had a heavy schedule of interviews, meals, and hospitality tours beginning the next morn-ing, and all we wanted was to sleep. About 5 P.M., I called Dr. Dutt to say I would have to break our date and replace it with a tele-phone interview sometime later in the month. It was an uncom-fortable task, and I got off the phone as quickly as I could. It rang not a minute later. Recovered from his surprise, Dutt insisted on coming to the hotel and seeing me anyway. If we couldn't have dinner, we could have a bottle of his wine in the bar and talk. He was only a few blocks away, he said, and was leaving on a long trip the next day. I could not hold out against his arguments, so I excused my wife for health reasons and, an hour later, went down to the bar of the venerable Arizona Inn.

Dutt arrived with a lady friend, and we asked the youngish wait-er for a bottle of the Sonoita Vineyards Cabernet Sauvignon. He had never heard of it, which did not go over very well with us. I asked to talk to someone else, who also shrugged in noncomprehension. We progressed through the ranks until we reached the restaurant manager, who kept his eyes on mine as he explained that the wine had been taken off the Inn's list some time ago. I got the message. He was being diplomatic, because there's generally a primary reason a wine gets taken off a restaurant list: it's not selling. He didn't want to say this in front of the winemaker. Instead he said that the Inn was "reevaluating the Arizona wines on its list."

Ultimately we ordered something from California and began to chat. When I asked Dutt to explain about starting his vineyard, he became more animated than I have ever seen someone in his late seventies. There was no need to ask questions. He poured out his story, with a passion so distracting I kept forgetting to write down what he was saying. It was mostly about fighting the odds, learning to make wine all on his own, without any infrastructure or industry around him, in an inhospitable environment. He wanted to make wine as good as the great Bordeaux wines he had tasted in France, and he argued strongly that he had achieved his goal. It seemed hard to believe, but there was no way to know.

An hour later, he was still talking, his eyes moist with emotion and my hand clasped in his. Apparently he was making up for a lifetime of being under-appreciated for his contribution to American viticulture, and I realized I needed to get back to my own agenda. The next time he took a breath, I seized an opportunity and got in a question. "The manager mentioned other Arizona wines," I said. "What are they like? Who makes them? Where can I find them?" This stopped him.

"There are a few others," he said. "We're the biggest and the oldest. We also have the newest facilities."

He had mentioned starting out in a small garage on his lonely vineyard property, and I asked what had become of it. He got a funny smile on his face and said he was renting it out to another winemaker. Perhaps he liked the idea that someone else was following in his footsteps. Or perhaps he took a kind of pleasure in the fact that someone else was suffering through the same hard conditions he had. In any case, I elicited the name of this individual, one Kent Callaghan.

In return, Dutt made me promise to buy his Sonoita Vineyard wines in Tucson and try them, and to come out to Sonoita to visit the winery over the upcoming weekend. I could not say no. No matter what else I had gleaned in our short time together, this man's passion for making wine despite all odds will never leave me.

And so, a few days later, I was rolling through the Arizona countryside, following instructions that said things like "cross the iron bridge, turn left at the gate, and follow the dirt road around the hill." I had with me my wife and our friend Bart, who lives in Tucson. Had Bart ever been to Sonoita to go wine tasting? He had not. "Everybody knows where the wine country is," said Bart, who moved to Tucson from San Francisco, "and it ain't in Arizona."

But it was.

When we came to the crown of the hill we saw a small vineyard, only a few acres in size but obviously more than a few years old. It was January, so the vines were virtually bare and about as forlorn as vineyards can look, even on a bright, sunny day appropriate for shirt-sleeves and sun hats. The landscape was rolling hills covered with long golden grass, hill-hugging trees, and the occa-

> The fact that the foothills of the state [of California] are admirably adapted to the culture of grapes particularly for wine-making purposes, cannot be too often repeated…
>
> The experience of scientific culturalists has demonstrated that while the loamy bottom lands produce the largest and most luscious grapes for consumption as fruit, the red gravel lands of the hills and high plains produce grapes which yield the best flavored and most lasting wines. If the majority of our miners, who are destined to years of toil, ending in poverty, at last would plant about their cabins a few acres of vines, they would find more profit therein ultimately than in the diggings which cause them so much anxiety.
>
> —Editorial, *San Francisco Bulletin*, February 7, 1861

sional abandoned barn silvered by relentless sun. We paused a moment in silence, taking in the incongruity of grape vines in this landscape almost devoid of human influence.

Finally we descended on the dirt track into a cradle between several hillocks. Down below we saw a shed-like building with a van parked outside, haphazard piles of metal and plastic equipment spreading in all directions, and absolutely nothing that said "winery." No sign, no barrels, no tanks, nothing. We had all but turned around when I realized that some of the metal had the vague form of a stemmer-crusher—an essential piece of equipment for winemaking. We rolled down to the shed and parked. I recognized other pieces of equipment. This could only be the original winery of Gordon Dutt, now the province of Callaghan Vineyards.

The man who greeted us, Kent Callaghan, was the polar opposite of his predecessor. He seemed uninterested in our visit, offered little in the way of welcome, and answered questions with the briefest of replies. I was used to trading on the notoriety of the magazine that had sent me to Tucson, because it made people open up and put their best foot forward. Certainly they were doing that in the restaurants and resorts all over town. But out here in the prairie lands—make that "wine country"—Callaghan seemed less than impressed. He was downright skeptical that anyone from a big-time wine magazine would be anything but trouble to him. I have since come to understand why people feel this way (and not just in Arizona), but at the time I almost took it personally.

Fortunately neither Bart nor my wife make wine or write about it, so they were just being their charming, engaging selves. Callaghan was not eager for me to see inside the building, so we waited outside while he produced clean, professional tasting glasses, set them down on an upright barrel outside the winery door, and proceeded to offer us a once-in-a-lifetime winetasting experience.

I was not in town to write a wine story, so all I wanted to do was see if grapes grown in Arizona could make top-quality wine. And the evidence, in this case, was conclusive. Standing in the warm winter sun, we savored a series of distinctive wines, some of them downright delicious. Callaghan knew they were good, and I knew they were good, and we somehow reached an unspoken agreement on that point without having to go through the usual song-and-dance routine between winemaker and wine writer. Out in the middle of nowhere, with the most rudimentary of means, this guy was single-handedly making great wine. It almost didn't matter what I thought of it: making wine at all was a considerable achievement.

Slowly, his manner warmed. When he went into the "winery" to get a sample of newly fermented wine from the previous autumn, he left the door open so I could follow him inside. As my eyes adjusted to the dim light, I was amazed. The room was clearly well organized into fermentation, storage, and shipping areas, but it was still more fit for bales of hay than barrels of wine. "You need a real winery," I said.

"We're building it," he said. "If people come all the way out here to taste wine, it shouldn't be too hard to get them to come to a nice new winery back out on the highway."

I asked about a designation on one of his labels: "Buena Suerte Vineyard." He explained that when he planted his own vineyard in the Sonoita area, he told a friend of his about the project and the guy said, sarcastically, "good luck, pal." So Callaghan named his vineyard "Good Luck" in Spanish. This puckish sense of humor turned up in a few other ways, and pretty soon everyone was having a good time.

By the time we left, it was too late to visit Gordon Dutt's current winery, which had closed for the day. But I did keep my promise to find his wines in town and try them. We found a shop that had what we were looking for, and I was amazed to see that the youngest wine for sale from Sonoita Vineyards was five years old. There were others on the shelf that were ten years old. In Napa, if you find wines that old they're locked in a special case and priced like jewelry. The man behind the counter eyed my purchases and asked if I knew what I was buying. I told him I had met Dr. Dutt a few days earlier. This seemed explanation enough. He handed me the bottles and we went on our way.

I was beginning to like this frontier approach to wine: unpretentious, understated, and unusual. I found out later that evening that it extended beyond the fledgling wine industry—or rather, that the local wine business was a reflection of the local approach in general.

While the others repaired to Bart's house to prepare a dinner party for friends—at which we would taste Dutt's wines—I headed across town to check out The Tack Room, one of Tucson's toniest upscale restaurants. The original property had been a huge dude range, racing stable, and resort in its pre-war heyday, before suburbs overwhelmed it and pared the property back to the rambling mansion and grounds that now housed the restaurant. It was dark when I arrived, strolled inside, and asked to see the manager. I was told that Drew Vactor, whose family had owned the property for generations, was presiding that night and would be out to have a drink with me in a few minutes. This was a piece of luck, and I reached for my wallet to get out a business card. No wallet. I reached into my pocket for my keys, so I could fetch it from the rental car. No keys.

With mounting dread, I went out to the parking lot and approached the car. It was locked. There inside I could see my keys in the ignition, my wallet on the passenger seat, and, in the back, the bottles of wine we had purchased that day. If I didn't get into the car, there wasn't going to be a wine tasting that night. I approached the valet station, but the two teenagers there just shrugged when I asked if they could help break into my car. I went inside, and while I was looking up phone numbers for locksmiths, the hostess came over and said she would send someone out. I went back outside and waited for him.

He appeared a few moments later. In the dark, I could see only that he was wearing a bomber jacket and had dark hair slicked back. He looked like the head valet to me, and carried the kind of tool you see crooks carry on cop shows: designed for the express purpose of breaking into cars. He seemed genial enough, but said little as he cased my vehicle. To break the ice, I asked jokingly if he also did domestic burglary work. He glanced at me with the merest hint of a smile and said, "They call me Cactus Andy."

I didn't know if that meant yes or no, but it took him all of about two minutes to get the car open. He headed back inside, and I proceeded to gather up my wallet, notebook, and keys before going back inside to meet the owner of the restaurant. The hostess seated me in the bar, got me a drink, and went to fetch her boss. I was preparing my speech of apology for locking myself out of my car and keeping him waiting, when in he walked. He had changed out of his bomber jacket into a suit jacket and tie, but the hair and manner were the same. "Cactus Andy" was Drew Vactor.

He gently accepted my bumbling thanks before changing the subject, and could not have been more gracious, welcoming, and informative about his family, its history, and the restaurant. It wasn't until I was walking out to my car an hour later that I remembered how he had responded when I locked myself out. Try pulling that stunt in Napa and see if the owner of the restaurant effortlessly undoes your error—and then has the good manners to act as if it never happened.

I got back to Bart's house, where the dinner party was just getting underway. By now I was prepared to like the Arizona wines we had purchased, no matter how they tasted. The first one, the five-year-old Cabernet Sauvignon, was nevertheless hard to enjoy in its current condition. If you have ever had a wine that made your lips pucker and your teeth feel chalky from too much tannin, you'll know what I mean. The others present were soon merrily dismissing the wine, its maker, and Arizona out of hand. "Why are we drinking this stuff?" someone asked, knowing that Bart would have plenty of juicy California wines stashed away somewhere.

I was about to throw in the towel, when I remembered that for many generations, British collectors of fine Bordeaux used a hard and fast rule: lay the bottle down for ten years before drinking it. Only time can tame the tannin like you used to find in the great clarets of Bordeaux, I explained, and, saying a silent prayer, opened Dutt's other bottle, the Sonoita Cabernet Sauvignon that was ten years old.

I could go on about the complexity, the bouquet, and secondary characteristics, but that would be a typical routine for a wine writer. So let's just cut to the chase.

Arizona, my friends, is wine country.

Thom Elkjer is wine editor for Wine Country Living, *has contributed to* Wine Spectator *in the U.S. and* WINE *magazine in London, and appears in Travelers' Tales volumes on Paris, Italy, Ireland, Food, humor, and personal transformation. He has also published a novel,* Hook, Line and Murder, *and is the author of* Escape to the Wine Country.

Foreign Exchange

What do you give to a wine country
that has everything?

THE PROBLEM BEGAN WHEN I FORGOT TO LEAVE THE CHARDONNAY for the Contessa. Or rather, I didn't forget, exactly. After all, you can't really forget you're transporting a bottle of wine when your luggage consists of a day pack the size of a briefcase. But my friends expected me to leave it behind, and I didn't know what to tell them. I didn't actually have to tell them anything just then because they'd left the day before — three rather substantial middle-aged ladies, two awkwardly growing children, and an impossible amount of baggage somehow arranged in a car about the size of a large bathtub — to drive from Florence to the Milan airport.

Being left behind, my job was to tidy up our rented rooms in the Contessa's *palazzo,* clean out the leftovers in the fridge (Florentine cooking is great, especially when you do it yourself), and pack for a cycling trip to Siena. Part of tidying up was to leave the bottle of wine, decorated with a bow, to indicate our appreciation. Except that because of some recurring problems with the "renovated" plumbing my appreciation was not what it might have been.

It only makes sense to take wine from California to Italy when you make it yourself, and we thought this Alexander Valley Chardonnay, from Cadd Ranch, had turned out rather well. My friends had suggested I bring it along, anticipating the egotistical pleasure of thanking our Contessa by pointing out that we were no ordinary American tourists. But now I looked at the wine, thought about the plumbing, and it occurred to me that the Contessa probably had more than enough wine already. Wouldn't a bottle of California Chardonnay be much better appreciated by some wine-maker along my route?

I had seen many signs for *"vendita diretta"* during my bike trips into the hills around Florence in the previous week, so I knew I'd have no trouble finding a likely candidate for my well-traveled bottle. No one I'd talked to in Tuscany seemed to have much interest in white wine. Still, I had fantasies that such an exotic bottle would be welcomed somewhere. I imagined myself communicating, maybe even conversing if I could assemble enough Italian and he enough English; casually mentioning that I was from California; that, oh yes, I made wine too, and that I just happened to have a bottle of it with me; and would he please honor me by accepting it in appreciation for the excellent wines I was tasting? From a backyard producer of wines of extremely limited distribution, I would rise to membership in the international fraternity of the winemaking elite. I imagined him opening the bottle, doubtfully of course, at a dinner party of local winemakers. They would all exclaim, stunned (or at least mildly surprised) at what a pleasing wine those crazy Californians could produce. I would be the Lone Ranger, doing my good deed and moving on. "Who *was* that masked man?"

I didn't have a particular route in mind; I vaguely thought I'd take my bike on the train as far as Poggibonsi, ride up to San Gimignano, and then take some of the back roads from there to Siena. But after I was thrown off the train (no bikes), I had to get serious about planning. There is a good network of secondary roads running through Chianti Classico south from Florence. But my eye went straight to SS 222, the Chiantigiana, through the heart of Chianti to Greve and Panzano, and then on to Radda and Castellina. These were all towns whose names I recognized from wine labels, and I was sure I'd find just the winery I was looking for.

I taly's unique distinction is preeminence in the grape-vine, so much so that this one asset enables her to surpass all the blessings of other countries—even with regard to perfume, because when vines flower, the pleasantness of the scent is unequalled. So far the best reputation is granted to vines indigenous to Italy. The rest have come from other countries. From Chios or Thasos there comes a light Greek wine comparable in quality to our Aminian vintages; the vine produces very delicate grapes in such small bunches that there is no point in growing it unless you have extremely rich soil. The Eugenia—its name tells us it is of high quality—was exported from the hills of Tauromenium and is now grown only in the region of Alba. This is because if it is planted anywhere else, it loses its personality at once. Some vines, in fact, have so great an affinity for a specific place that their reputation is totally dependent on it.

—Pliny the Elder, *Natural History, Book 14*

Heading south from Florence is a long climb. The road plays roller coaster along the ridges, past the Ugolino golf course (something I didn't expect to see in the Tuscan countryside) and the brown and beat-up soccer stadium. It was Saturday, and I was being passed by small, fast cars with numbers taped to their sides and by clots of cyclists in heavy lycra on wispy bikes. By midday the bottle was getting heavier in my pack.

I hadn't yet found an open winery—signs were hanging out but the doors were bolted. In the small towns all the shops were closed. This was puzzling. I knew the Italians kept rather fanciful hours, but wineries closed on a Saturday? I had read that Greve had a well-known market in the piazza on Saturdays, but when I coasted through town in the late April heat the piazza was nearly deserted: just a few German tourists sitting around in the shade. I checked out the charmless Amerigo Vespucci monument, filled my water bottles, and found a *gelateria*.

Climbing the hill south from Greve I passed

Querciabella, a prosperous-looking winery with a beautiful view: closed. Was I doomed to travel forever through the land of the closed wineries? Onward, and my weary legs began to feel as if they were carting a case of wine through the Alps. Near the crest I stopped at the junction heading off to Panzano, a mile west. The view was picture-book Tuscan, the walled town hazily crowning a small hill. In a last burst of optimism I pulled out my map to see if I might have time for a side trip. Fontodi was there, and I admired their wines.

A couple in a small red car pulled up and got out to stretch and enjoy the view. They were from Florence, out soaking in the warm spring weather. Wasn't it wonderful that, since everything was closed because of the holiday, the countryside was so quiet. Holiday? Didn't I know? Liberation Day, of course. They were congenial, but seemed surprised and aloof at my obliviousness to one of their most significant national holidays, apparently a combination of Fourth of July and Memorial Day. There was an awkward silence while they drank some bottled water. He must have noticed the way I was slumped over my bike, because he suddenly smiled and said *"coraggio."* Then they got back in their car and waved as they set off for Radda.

I reluctantly decided no to Panzano, and followed them toward Radda. At least I had my answer. Bad luck to be cycling through Chianti looking for wine tasting on Liberation Day. Bad luck to be carrying a bottle of wine on my back for thirty miles. But I had some downhill ahead of me through the cooling air, the scenery unfolded from vineyard to olive grove to wooded hillside, and I could make it to Radda by evening.

After yet one more climb to yet one more fortified hilltop, I wobbled into Radda just in time to confirm that the little winery shops in the center of town were no exception. I was imagining carrying my homeless wine all the way to Siena. Perhaps I'd surprise some attractive stranger with a gift while strolling Il Campo. More likely I'd find a seatmate on the train to Milan tomorrow who was willing to take this poor Chardonnay home.

In the meantime I needed to find lodging. I went back out the town gates and down the road toward Castellina. There were a few houses along the road and some signs out advertising *"camera"* and *"zimmer."* I wheeled slowly down the drive toward voices coming from behind a house built in the modern rustic style. Two women stood in a vegetable patch talking animatedly. When they saw me one of them waved and walked up toward me. The Signora was wiry and vivacious, with striking dark features, and, yes, she did have a room available. When she found out I was from California she told me, in Italian, about her daughter in Seattle. I tried to tell her, in Italian, about my winetasting frustrations. But she herself made wine; would I like to try some?

Her casual generosity caught me off guard, and my paltry Italian completely failed me for a moment. My little speech coyly mentioning my own winemaking skills had flown from my brain, but I reached into my pack, and, among the spare shoes and clean pants, found what I was looking for. My *"grazie"* must have come out just as I held my overheated Chardonnay out to her, and it was her turn to be surprised. She looked at me with puzzlement and a hint of suspicion. Then her eyes turned to the handwritten label and she broke into a grin. "You too?" she said. I laughed with her out of unexpected kinship, and out of relief. I held my bottle out again, she took it, and we impulsively shook hands. My problem was solved.

She brought a bottle of her wine to my room as I settled in. She'd bottled her dark red wine in a Ricasoli white wine bottle, label intact. I found myself wondering whether she'd poured the original wine down the drain in order to free up the bottle; she didn't seem the white wine type. I could just see my Chardonnay going into tomorrow's *ribollita*. She wanted to talk about travel and the United States, but I could understand only a tenth of what she was saying. Finally I tried to ask her where she got her grapes. She shrugged her shoulders and said, "around here"—it was clear that for her, wine was something to be drunk and not discussed too much. I was not keeping up my end of the conversation, and so we thanked one another again and she went back upstairs to her family.

After my shower I took my hostess's wine to the deck looking out over the valley. I poured a little into the glass and swirled it in the pale golden light. Finally I was drinking a Chianti at the winery—from a backyard producer of wines of extremely limited distribution. The evening birdsong came up as I sipped my glass of cherries and dust. In a few minutes I would walk back into town for dinner, but right now the warm, dusky air was enough. It turned out that I was already a member of an international fraternity in which my presumption, my grandiosity, was irrelevant. How earthy, how satisfying, how Italian.

Michael Durphy practices psychiatry and winemaking in San Anselmo, California. If his profession and avocation haven't taught him humility, travel certainly has. When he's not involved in one of these activities, he enjoys early music and late-season backpacking in the Sierra Nevada.

ANTONIA ALLEGRA

The Biggest Bread
in Sancerre

A loaf of bread, a jug of wine, and ...

MY MEMORY STILL FLOODS WITH THE RICHNESS, THE SLIGHTLY
moist crumb, the yeasty goodness of every bite of the bread of
Sancerre. It was not only the best bread in the world; surely it
was the biggest, at least in that region. At the turn of the year in
1973, we traveled with our three children from our home in
Palaiseau just south of Paris to visit friends in a five-dog town
southeast of Sancerre. We stayed at the family home of a colleague
of my husband. That home had started its life as a *relais* (inn) in the
1600s. The limestone soil was icy cold, colored only by the deep
umber trunks of occasional leafless trees lining the vineyards. Frost
lined the edges of a small bowl set out for the family dog who
howled into the night, unable to lap from his thick wooden bowl
of frozen water.

We needed bread for the family to go with cheese—local
Pithiviers and Gien were our favorites—and to accompany the
wonderfully crisp Loire Valley white wines. So, we asked around for
the best source. All leads pointed to the stone oven of an older gentleman baker and his son living in the hills outside the village. We
chipped away at the opaque freeze on the windows of our Citroën
and off we went to find the *pain de campagne*.

Following our noses, we sought the renowned bread. We climbed a hill stretching up from the main dirt road. There was a pungency that absolutely overtook us, a smell of the best bread in the world, a smell that wended its way deep to the marrow. By the time we arrived at the crest of the hill, the children were pink and wide-eyed, hopping like small birds on the cold ground. Then we saw the bread. It was the biggest bread we'd ever seen. It was almost as high as Paul, our two-year-old, nearly three feet. The flour-encrusted young *boulanger* guided earthy round loaves from the steaming outdoor oven to a stone side table and then handed a cooled loaf to us. The father baker tore off pieces of the loaf and handed them to us. I still recall the sour, toothy crunch of crust and core of that bread. We talked a while, sipping Sancerre and learning that the people of the town used chunks of the bread to thicken soups and as salad croutons once the bread staled.

As we walked down the hill, the huge round of bread in hand, I chatted with the kids while my husband spoke with the bakers. It was only after we were well on our way back to Palaiseau that he told me that the senior *boulanger* had offered to negotiate a wine country trade: a loaf of his bread for a roll in the hay with madame.

Antonia Allegra writes about food, wine, and travel. She lives in St. Helena, California, where she also works as a career and writing coach for professionals in the wine and food industry.

TIM PATTERSON

The Impossible Port

Wine in the woods beats claret in the kitchen.

OF ALL THE INHERITED WISDOM IN THE CULINARY WORLD, NO
maxim may be older than the chestnut, "Food always tastes better
outdoors." (Indeed, some food historians feel this hoary insight likely dates to an era in which there was no "indoors" worth mentioning.) At one time or another, nearly everyone has enjoyed glorious
al fresco meals that corroborate this deceptively simple adage. But
can anyone explain why?

Time and again the mystery unfolds. What transforms a so-so
cook into a three-star chef the minute the Coleman stove gets
cranked up in a state park? Why does a casserole that routinely produces yawns at the dinner table suddenly inspire free-run saliva
when it's reheated over a campfire? What makes the tuna salad
sandwiches come alive when they're taken out of the cooler, and
the premixed iced tea sing in the glass?

Perhaps there's nothing more to it than the salutary effect of
abnormally clean air. Giving the lungs a vacation from smog, even
a temporary one, could well sharpen the senses and bring out previously hidden flavors in that leftover fried chicken. Or maybe it's
the sheer presence of Nature, the banishment of urban artifice, that
frees up the sous-chef in all of us and sparks so much creative cook-

ery, things like coffee with crunchy grounds, or morning toast charred on one side and still cold on the other. The natural camaraderie of the wide open spaces also likely plays a part, infusing the chow with the good vibes of the chow hounds.

Let me advance a much simpler answer: desperation.

Nine times out of ten, food and beverages outdoors are consumed by people on the edge of starvation, dehydration, or emotional meltdown. The vast majority of open-air meals (leaving aside things like afternoon tea service on yachts) arrive on the plate only after the debilitated diners have worked their way through some rustic appetizers: unusual levels of physical exertion (and discomfort), tussles with racoons, crows, and ants over control of the food supply, multiple failures at fire starting, ineffectual mosquito abatement, the abrupt descent of total darkness, discovery that crucial cooking implements were left at home, harrowing trips back into town for additional propane, firewood, or lantern mantles, and the consumption of excessive volumes of beer.

We've all been campers on this trip. Yet as a worshipper of the grape, I was somehow blind to the subtle interplay of location and libation, the many ways in which wine in the woods is different from claret in the kitchen. It took the following true life experience to convince me of the obvious: that desperation equally accounts for the wondrous qualities of certain beverages in the outdoors.

Some years back, my wife and I took up the civilized custom of unwinding after dinner on Friday evenings with a round of blue cheese, sliced pears, and good Port. We make no claim of originality here; on the contrary, half the fun was participating in a time-honored gourmet tradition. Week after week, we roamed through the fields of blue, from Roquefort to Maytag, from Gorgonzola to Castello to Stilton. Depending on the season, we varied the pears from Bartlett to D'Anjou, sometimes throwing in a Gravenstein apple instead. And depending on our budget, we sipped basic blended Port or treated ourselves to a well-aged tawny or the occasional vintage bottle. Endless variations on a familiar theme.

When summer came along, we simply carted the practice outdoors on weekend camping trips. Under the stars, the combination took on just enough decadence to seem extra delicious. We would sit by the campfire, let the aromas and flavors expand our senses, and pity the poor folks at the adjoining site making do with Cheetos and Bud Light.

In the early fall one year, we headed down the Northern California coast to one of our favorite spots, a gorgeous redwood-lined campground in Big Sur. Though we normally brought pretty basic Port on these camp-outs, this time I had decided to up the ante with a tantalizing 1984 Late Bottled Vintage Character Port from Quinto da Infantado. My interest was piqued by knowing that Quinto da Infantado is one of the few Portuguese-owned Port houses, and further aroused by a hearty recommendation from a trustworthy wine shop. To accompany it we had two Bosc pears (purchased a day or two earlier in order to ripen them fully), a savory, slightly funky wedge of imported Cambozola, and a box of crackers.

Arriving in the morning, I found a good shade spot for the Port, and stood the bottle upright to settle the sediment. We spent a glorious day taking in one of the most lovely stretches of surf and turf on earth. We made dinner, lit a fire, took the cheese out of

F or Port—*red* Port, as one of its earliest celebrants after the Methuen treaty no less justly than emphatically calls it, white Port being a mere albino—is incomparable when good. It is not a wine-of-all-work like Sherry—Mr. Pendennis was right when he declined to drink it *with* his dinner. It has not the almost feminine grace and charm of Claret; the transcendental qualities of Burgundy and Madeira; the immediate inspiration of Champagne; the rather unequal and sometimes palling attractions of Sauternes and Moselle and Hock. But it strengthens while it gladdens as no other wine can do; and there is something about it which must have been created in pre-established harmony with the best English character.

—George Saintsbury, *Notes on a Cellar-Book* (1921)

the cooler to warm up properly, and got ready to rock and roll. Smugness was thick in the seaside air.

By lantern light, we both admired the bottle's label, consciously old-fashioned in its plain design and faux-faded color scheme. After removing the capsule, I plunged the point of my double-winged corkscrew into the cork, gave it a couple of twists, firmly grasped the wings—and broke off the shaft, leaving most of the screw securely lodged in the cork, which had raised not a centimeter.

No problem, I thought. I had brought along a double-pronged cork remover (a souvenir from some tasting room) as a backup, and was confident that the application of a little torque would do the trick. I soon discovered that serious Port bottles are stuffed with truly tight corks. (My personal theory is that because Portugal is home to nearly all of the world's natural cork, its homegrown wines get the best stoppers.) This particular plug was stubborn enough that the prongs stayed resolutely put while my wrist flailed in ever more exasperated motions. The result was a metal tangle worthy of the Museum of Modern Art…but still no Port.

Sensing the direction of things, Nancy turned her attention to the Cambozola and pears. Unwilling to compromise, I turned to my last remaining option, the pathetic screw blade on my ancient pocketknife. I might as well have used my elbow. I hacked with increasing fury at the recalcitrant cork, twisting and yanking, achieving only a dusting of cork shavings and a near-hernia. Utterly defeated, even our late-night game of strip poker (another camping ritual, considerably less fattening) failed to console me.

Late the next morning, after breakfast, Nancy drove the quarrelsome Quinto over to the upscale Ventana Inn restaurant. The sommelier immediately complemented her on the quality of our selection, deftly removed the cork, and put a user-friendly stopper in the bottle.

And so on our second night, we laid out what was left of the cheese and fruit and poured the Port. By now, thanks to the previous night's epic struggle and the bumpy trip to and from the restaurant, every bit of sediment in the bottle had been stirred up. The mouth-feel resembled giblet gravy, and Nancy and I both felt compelled to floss by lantern light before retiring.

But I swear to you: that Port tasted fabulous outdoors.

Tim Patterson lives in Berkeley, California, where the wine country meets what's left of the 1960s. He writes about wine and spirits for a number of national and regional magazines, and prides himself on a soft spot for the underdogs: unglamorous regions, under-appreciated grapes, wines normal people can afford. He makes his own award-winning vino in his garage (reds) and basement (whites).

Wood Nymphs and Viagra

A Greek idyll, with retsina.

COLD, WET, AND DISCOURAGED.

These are not words from Lawrence Durrell or Henry Miller or any other expat writer enjoying the good life in Greece. But my first day on a Greek island was hardly a languorous tale of a taverna-by-the-sea. My boyfriend and I were tromping around Hydra in the rain looking for a place to live for the winter. Through narrow alleys that snaked past whitewashed houses and fuchsia clouds of bougainvillea. Up slick stairways traversed by donkeys bearing stacks of terra cotta roof tiles and bags of cement—even a washing machine in a soggy cardboard box. And down paths that hugged the mountain and overlooked the choppy sea.

Apartments for the winter should have been cheap. But this was Hydra, where cars and motorbikes were forbidden, where goods arrived by ferry and were dispersed by "water taxis" or donkeys. This was the island that teemed with artists and their sycophants, wealthy Athenians and their yachts, Japanese day-trippers and their Nikons, and stars like Joan Collins and their helicopters. Hydra, then, was expensive. And judging from the apartments we'd looked at, even a grungy space on this half-deserted, wind-blasted island with its boarded-up tavernas was going to cost us dearly.

So that's how Linda found us: cold, wet, and discouraged. Her ratty tennis shoes and faded rain slicker showed she was prepared for rugged island life; her wide grin, framed by short, graying hair, suggested she throve on it. After greeting a passing donkey with an affectionate torrent of Greek, she turned to us.

"Where you kids from?"

"San Francisco."

"Duluth," she rejoined, "and I miss it!" She'd married a Greek, Tassos, and they'd lived on Hydra with her mother-in-law for the past ten years. We followed her uphill to a corner market where she bought bread and plunked a large, empty plastic water bottle on the counter. I was surprised Hydra practiced recycling.

"Oh no," Linda said. "This is for the wine, from the barrel out back. My husband makes me buy his wine," she whispered. "He won't come in here because he thinks the owner is a cheat. They're cousins, haven't spoken to each other in years." She rolled her eyes.

The shop owner's wife generally ran the store, but for the wine-pouring duty, she had to fetch her husband. He would not allow her to touch the barrel. While we waited in the tiny store for him to appear, I enjoyed a respite from the rain and studied the goods stacked from floor to ceiling. Toilet paper, spaghetti, olive oil, sheep cheese, goat cheese, cow cheese, small notebooks covered with dust, cartons of cheap ballpoint pens, plastic brooms, Fanta, Mars candy bars, buckets of fresh olives and tangy pepperoncinis, wilted spinach, potatoes caked with dirt, bruised tomatoes, plastic containers of *tzatziki* (a Greek yogurt and cucumber dip), and an ancient bottle of tequila dwarfed by several 1.5 liter bottles of Metaxa, a Greek brandy.

On the off chance that Linda might be able to help us, I explained our urgent need to find a reasonable place for the winter.

"Yanni might have a place to rent, but he's drinking with Tassos." She paid the shopkeeper and we followed her through the labyrinth of miniature streets and up another steep hill, to an unassuming, dark, wooden shed. I heard muffled laughter before Linda opened the creaking door. My eyes needed a few seconds to adjust to the musty darkness inside.

"This is Steve and Erika. They're American," Linda announced. "That's my husband," she said, pointing to the big-bellied guy in the red flannel shirt and baseball cap who'd already risen to shake our hands.

"I hate America," he said. "But I like you." We all laughed. Linda explained our plight and Yanni nodded. "Business later. First, we drink. Sit." I feared the saggy canvas chair I sat on would break. Like the men, it was past its prime. Yanni introduced himself before hunting down two more glasses. He had silver hair and dark, sparkly eyes.

"He is a poet," Tassos announced. They'd known each other since they were kids.

"Tassos is my light," Yanni said. "I would be sad without him."

Yanni put a tiny glass before each of us, poured some white wine from the water bottle into a small copper pitcher, then, using the pitcher, filled our glasses with wine. This was retsina, a much-disparaged wine that could be traced back to the

Resin found its way into wine in the Mediterranean when the Greeks were first transporting wine in earthenware jars call amphorae. Even the best-made amphora was not watertight, so sticky tree sap was smeared on the inside. This kept the wine from leaking out, and kept air from leaking in and spoiling the wine. By the time of Pliny, in the first century of the Common Era, the flavor of resin was considered one of the charms of wine, and winemakers developed various techniques for adding it. When the Romans shifted to wooden barrels in the third century, most other winemakers in the eastern Mediterranean did too, but Greek taste buds were not to be denied. Today retsina gets its resin flavor from the Alep pine. Bits of pine resin are added to the grapes just after they are crushed, and they stay with the wine until clarifying steps are taken later in the winemaking process. This technique goes back to the ancients, who also had a related rule: the best wines should not be resinated at all.

—TE

ancient Greeks. What tasted to many Americans like Pine-Sol was actually the beverage of choice for Odysseus. Back then, wine spoiled quickly, so additives like seawater or, in this case, pine resin, were used to preserve it. When I'd had retsina in the States, it had resembled paint thinner more than Homer's "honey-hearted wine." But in this wine, the color of watery, winter sunshine, the hint of pine was refreshing, not overbearing. Now I understood why Greeks had given retsina a more romantic name: wood nymph tears.

Greek custom requires that the glass never be empty. Both host and guest collude on this, with the guest never swigging down that final mouthful, and the host relentlessly topping off the guest's wine, until every drop of wine is gone. The dangerous element of this game is that the better the wine, the smaller the glass, and the more vigilant the host, the less aware one is of how much wine one is ingesting. I came to think of this as "retsina creep," a term that doubled as a reference to some of the opportunistic local men I would later drink with.

From the looks of it, Tassos and Yanni had been at it all afternoon. Now the drizzle became a deluge, thrumming on the roof. These aging men teased each other like teenage boys, told dick jokes tirelessly (mostly in English for our benefit), and laughed until they cried. Impotence was a favorite topic. "We used to drink in this shed when we were fifteen," Tassos said. "In this shed you have everything you need. A bed," he pointed to a folded cot in the corner, "a thing to look at the sea," he indicated a small telescope on a tripod, "and even this…" He gestured to an empty condom display that looked to have been snatched from an old drugstore. I didn't ask. Tassos leaned in close and confided, "He stole that! But look. All the condoms: finished!"

Yanni: "Tassos doesn't need them—he is too old to make sex now! He needs Viagra!"

Tassos: "Wife too fat. Need young girl to make me go again!"

One joke flew by in Greek, causing the men to collapse in giggles. I asked for a translation. "Or do I not want to know?"

Tassos: "Is better you not know."

Linda (who wasn't drinking): "Tassos said his dick leans to the left. Yanni said that's because he's a communist!"

Yanni kept repeating, "No, you don't understand: I love this guy! I like this guy!"

They apologized profusely for having eaten most of the food. All that was left of the grilled fish were charred fish heads attached to skeletons picked clean. They handed me a plate with a few pieces of grilled octopus.

"Tassos caught this," Yanni said. "He is a fisherman."

"I work only for wine now," he said, "for my friends."

They passed around a plate of olives swimming in olive oil. "From my trees," Tassos said. We broke off chunks of bread and swabbed them in the olive oil, laced with raw onion. Despite the dirt floor and drafty walls, it was cozy. One overhead bulb poured a yolkey glaze over the windowless interior. I asked the men where they'd learned English. Their stories paralleled the story of the island since Hydra's fortunes were tied to the sea. In the nineteenth century Hydra became a maritime heavyweight, famous for it shipbuilders; today the island was home to the merchant marine academy our hosts had attended. Yanni and Tassos had traveled the world and picked up English this way before returning to the tranquility of Hydra, to their families and old friends, to their beloved wine. They would never leave, they said. They would miss their wine too much.

Now we were their friends too, they assured us. "You must come back and we will do the whole thing, the food and the wine, and next time, we will sing."

The next day the gods were smiling on us: we found an airy apartment in a deserted village, roughly a forty-minute hike from the harbor. This rental, located above Antigone's Ouzeri (closed for the winter) was available at a significant discount due to the laziness of foreigners—no one wanted to have to hike into town for groceries. Yanni's parting words had been, "If you no take my apartment, no problem: we still be friends. My house is your house." True to his word, he didn't seem bitter that we'd drunk his wine and then moved to the hinterlands. However, living outside of town encouraged a hermit existence, so we rarely saw the trio. Then, like many of the islanders, they left for the holidays. I knew they'd be back in the spring. After all, they couldn't live without their wine.

Nor could we. On sunny days, we hiked to town to buy our own retsina at that corner market, hauling it home in our backpacks. We would sip it while we sat on our terrace overlooking the sea. But the wine always tasted a little over-the-hill, a little vinegary, a little sticky with resin. Sometimes there were insects floating in it (I like to think they died drunk), which added an authenticity you just can't buy in Provence. Alas, even when the wine was bug-free, it wasn't the same as that day in the shed with the fisherman and the poet, with Viagra jokes and wood nymph tears.

Erika Trafton has traveled in thirty-five countries and worked as a writing instructor, dishwasher, hotel painter, legal file clerk, substitute science teacher, personal assistant, recipe translator, prep cook, tutor for the learning-disabled, and dog-walker. Once she was paid by the hour to entertain a pair of cats. She lives in the San Francisco Bay Area where she is writing a book about traveling around the world while coping with bipolar illness.

ALAN GOLDFARB

Chewing on Chile

*Chilean wine country offers a
tasty collision of cultures.*

"THE FRENCH HAVE GOT THE BALLS AND THE CHILEANS HAVE the wine."

That statement, made by an expatriate Canadian working in the wine business in South America, specifically concerned the French, who are buying up cheap Chilean vineyard land faster than a grape picker works on a cold harvest morning. It applies just as well to the untold amount of foreign money being poured into the Chilean wine industry from a number of countries, including the United States.

There was plenty of it on display when the Baroness Philippine de Rothschild—who inherited the Bordeaux first-growth estate Château Mouton Rothschild—climbed from her fire-engine-red helicopter after it set down in the middle of her new vineyard in central Chile's Maipo Valley.

Chileans had never seen anything like it. They'd never seen such opulence, with Santiago's high society—represented by the monied class, dignitaries, and high government officials—joined by dozens of members of the international wine press (myself included), for food, wine, and fireworks that obliterated the star-filled sky. The occasion on this splendiferous late-summer night was the inauguration of Chile's newest and most expensive bodega, called Almaviva. The opening of Almaviva, a joint venture between Mouton Rothschild and Chile's Concha y Toro, spelled the end of Chilean wines' run as the best bargains in the world.

But what did it matter that interlopers from half a world away were suddenly investing in Chile as if it were some red-hot IPO, and charging $70 at the opening bell? I was there, in the country, on the ground. I had had it up to here with the swells, the dignitaries, and the high-priced frou-frou meals laid on to impress the foreigners. I wanted to find the real Chile.

I found it when I stumbled upon Derek.

Derek is a suave, darkly handsome expat Canadian with jet-black, slicked-down hair parted in the middle. Two long thick strands cascade down either side of his forehead in a rakish sort of way. The hair seems to give him confidence as he knocks on the scarred, wood-slatted door of what he calls an "anti-restaurant."

We have approached the place by walking down Purisima Street on the fringes of the teeming Barrio Bellavista, on a warmly delicious Monday night at the beginning of February. With no sign of any sort to announce its existence or purpose, save for some graffiti on its green-walled exterior, I get a feeling right away that our destination, the El Carmaño, must have harbored a left-leaning clientele who sought refuge from the darkest period in Santiago's modern era, under the repressive regime of Augusto Pinochet.

In fact, as Señor Vicente Góme, El Carmaño's sixty-year-old proprietor, tells it, he opened the restaurant during the height of Pinochet's rule "because food was taken off the table. Generations had missed out on the real thing. It was the death of Chilean food. Anyone was allowed in here except the monied classes and the drunkards. That's why you have to knock on my door."

Thus, the "anti-restaurant." Anti-Pinochet writer Julio Cortazar once read his work here, as did poet Nicanor Parra.

It's half past ten and the El Carmaño is just beginning to fill up. Its rabbit warren of rooms, however, seems to be stuffed to the gills with wooden chairs inexplicably hanging from the ceilings and with hand-written messages of love, politics, and greetings scrawled on every conceivable surface from floor to ceiling. The latter seems to be the custom in restaurants and bars all over the country, as Chileans take advantage of the freedom of expression they were so long denied.

Gómez has no freezer in his kitchen. Everything is served fresh. The eight-page handwritten menu consists mostly of fish: the staple of this long, thin wisp of a country, whose entire 2,700-mile western edge is lapped by the Pacific Ocean.

There's no Chilean sea bass. Most of it, called *congrio* here, is shipped out to the United States. What you'll find at El Carmaño, or during the day at the 100-year-old Eiffel-designed Mercado Central, the magnificent central marketplace on Calle Puente, are fish called *corvina, merluza, reineta, lisa, sierra,* and *mariscos* such as barnacles, whose ugly gray-mottled six-inch girth reveals a most delicious creature, which when steamed tastes reminiscent of crab.

Gómez relentlessly sends out an array of such wonders as *reineta,* a flat-bottomed Pacific fish, pickled and served with whole black peppercorns. In another dish, it's baked in foil with clams and bacon. We follow that with baked pureed crab (or is it barnacle?) with gouda, and what Gómez calls a "pure" *chupe* of clams and mussels. With glee we consume grilled goat cheese and then stewed lamb with bell pepper sauce. The dessert is made from a variety of Chilean fruit, including dried and reconstituted peaches with what, we are told, are wheat hulls with stewed figs, papaya with *lucuma* sauce, and carmelized *alcayote,* which has the consistency of marmalade. We wash it all down with a bottle of very local Carmenère made by Alvaro Espinoza, who is in our party of six. The wine label depicts a Mapuche *kultrún,* a drum of Chile's native Indian people.

After two and a half hours, this gringo is sated. But Derek, a young entrepreneur working on the fringes of the booming Chilean wine business, is ready to move on. So, as we leave El Carmaño, Derek and his Chilean-born wife, who is struggling to become a winemaker, squeeze back into their red 1959 Volkswagen Beetle to whip me around Santiago. It's one o'clock in the morning.

We scoot to the other end of the Bellavista Zone, a thirty-square block area on Santiago's north side. It's the oldest part of the city and it most resembles New Orleans's French Quarter. But unlike the Quarter, things don't get going here until ten or eleven at night and continue until the sun begins to peek blush-pink over the Andes to the east.

At the entrance to Parque Metropolitano, where you find the best views of Santiago, you also find the highest concentration of restaurants, nightclubs, *cerveza* halls, and discos. The streets themselves, particularly on Pio Nono, resemble an outdoor bazaar with cigarettes, lighters, lava lamps, gin flasks, playing cards, and photos of Elvis being hawked from Mapuche blankets laid out on the sidewalks. The scene—complete with tarot readings and tie-dyed shirts—is not unlike that on Berkeley's Telegraph Avenue.

The streets are jumping with the sounds of music and people. The courtyard at Mundano, a restaurant at Dardignac and Constitution streets, is packed. So is the mysterious Etrinko wine bar where a knock on the door

---

The explosion of interest in Chilean wine in the 1980s exposed the fact that many of the country's best Merlot vineyards contained a grape that was not Merlot at all, but Carmenère. This grape was killed off in its native Bordeaux by phylloxera in the late 1800s, but not before it had been exported to Chile and found a much more hospitable home. Its reputation restored, Carmenére is now being made on its own, and it's one of Chile's more intensely pleasurable red wines.

—TE

---

may or may not get you in. The Alcol Profunto, a nautical-themed coffee and cognac bar, makes me think of a Greenwich Village coffeehouse in the late '50s.

In Bellavista, for the serious wine drinker, it's the Kilométre 11680. The name refers to the distance between Santiago and Paris. For this is as real a French wine bar as you'll find in Chile. The 100-selection wine list at this bistro features mostly French wines but has four Carmenères, the varietal which will eventually elevate Chilean wines out of the bargain bin. The "list" is delivered on a sizable wooden plank, I suppose to show that at Kilométre, they are serious about wine. The food, on the other hand—with a "smiley face" stamped next to dishes such as *foie gras* with caramelized onions, to show it's in short supply—I find wanting.

Derek picks me up the next night at around ten. So as not to make me feel as if I missed anything, he takes me to the El Bosque Norte district in the north central part of the city, for a light meal at Liguria. Luckily we score a seat at on an outdoor table but the cigarette smoke nevertheless is intrusive. We wash down small plates of mussels and grilled *congrio* with a Casablanca Sauvignon Blanc. It's all wonderful.

We then jump back into the Bug and head for the nearby Plaza Nuñoa, a live theater district. Its outdoor cafes cater mainly to actors, who come for a late-night *Vaina*, a popular Chilean concoction (sometimes referred to as a "grandma" drink because of its sweetness) consisting of Port, Cognac, and an egg yolk. We end up at Las Lanzas for a punch-like aperitif, which contains white *vin ordinaire* with ice, sugar, and canned peaches. It reminds me of bad white Sangria.

The "treat" here, insists Derek, is a hot dog topped with mashed avocado and gobs of mayonnaise. It's called a "Hot Dog Italiano." Next comes strips of beef with julienned stringed beans and tomatoes on white bread, whose crust has been cut away. I can't tell if it's the cigarette smoke or the food that drives me back into the VW for a quick ride to my hotel. I need to regroup.

Thank goodness I'm on my own the next night, because Derek has worn me down. I walk to the more subdued and decidedly upscale Providencia district. Here on Avenue Suecia, every business seems to be a nightclub, a restaurant, or a bar. Discos such as Mala Junta with twelve-foot-high faux-bronze "Oscars" out front, share the street with The Big Box, The Green Bull, Mr. Ed, Entre Negro, Casbah Discotheque, and finally the Louisiana River Pub, where you can get a "Coney Island Twist," a platter consisting of *papas fritas* with hot melted cheddar cheese. I was brought up near Coney Island and have never seen French fries treated like this.

It is midnight now on a Wednesday night and the clubs haven't even opened. I figure I'll quit while I'm ahead, walk back to my hotel, and settle in to dream of the good peasant food of Santiago, a city of clean, safe streets that seem to have left Pinochet, the Andes, and the Mapuche Indians far behind.

Alan Goldfarb has been the wine columnist for the San Francisco Examiner, *a contributing editor for* Epicurean Magazine, *and a contributing writer for* Wine Enthusiast, Appellation, *and the* San Jose Mercury News. *He is currently wine director at restaurants Via Centro and Santa Fe Bistro in Berkeley, California, and Nirvana Restaurant in San Francisco.*

Scents and Sensibility

It all comes down to you and your nose.

SMELL HAS ALWAYS BEEN THE COMPASS BY WHICH I HAVE NAVIGATED through life. Having hippie parents in the 1960's guaranteed a childhood filled with a vast array of smells. Showers were uncool, incense was cheap, and the older and funkier your truck, the better. I was intimately familiar with the smell of cannabis by the time I was six. My friends and I fantasized about the suburban life. In our minds, nothing was sexier than wall-to-wall shag carpeting, station wagons, and the smell of air conditioning. I grew up secretly admiring the sterile aromas of swimming pools and malls: my personal revolution against the aromatic tyranny of the hippie. But by the time I was a young adult, I found I could embrace both the feral and the sanitized.

During college in New York, in an effort to please my father, I hatched a plan to become an attorney. It is a good thing I did not succeed, as the smells of law libraries and courtrooms would not have suited me. Instead, I plodded away at a newspaper job and several restaurant positions until one day a sommelier shoved a 1978 Échézeaux under my nose. Like a lifeline, the aromas of the wine lifted me from the throes of my career ennui, and I immediately signed up to apprentice with the wine steward who had rescued me.

Over the next year, he opened countless doors in my brain with a flick of a corkscrew.

I moved to Washington state and took a job in the cellar of a small winery. Among the tanks, barrels, and pumps my nose began to catalog a slew of aromas that I had not yet discovered in the bottled wines of the restaurant world. Esters rising from fermenting Chardonnay smelled like banana candy. Tan-colored lees running out of bung holes filled the cellar with yeasty, primal smells. Gaseous, fermenting Merlot must emerged from tanks with prickly, fruit-driven heat. Each barrel smelled different, a crash course in caramel, resin, and spice. Not all of the aromas were pleasant. As I helplessly watched a struggling fermentation produce a horrid, sulfurous smell in our Chardonnay barrels, I felt remorse for the careless criticism I had leveled at wines in the past.

When I worked in Burgundy for a summer, I encountered an entirely different pastiche of smells. Descending into one dark cellar after another, my eyes would slowly adjust to the low light while my nose sifted through the many layers of perfume. I was accustomed to the smell of bleach in American wineries—the antimicrobial insurance we took out so that we could sleep at night. These Burgundian cellars were evolved, fauna-filled testimonials to the complex interaction between yeast and juice. For all of their Cartesian sensibilities, the French approached their winemaking with aboriginal abandon. I was mesmerized.

Later, when I moved to California and traveled around the country as a wine educator, it became clear to me that no two people have the same smell memory. This in turn showed me the hubris of presuming to describe wine for other people. I would pour wines for groups of people and elicit their comments about the smells coming from the glass. Suppose that they were tasting a fruity white wine. If they had grown up in Connecticut, they surely were familiar with the smell of green apples and had been so since childhood. But in the restaurants of Miami, many of the assembled servers hailed from Cuba, Mexico, and Puerto Rico. Their faces lit up in recognition only when I asked if anyone smelled mango.

During these olfactory exercises I saw the lights go on, more so than in any other facet of wine education. Human beings are capable of detecting nearly ten thousand different smells, but most of us catalog only a thousand or so. Our olfactory memory is located in the front of our brain, in the limbic system, where our emotions are stored. Many believe that this is why certain smells can bring sudden tears to our eyes as they resurrect emotional moments from the past. I acknowledged that this was very personal terrain, and asked my students to search for individual metaphors from their own smell memories. The responses were illuminating. Like sparks from a fire, out burst descriptors ranging from cumin to Barbie legs, from Playdoh to star fruit.

I continue to thrive on aroma-steeped sessions with wine. My husband, also in the wine business, is as much a fragrance hunter as I. A glass of older Riesling from the Mosel can stop us both in our tracks, the steep shale hillsides translating to diesel, lime peel and white smoke in a moment.

As my palate evolves, I approach wine differently. It has taken me years and thousands of wines to discover that

As tastes and smells reside not in the objects themselves, but in the senses by which they are perceived, so they are liable to be modified by the habits and conditions of these organs. The difference of tastes, in this view of the subject, is proverbial; and much of the diversity undoubtedly proceeds from the way in which the palate has been exercised. Thus, strong liquors blunt its sensibility, and disqualify it for the perception of the more delicate flavors of the lighter wines. A person accustomed only to bad wines will often form but a very erroneous estimate of the better growths, and sometimes, even, give the preference to the former. Whole nations may be occasionally misled by this prejudice.
— Alexander Henderson (1824)

the most delicate aromas are revealed slowly, after my nose has been in the glass three, four, five seconds. Bergamot, violet, or musk may be hiding behind the more assertive smells of oak lactones, spice, or fermentation character. I suspect it is akin to an archeological dig, where first a carapace emerges and then, after careful digging and brushing, finger bones, beads, and finally the paint and letters on clay come to light.

I am worried that our world is no longer patient enough to wait those extra few seconds. The computer chip has extracted a terrible price for its immense power and speed—we no longer have the patience for long scenes of dialogue in movies, handwritten notes, or wines that beg for contemplation. Our wines, like our forms of communication, music, and food, have become more powerful. Reprising my childhood stand against fragrant hippies, I rebel against the tyranny of Big Wine by delighting in subtle wines instead, searching for quiet communiqués from soil to air to nose.

After beginning her career as an assistant sommelier in 1987 in the Finger Lakes region of New York, Gilian Handelman went on to work in wine production in Washington state, Burgundy, and California in a number of wineries both large and small. After seven years in the cellar, she was hired as Kendall-Jackson's Trade Education Manager for the National Market. She now plies her skills and experience at PPC WineCom, a California-based communications firm serving the wine industry.

PART FOUR

IN THE SHADOWS

ROBERT HOLMES

Strictly Kosher

Wineries — and winemakers —
come in all kinds.

IT WASN'T THE AK-47S THAT SEEMED OUT OF PLACE. I WAS USED
to those. Every group of school children I had seen in Israel had
a couple of heavily armed guards accompanying them. What surprised me was their destination. For a Westerner living in a
country that never seems to have fully come to terms with the
repeal of Prohibition, the idea of young children going on a school
field trip to a winery is enough to drive you to drink. Here was a
large group of fifth graders following the rabbi around Carmel
Winery with the ever-present rifle-wielding guards following
close behind.

I too was introduced to wine at an early age. I well remember at
the age of thirteen being served red wine diluted with water in the
school cafeteria just outside Paris. The experience was memorable
for the medicinal quality of the mixture, whose finish was so big I
can still taste it forty-five years later. It was enough to launch a life
on the wagon.

Had I not persevered and struggled to overcome my initial dis-
taste of the fermented grape, I would not have found myself in the
heart of Israel's wine country as one of the photographers invited
to shoot for the book, *A Day in the Life of Israel*. My assignment to

203

the Shimshon region located between Tel Aviv and Haifa resulted from my well-known epicurean passions.

I had never thought of Israel as a wine-producing country. Serge Hochar of Château Musar produces a wonderful Bordeaux-style red from bomb-ravaged vineyards in the notorious Bekaa region of Eastern Lebanon. I love the wines of Château Musar but always thought them an exception in the Middle East: a geographic accident.

Wine has, of course, been made in the region since well before the birth of Christ. According to the Bible, wine made from grapes smuggled out of the Promised Land sustained the Israelites on their forty-year journey through the wilderness. As improbable as this tale may seem, the wine was undoubtedly so bad that a little went a very long way. In fact, high quality has never been a necessity for the successful export of wine. Israel was probably the first country to develop overseas markets in the expanding empires of Rome and Egypt, where the ancient Egyptians used a mixture of honey, pepper, and juniper berries to make it more palatable. One of Islam's great legacies to the world was the conquest that put the local wine industry out of business in 636 A.D.

The kosher wine industry has benefited from advances in the wine business generally, and it's now possible to buy kosher wines that hold their own with the best of the rest. My favorite kosher producer is California's Baron Herzog, which offers a Lodi Zinfandel among other delicious varietal wines. Gan Eden and Hagafen are two more top California kosher wine producers. The august Lafite-Rothschild family of France makes what is probably the world's best-known kosher wine, produced in Bordeaux by Baron Edmund Rothschild not far from the family's famed first-growth Chateaux. It's called Baron Rothschild. Israel also sends a number of excellent kosher wines to the U.S.—wines you don't have to be Jewish to enjoy.

—TE

When Baron Edmond de Rothschild revived the industry in 1875, the product bore little resemblance to the wine made at Château Mouton Rothschild in France. British Prime Minister Benjamin Disraeli commented that the wine tasted "not so much like wine but more like what I would expect to receive from my doctor as a remedy for a bad cough." Cloyingly sweet kosher wines remained the staple of the Israeli wine industry for the next hundred years. I had never tasted kosher wine; moreover, the tales I heard from Jewish oenophile friends convinced me that I never wanted to.

I drove north from Tel Aviv with minimal expectations. My first impression was how normal everything appeared. No bomb craters. No terrorists lurking in the undergrowth. It could have been California. I felt immediately at home. Rolling vineyards covering gentle hillsides beneath clear blue skies, punctuated by small boutique wineries that could have been in any of the world's great wine growing regions. There was an air of newness to everything, from shiny stainless fermentation tanks to the latest state-of-the-art bladder presses, yet it still looked like the wine business I knew and loved in the U.S. and Europe. But what about the wine? Even that was a pleasant surprise. It certainly wasn't a *premier cru* Bordeaux, but it was a damn sight better than most French "house" wines in pretentious restaurants.

Things were looking up. I had been assigned to Baron Wine Cellars, a small, family-operated business founded in 1984. It was the kind of winery I have shot photographs in all over the world, and I knew exactly what to expect. Or so I thought. I had not anticipated the rabbi.

The majority of wines produced in Israel are kosher. This means that they have been produced in strict adherence to all aspects of the Jewish religious laws called the Halacha. Anyone who has had any exposure to Judaism will know the complexity and, dare I say, wackiness of some of the more esoteric elements of the Halacha.

In the first three years after a vine is planted, the flower buds must be removed to prevent the formation of any fruit. According to the Torah, it is absolutely forbidden to consume this fruit in any way. Only grapes from the fourth year onwards may be used in winemaking. Every seventh year, called Shmita, the fields must lie fallow. Orthodox Jews will not buy any agricultural product grown in Israel during a Shmita year.

From the time the grapes arrive at the winery, only male, Sabbath-observant Jews are allowed to work on the production of the wines. It is not unknown for a winery owner and winemaker to be banned from their own facilities. All substances used in the production of the wine must be certified as strictly kosher for Passover. Finally, a tithe of 1 percent of the wine produced every year is poured away in the presence of prominent rabbis and schoolchildren, symbolizing the tithe given to the priests in the time of the Holy Temples. Imagine Château Petrus doing this!

Traditionally, kosher wine has always been pasteurized. This explains its dubious reputation: The wine was literally boiled. I had always thought that pasteurization was necessary for the wine to be kosher but, for a gentile, the reason is even more bizarre. A wine will be strictly Kosher if made according to the Halacha, which does not allow for pasteurization. However, if a non-Jew opens the wine, it will no longer be considered Kosher unless it has been pasteurized. Pasteurization lives on but fortunately boiling is a thing of the past. As a rabbinical law, it has evolved over time and now, as long as the rabbi sees steam over the wine, it is usually acceptable. This flash pasteurization seems to have little effect on the wine in the short term, but I wouldn't plan on laying down a case for my kids.

Baron wines were kosher, so before I set foot in the production area I was told the rules, most of which concerned touching equipment with my feet. Like any winery, it had pipes and tubes carrying various fluids all over the place, and if I so much as brushed my foot against one of these obstacles the whole production would have to be destroyed. As the potential for disaster was thus made known to me, I was introduced to the rabbi.

To make sure I obeyed the rules, he was to accompany me the whole time. He appeared to have come straight out of Central Casting, dressed entirely in black, with a long black beard and black ringlets under a black hat. As far as I could tell, he was utterly humorless. His piercing eyes, behind glasses with thick, Coke-bottle lenses, never strayed from my feet as I maneuvered through the pipe-strewn floors of the winery. It was like walking on eggshells.

There was no conversation. Occasionally a few words of Hebrew passed between the rabbi and a winery worker. I struggled to concentrate on taking photographs, continually conscious of the fact that a clumsy slip would result in several hundred gallons of wine going down the drain. Two hours seemed an eternity and I have rarely been more relieved to finish a shoot. The rabbi seemed even more relieved.

In spite of all the modern equipment, observing the Halacha while in the winery conjured up a strong feeling of tradition and history. It felt as if these men had been doing this for centuries, in the same ways, according to the same rules. I asked the rabbi how long he had been involved in the wine business. In a strong Midwestern accent he told me, "For about two months—since I moved out here from Chicago."

Oy vey.

Robert Holmes is widely acknowledged as one of the world's finest travel photographers. His photographs have appeared in virtually every major travel magazine, beginning in 1975 when he covered the successful British Everest Expedition for Paris Match *and* Stern. *He has searched for snow leopards in the remote valleys of western Nepal for* National Geographic, *journeyed into the rainforests of Borneo with Penan tribesmen for* Islands *magazine, and crossed the Great Indian Desert on a camel for* Departures. *He has twenty-eight books in print in addition to being featured in the acclaimed* Day in the Life *series and many similar publications.*

LISA SHARA HALL

The Test

In which a winemaker turns the
tables on a wine writer.

PERFORMANCE IS NOT MY STRONG POINT. I DON'T PLAY A MUSICAL instrument or dance. I get nervous when making speeches. I will always raise my hand to answer a question if I'm sure of the answer, but I live in fear of being called on if I am uncertain—that's when I want to slither under the table and become invisible.

Most of time, wine writing and traveling don't require that I entertain people or have answers to all the questions. That's why I travel in the first place, so that the vintners I visit will supply the answers. Tasting wine with the winemaker is my preferred opportunity, a chance to understand the personality that produces a product. Here's where I can ask cause-and-effect questions, compare vineyards, learn vintages, and get a handle on the wine. When I travel, I always try to make appointments with the winemaker because that's the best way to understand and capture everything I can about a wine and a region.

Recently I spent a magical two weeks in pursuit of Riesling, traveling along the Rhine, down to the Mosel, and then into Alsace. I had prearranged visits at most of the top wineries in each region. As a Riesling lover, I looked forward to an educational and particularly delicious trip.

I learned from Georg Breuer in the Rhinegau, tasting his steely *trocken* (dry) wines, tromping through the vineyards, sampling fine older examples of magnificent *terroir*.

On the Mosel, I spent time with the great names—Loosen, Selbach, von Kesselstatt, and Prüm—seeing for the first time the impossibly steep terraces in the vineyards, experiencing the unusual climate for grape-growing, and finally understanding the Oechsle system of ripeness. And tasting all those marvelous fruity wines: the Kabinetts, the Spätleses, the Ausleses, and the spectacular, botrytised dessert wines.

But a late-afternoon visit to J. J. Prüm nearly blew my credibility and came close to shaking my confidence.

I was sitting in the living room of Manfred Prüm and his wife. The windows of the room face the beautiful Mosel River and signature Prüm vineyard on the other side of it: Wehlener Sonnenuhr, with its famous sundial. We were tasting wines and talking, not only about the wines but also about travel, people, history, life. It was the kind of appointment I always hope to have and only occasionally get, a warm, intimate visit with a winemaker and his wife, learning more about their wines than a tasting alone could ever disclose.

After we tasted a number of his wines, Prüm disappeared again to fetch another bottle from the cellar. He returned to the room with one bottle. It was wrapped in a jacket, hiding its label. Prüm poured a glass for me.

"I have been telling you about each of the wines we have tasted. Now it's your turn. I want you to tell me about this wine. What is it?"

This is the moment winemakers love, and wine writers dread. The tables are turned, and those of us who ask questions all day long are faced with the hardest question of all: identifying and describing a wine without knowing what it is. Suddenly I was that classroom schoolgirl again, hoping for all the world to be able to disappear or slink down low and not be noticed. What if I got it wrong about Prüm's mystery wine? I was having a perfectly lovely time, and now I might blow it completely. Yikes!

I started my analysis, using the approach I was learning in my study for certification as a Master of Wine. The color was advanced, a deep golden hue. That was a good clue, a sign of some age. The wine was thick, with higher than usual viscosity. That was a sign of serious sugar in the wine.

I swirled and sniffed, sensing apricots, a strong diesel odor, and honey. All these are classic markers for a Riesling with some age.

Finally I tasted that luscious nectar. More apricots, peaches, honey, minerals, searing acid, and a rich, fat mouthfeel. Lower alcohol of about 8 percent. Sugar more than 100 grams per liter. An older wine, certainly.

But *how* old? Prüm's cellars are cool and deep, which can greatly slow an aging process.

At this point, sweat was beading on my brow. I started speaking.

"Well, this wine has age. The ripeness and structure suggest a good, fine vintage, at least eight to ten years ago, but not too much older. It's not fat enough to be a 1990; there's not enough botrytis to be 1989. I don't think the color suggests *much* older than that, though. So I'd have to say this is a 1988. A very good vintage that wouldn't be confused with an even older wine such as a 1985."

By now, my entire forehead was wet.

Prüm said, *"Ja."*

In a 2000 article in *Harper's Magazine*, William Langewiesche argued persuasively that Robert M. Parker, Jr. is the most influential critic in the world. Parker's eminence is based on his exceptionally sensitive (and durable) palate, his apparently limitless memory for previous tasting experiences, and a stubborn reliance on his own taste buds to tell him what's good. His newsletter, *Wine Advocate*, is widely read in the industry, and his power to "move" wine (create a run that sweeps stores clean) is legendary. Retailers made so much of Parker's numerical ratings, in fact, that he sued them to stop it—proof that however modest the man may be, he knows how much power he has. Imagine what it would be like to have someone that powerful in the travel business.

—TE

I breathed a sigh of relief. I had passed the test!

Then he said, "Keep going."

Keep going? That wasn't enough? What more did he want? I put my attention back on the wine. Hmm. It came to me: the ripeness level. This is one ripe wine. With the level of sugar I perceived, this wine could be a Beerenauslese, which is generally the second-ripest category of sweet Rieslings, riper than Auslese but not as ripe as Trockenbeerenauslese. But was it *that* ripe, with *that* much sweetness? I hedged my bet: "This has the ripeness and concentration of a Beerenauslese, but maybe it's been declassified to Auslese."

Prüm said "*Ja*. Gold label. Declassified to Auslese. *Gut.*" But he still looked expectant.

"And," I said, "it has to be from Wehlener Sonnenuhr."

The same minimal reply from Prüm: *"Ja."*

I passed!

Now sweat was running down my cheeks: very attractive, I'm sure, but I didn't care. The friendly conversation picked up right where it had left off before my performance, as if the examination had not occurred. But we both knew the test had taken place and that it meant something special: I would be welcomed back in the Prüm household anytime.

Lisa Shara Hall is the author of The Wines of the Pacific Northwest *and the co-author of* The Food Lover's Companion to Portland. *She serves as senior editor for* Wine Business Monthly *and also writes for* The Oregonian. *She has contributed to numerous books including the annual* Hugh Johnson Pocket Guide to Wine, The Oxford Companion to Wine, *and* The Hugh Johnson/Janus Robinson World Atlas of Wine.

DAVID DOWNIE

Braving Barolo

Gastronomy and religion can be
a dangerous combination.

THE RIBBON OF BLACKTOP TO MONFORTE D'ALBA UNFURLED
crazily beneath us as we slalomed through Piedmont's lumpy
Langhe hills south of Turin. We'd corkscrewed up from Alba, a
medieval town of white-truffle fame, our base camp for the gastronomic tour we'd mapped out. Alba crouches in a valley fifteen
scenic miles from Monforte as the crow flies but three times that
distance by roller coaster road. A tepid fall sun filled the sky above
the castle-crowned hills around us, hills dwarfed by the distant,
snow-capped mandible of the Maritime Alps. Each rise shimmered
with russet and amber vineyards recently shorn of their Nebbiolo
grapes—the essential ingredient of both Barolo and Barbaresco
wine. Above the vineyards rose the requisite perched villages and
solitary campaniles. Below them the Tanaro River valley teased out
its dark meanders.

In *Piemontese* dialect "Langhe" means "tongues." Here they roll
in all directions, like so many soft Italian "r"s. Tongues—aided by
keen noses and palates—are the most vital of Langhe organs. This
is foodie heaven.

"I don't think I'll be able to eat anything at all tonight after that
lunch," groaned my wife, Alison. A professional photographer, she

212

strained to keep her heavy camera bag from flopping over as we swerved down the road. "And unless you slow down I'm going to be sick."

We swung through clusters of damp stone houses strung along the highway. I eased up on the accelerator. According to our map, Monforte d'Alba, the Pagus Romanus of Antiquity and Mons Fortis of the blood-soaked Middle Ages, lurked around the bend.

I reminded my wife that she wasn't here to indulge her artistic sensibilities and shouldn't waste our precious time shooting in artistic black and white. We hadn't come all this way to document Monforte's history, art, or architecture. If anything, those topics would be trimmings on the colorful, bright, good-news food-and-wine features we had been assigned by luxury travel magazines in France and America.

In a week we'd wallowed through two Lucullan feasts a day in Alba, Neive, Costigliole d'Asti, and other sites of oenogastronomic pilgrimage. We'd slurped gallons of red nectar from musty cellars in Barolo, La Morra, and Barbaresco. We'd suffered through tastings of flinty Pelaverga wine and grappa from Verduno, and choked down grotesquely oaky Chardonnay from fashion-conscious Langhe vintners hoping to cash in on the American market's demand for fruit-pump whites. *Facciamo questo qui per voi*, they'd cluck. This stuff we make for you.

Over-indulgence had begun to take its toll. Despite her athletic build and normally healthy appetite, Alison had not eaten much in the last two days. She'd turned that shade of green worn by long-suffering saints in waxy, Seicento paintings. Had there been saints martyred by food, I wondered?

"If we don't try this place tonight," I said, thinking aloud while trying to gauge the depth of her liverishness, "how am I going to spend the rest of that expense money? Remember what happened in Scandinavia when I economized? My editor was furious."

She nodded. "But we've already eaten at a two-star restaurant today."

"A one-star," I corrected. "And I didn't spend enough."

As far as the American magazine was concerned, writer's hell awaited those who failed to gluttonize and guzzle away their entire expense allowance. Failure to drain the budget meant there wasn't enough luxury at the proposed destination, or, worse, the offending writer was incapable of ferreting it out. And without enough luxury there was no story. Hence luxury was always found, even in the most unlikely places.

We tumbled out of the car in Monforte's main piazza—a misnomer. It was a parking lot facing leprous gray buildings. As in many of the Langhe villages we'd seen, the houses here looked as if they'd last been painted circa 1900. These hill towns possessed what a romantic traveler might call a rough, weathered beauty. However much I might like them, though, they wouldn't necessarily come off well on glossy pages. For one thing, the ruins surrounding us were authentically rundown and occupied by unfashionable natives, some of them in rags. The town looked semi-abandoned.

This, we'd heard, was common in the Langhe. Entire villages had decamped fifty miles north to Turin after the Second World War, when Fiat was hiring assembly line workers to build cars. Only old fossils and the feeble-minded stayed behind to hold down the family fortress.

Though well-heeled Turinese had begun to return and gentrify a handful of hewn-stone hamlets near Alba and Bra (a prosperous small town), many farther-flung villages remained in the realm of the roughshod. Visitors to Monforte were therefore entitled to wonder, as we did, how three highly touted gourmet restaurants could survive in this town of a few thousand souls. The locals couldn't provide enough custom. And people from Turin would have to come too far for spur-of-the-moment indulgence.

I also couldn't help wondering why the Langhe in general had become a resort area—if indeed it was one, as the guidebooks claimed. In a week of touring we hadn't seen many holiday hot spots. There were no lakes, no ski slopes, not even a sizeable forest at hand—just mile upon mile of vineyards surrounded by scruffy oak and chestnut woods. Here an unsuspecting hiker might be frightened away with grapeshot for encroaching on someone's jealously guarded wild porcini mushroom or white truffle territory. After all, real white Alba truffles (as opposed to faux specimens from

Acqualagna or Eastern Europe) are worth about $150 per ounce.

Food and wine are the Langhe's only real tourist attractions, it seemed. What the area in general and Monforte in particular might lack in posh boutiques, museums, and *palazzi,* it compensated with great gastronomy. One connoisseur of regional cuisine I'd button-holed at Alba's annual International Truffle Fair had tremulously pronounced Monforte d'Alba an "epicurean's paradise." His mouth had watered, his bee-stung lips quivering at the very mention of the village's name.

Strange: the place seemed gloomy and unappetizing. Maybe it was the damp fall weather or the darkening hour of the day, or the almost palpable shades of Monforte's gory past about which I'd read with fascination while planning our trip.

Monforte is stewed in history like the local beef is braised in Barolo wine. In addition to the dizzying succession of homegrown and foreign tyrants who plagued the whole of Piedmont, in the eleventh century the Càtari had thrived here. The Càtari (related to France's Cathars) were a heretical Christian sect of proto-vegetarians led by a master Manichaean killjoy named Contessa Berta.

It's a pretty gruesome tale. Epicureans the Càtari were not: their main source of pleasure was denial, denial of natural appetites. They allowed themselves no meat. No sex. No private property. No money. And no worship of icons or images.

That's fair enough, you might say, if you, like them, don't believe in the divinity of Christ, in the Catholic mass, in baptism, or the existence of Purgatory. But how on Earth could anyone fast in the Langhe? How could anyone in his right mind shun the milk-fed veal, white truffles, porcini, and wine, all famed even in Roman times? Denying the divinity of Christ was one thing. Denying the virtues of Langhe gastronomy was another. That seemed heretical indeed, and maybe it explained why the Church authorities in the Middle Ages dealt so mercilessly with the Càtari: they were roasted alive in front of Milan's city gate like spitted oxen, a punishment right out of Dante's *Inferno* (even if the Florentine poet hadn't yet written his masterpiece).

Certainly the Càtari's attitude couldn't have been good for foodie tourism, such as it was 950 years ago. That, I reflected, was something for me to keep in mind. It was a call to duty, a reminder to successfully carry out my assignment lest I be roasted by my editor, who was less interested in history than in good times. Amid the tumbledown rusticity of modern Monforte, we would have to single out and sing the praises of the most luxurious, the most sumptuous, the most expensive gourmet establishment in town.

But I'd driven much faster than I'd thought. We had an hour to kill before dinner. At the mournful tolling of a church bell we turned our eyes toward the mossy campanile perched atop Monforte's hill, a finger thrust recriminatingly at the bruised cloudscape. My wife bounded across the highway with her cameras. I saw her reload one of them with black and white film. Now that she knew we were early, there was no stopping her from exploring the ungentrified aspects of town. A landslide of fixer-uppers clung precariously to the slope—windows out of kilter, rusted balconies, and humpbacked tile roofs cascading toward the highway and the lower, slightly less ancient section of the village where we'd parked our car.

Among the ruins glided a man wearing tattered black pants, a tattered black coat, and a dusty gray fedora. Coiled around his neck was a bright red scarf that leaped out to catch the dying sun. Alison machine-gunned him mercilessly through her telephoto lens, then cursed as he disappeared around a corner before she could switch cameras. No matter, I thought: tattered clothes and rutted roads didn't quite fit our brief. What we needed here was a handsome pair of lovers mauling each other in front of a panorama, with a brilliant blue sky warmed by sunset tones. That was what one of the photo editors had said he'd wanted. "It's Italy, right? Bring me blue!"

To such postcard shots he would match others showing a feeding frenzy of ecstatic eaters slavering over mounds of steaming *tajarin* (taglierini pasta) and *agnolotti* (jumbo ravioli); roasted pheasants and stuffed bell peppers; bubbling *bagna caoda* fondue and boiled beef topped with bright green sauce; wild mushrooms and pockmarked, pungent truffles; and bottles of brawny Barolo, Barbaresco, and Barbera arrayed like organ pipes behind an altar of delicacies…I could just see the opening shot: a paean to Epicurus.

With my mouth watering and happy thoughts in mind, I followed Alison up a series of serpentine paths to the village castle. According to the books I'd read, in an earlier incarnation this had been the fortified aerie of Contessa Berta. Here she and her nutritionally-challenged followers, many of them noble men and women, would mortify their undernourished flesh. In my mind's eye I could see them burning their fingers on roasted carrots and fresh-baked seven-grain bread, perhaps pausing for some friendly flagellation with a spiky artichoke.

Could Monforte's proto-vegetarians have lived nine centuries ago in these same cave-like houses of brick and stone? It wasn't impossible. Relatively little has changed in the upper village in the last thousand years. Mons Fortis, reported my sources, was fortified by the Lombards, reinforced by the Carolingians, and then left to the vagaries of time. In other words, it was damned old and in need of repair. Here, as in countless other Italian fortress-villages, humble dwellings sprouted like fungus on the thick town walls, walls that had once kept the Barbarians out and the serfs in. Tiny windows gave on a tangle of passageways an arm span wide, turning blind walls to the gorgeous panorama. Out there, in the world beyond, every imaginable kind of intruder lurked with hunger in his heart.

No surprises then, if, in 1028, when the bloody-minded Archbishop Ariberto d'Intimiano and his soldiers clattered up to Monforte from Milan, the village heretics quickly shut the town gates and hightailed it. Scrambling up the steep slope with what little they could carry, the Cathars found refuge in Contessa Berta's castle. But not for long. Gazing, breathless, from the panoramic *piazzetta* that spills in front of the castle we immediately appreciated what Monforte's military value must have been during the civil and religious strife of the Middle Ages. The view floats out as far as the Alps, taking in the Cadibona Pass and the hulking Monte Rosa a hundred miles away. The Tanaro River coils at Monforte's feet, a thousand vertical feet below where we stood. Along the valley, where today the freeway sweeps, ran the ancient roads linking the Italian Riviera to Turin and France.

Archbishop Ariberto and his men knew those roads well. As

Christian soldiers, veterans of the Burgundian campaigns against heretics, they'd fought the Devil wherever he'd reared his head. On that fateful day in Monforte in 1028, Lucifer had reportedly taken possession of Contessa Berta's young body. Rumor had it she and her fellow Cathars not only rejected the Langhe's culinary wonders and the tenets of the Church of Rome, but that they were also fornicating indiscriminantly and running amok. Some pious spies swore that this particular bunch of Cathars were heretical Manichaeans, disciples of dreaded Bogomiles from Macedonia and Bulgaria. The Bogomiles were a dualist sect that viewed the material world as a manifestation of evil and only the hereafter as good. Therefore they shunned riches, honors, and titles—not a particularly wise thing to do in medieval Italy. Other commentators maintained that Berta and her gang were harmless homegrown loonies fed up with the corruption of the Church, and though they ate only vegetables and foolishly renounced their worldly goods, they were neither sexual deviants nor heretics.

In either case, reasoned Ariberto, the subversives had to go. A siege was ordered. Monforte put up little resistance. This made sense: the Càtari believed there was no point keeping body and soul together. Martyrdom was true salvation. Contessa Berta's castle was expunged and torched. What was left of the Cathar community was rounded up and carted off to Milan. There they were shut in cages in a public square and left to reflect upon their sins. Archbishop Ariberto, having slipped out of his chain mail and into comfortable robes, waved his crosier and gave the heretics a charitable choice: either return to the fold or feed the barbecue being prepared just outside the city gate. Naturally, given their beliefs, they leaped gleefully into the flames. Certain chroniclers speak of horrible tortures and dismemberment, of mutilated Cathars being paraded half-dead around Milan before being burned at the stake. All the histories I consulted seem to agree that the execution took place outside the city gate which came to be known as Porta Monforte. The gate no longer exists, but the road leading from it into the heart of Milan is still called Corso Monforte in memory of the event.

At this point the tale becomes hazy. The castle of Monforte

seems to have been rebuilt a century after the massacre. It then passed through the hands of the Commune of Alba, the Viscontis of Milan, Emperor Frederick I, Charles Emmanuele III King of Savoy, and the powerful Carretto family. Its owners at the time of our visit were the Marchesi Scarampi del Cairo, a reclusive bunch of aristocrats. As if to cleanse the spot of its earlier associations, in the thirteenth century a Romanesque church was built in the small square in front of the former fortress, interposed between it and the village. Of this church only the bell tower remains, flanked by the unremarkable eighteenth-century twin churches of the Confraternita delle Umiliate and Sant'Agostino.

Alison and I now stood in the square as the sun set, thinking of old Contessa Berta. Mist welled up from the valley. Alison had managed to take only a few moody dusk shots, blighted by a clutter of TV aerials and garbage cans. No lovers had appeared on the parapet to take in the view. No one had come at all. Upper Monforte seemed deserted. Save for a ghostly creaking of wooden floors in the church and the slamming of unseen doors down dark passageways, there was no sign of life. Who knows how many eyes were staring out at us from the shuttered windows, though? How many old men and women in tattered black clothes hid from us? We, the intruders…

With such fanciful thoughts in mind we picked our way down the pitted alleys, dribbling from one puddle of yellowish lamplight to the next, escorted by our own long shadows and the hollow boom of church bells. We were just beginning to enjoy the spine-tingling mood when we reached the highway. Like wraiths in the twilight, headlights raked the mist, first one set, then a second, then a third and a fourth. It was a posse of powerful cars, and they all pulled over in front of the same famous hostelry we had come to write about and photograph.

The restaurant, operated by a third-generation Langhe chef, his wife and son, is renowned for its food and its cloistered garden. It was too late in the season and too cold to sit outside, so we'd reserved a table indoors. We joined the crowd of Turinese, Japanese, and fellow Americans in the flower-filled dining room. Luxury at last! Certainly the menu—scented with platinum truffles—was expensive enough to satisfy the most spendthrift of editors. I had been made to understand before leaving for the Langhe that at this restaurant the food was Good, with a capital "G." If by some unlucky stellar conspiracy it wasn't Good, Those In The Know didn't want to hear about it. Damn the place by silence, in other words. As the meal progressed at a gruelingly slow pace I began to wonder if our hosts weren't themselves descendants of Contessa Berta, who by a perverse twist of fate, had become restaurateurs. Where was the Epicurean abundance and joy? Where were the savvy locals? The tongues susurrating around us were foreign.

Unsmiling servers delivered a series of insipid imitations of French *amuse-bouches*, pâtés, and game mousses. The pasta dishes—rough-cut *tagliatelle* with wild mushrooms, and purselike *agnolotti* topped with truffle shavings—were no match for those we'd had in more than one local trattoria, where the simple, traditional food was unerringly delicious. An off night, perhaps? It happens. The chef was doubtless a talented host, otherwise how could he be famous and star-spangled? Nonetheless, I couldn't help thinking of the Cathars. Had they cast a spell on the place? On us?

The night I met Alfredo Currado, a legendary *Piemontese* winemaker, was one night after I contracted a vicious case of food poisoning in Germany. The effects were slow to leave me, and when I sat down with Currado and his wife in a restaurant in Monforte, my intestines were not ready. I faked my way through the *antipasti*, sniffed at the soup, and pushed the pasta around on my plate. Suddenly the chef was standing over me, demanding to know why I did not eat. My story tumbled out. He turned on his heel. The Currados were silent. A moment later, the chef arrived with a small plate of coarse powder. It was…yeast. The kind bakers use for bread. I ate the yeast, and though I ate little more that night, I was completely cured by next morning.

—TE

We watched now with grim satisfaction as a pencil-thin solitary diner two tables away sent his *agnolotti* back for the second time. Half an hour later he rejected the main course too—I couldn't see what it was. Finally out came the chef, toque in hand, visibly nervous. He sat down across from the thin man—a gastronomic guidebook inspector? Soon the man's table was overflowing with a sampler of house specialties. Bottles of wine appeared.

A few minutes later, seemingly shaken by the thin man's words, the chef disappeared into his kitchen. He reappeared several times over the next hour to see how the thin man was faring, never once glancing at other patrons. Meanwhile the butter began to congeal on our plates. The candles on our table guttered. We remained uncomplaining and anonymous—we had not yet introduced ourselves. We, like the restaurant's other diners, might as well have vanished. After what seemed several millennia we got the bill, paid up, and slipped out. By then Alison, utterly uninspired, had decided not to take photos anyway. Something had gone very wrong with our meal. At least I'd spent a lot of money, I said cheerfully as we scuttled away.

We debated whether to return to the spine-tingling square on top of the hill for a final view of this bizarre town. We'd come to love it for all the wrong reasons—for its rundown soulfulness and the tangible history I would, of course, have to soft-pedal in my articles. But it was late now and we'd been on the move for sixteen hours. As we picked our way back to the car between the crumbling houses, the mist rising and the campanile floodlit above for some passing ghoul, we suddenly heard blood-curdling croaks coming from a dark alley. Covered with gooseflesh we froze, fully expecting to see phantom Cathars swirling above our heads. The shadows slowly took human form. The horrible croaking stopped. A purple-faced man emerged from the gloom, dabbing at his mouth with a handkerchief, then dashed off in the direction we'd come from. His raincoat flapped like a monk's robe. The Cathars' curse again? Or too much beef braised in Barolo? We wondered which of Monforte's three great restaurants he'd been martyred in. Happily, there was no way of knowing.

*David Downie, a native San Franciscan, has lived and worked in France
and Italy since the early 1980s. His articles about European travel, culture,
and food have appeared in* Departures, Condé Nast Traveler, Travel &
Leisure, Saveur, *the* Los Angeles Times Magazine, *the* San Francisco
Sunday Chronicle, *and many other American and European publications.
His nonfiction books include the* Irreverent Guide to Amsterdam,
Enchanted Liguria: A Celebration of the Culture, Lifestyle, and
Food of the Italian Riviera, *with photography by his wife Alison Harris,
and* Cooking the Roman Way *[a cookbook featuring contemporary
Roman cuisine].*

TIM   RUSSO

Wine Country at
the Crossroads

A fragile democracy evolves in a series of toasts.

SOMETIMES A GLASS OF WINE CAN REVEAL A GREAT DEAL ABOUT A
country. When strands of history fortuitously meet amidst the
sound, smell, and taste of timeless tradition, along an old route of
traders and tyrants, princes and kings, mountains and castles, then a
glass of wine raised in a toast can tell you about a country's past, its
present, and the prospects for its future. This particular glass of
wine I saw in a place called Borjomi, in the former Soviet Republic
of Georgia.

Borjomi is a low mountain village west of the Georgian capital
Tbilisi, a drive of about two and a half hours through the slowly
receding plains and into the foothills of the Caucasus Mountains. To
get there, you have to drive along the main road from Tbilisi to the
west. For centuries, this road was part of the ancient Silk Route that
spanned Eurasia. Traveling westward through these mountains, caravans would pass along the Mtkvari River until it wound through
the range and out into the lush open spaces of western Georgia, and
onward to the Black Sea coast to the ports of Poti and Batumi.
From there, the caravans would load their cargo onto ships bound
for the Bosporus, which would take the cargo into the
Mediterranean to the rest of Europe.

The route to Borjomi was once a main channel of invasion for Ottoman Turks out of eastern Turkey. As a result, all along the road are ancient castles and fortifications. Settlements grew up around them; medieval churches, in characteristic Georgian orthodox architecture, punctuate the landscape, like the one at Igoeti, about an hour west of Tbilisi. Local tradition holds that to travel this route safely, one must throw some money out of the car while passing the church at Igoeti.

Today the route is a narrow two-lane asphalt ribbon for most of its length, and despite poor maintenance remains a main artery for trade. Trucks from Turkey filled with consumer goods head to and from Tbilisi. Georgian farmers, desperate for every inch of possible space in which to transport their goods, remove the seats from their Lada sedans, fill them with fruit or vegetables, and head down the road to market. Cars filled to the roof with oranges, potatoes, carrots, and other produce are a regular sight on this road, crawling slowly along under the weight. Shiny new gas stations have popped up along the route, contrasting jarringly with the mule-drawn carriages and flocks of sheep which still make up a portion of the traffic. The new stations service the modern vehicles now using the route to support construction of new oil pipelines which will take Caspian Sea oil from neighboring Azerbaijan through Georgia, along the ancient Silk Route, to ports on the Black Sea.

There is something about this Caucasian former Soviet republic that makes you want to come back, stay longer, learn more. It is a place where the sense of history surrounds you, where it is easy to imagine the comings and goings of kings and princes, czars and dictators, travelers and tradesmen. It is marked by alternating domination by Romans, Armenians, Persians, Turks, and Russians. Ethnic Georgians themselves are a bewildering mix of individual cultural identities with names such as Mingrelians, Svans, Abkhazians, and Adjarans. Georgia's mountainous terrain gave rise to the development of some of the most obscure languages in Europe, which still survive in isolated highland villages.

Georgia is also a place where wine is an ever-present companion. Georgians like to say that they invented wine, claiming a wine culture that goes back five thousand years, a claim indeed backed up by some archeological evidence of ancient wine casks scattered across the country. Wine is as much a part of daily sustenance in Georgia as it would be in France or Sonoma, like bread or salt or water. If you work in politics in the former Soviet Union, particularly in Georgia, you quickly gain an appreciation of this. Every political meeting has the potential to lead to a *supra*: a grand, traditional Georgian meal complete with vast quantities of local wines. The wines come red and white, dry or sweet. Most often they are poured from big jugs rather than typical bottles; they vary in quality but are almost always perfect with the food that is served.

Most Georgians who don't make their own wine buy it in bulk from local markets. At a *supra* it will be served from pitchers, as glasses empty rather quickly due to the Georgian tradition of constant toasting throughout a meal. The tradition has a set of rules that calls for certain people to give certain toasts at certain times, a structure which lends itself well to political dinners. Borjomi hosts more than its fair share of these.

There are natural springs in Borjomi which have given

Persia is often cited as the likely source of today's *vitis vinifera*—the species of grape used to make the vast majority of commercially produced wine. Wherever it came from, all the ingredients for the world's first wine were present with the grapes themselves: sugars in the grape pulp and juice, acids in the skins, and yeasts on the outside of the skins. The yeasts consume the sugar, which produces alcohol, and the acids keep the resulting liquid in a pH range that makes it palatable for drinking. We'll never know which hunter-gatherer put a load a grapes into a container, left it in the sun, and forgot about it long enough for the liquid that collected in the bottom of the container to ferment into wine. It seems, though, that the process was destined to be discovered somehow, by someone, somewhere.

—TE

rise over the years to health resorts. The spring water is bottled, named after the town, and sold throughout the Caucasus and former Soviet republics. During the years under the Russian czar, and continuing through the Soviet years, Borjomi was a popular spa resort, a good place to relax and take in some fresh air.

The spas in turn attracted famous visitors. At the beginning of the twentieth century, the Romanov family built a giant dacha complex along the river, called Lekani, where the last czars and their families would come for holidays. After the Soviets took over, it became a state dacha for leaders of the USSR. The most famous visitor was Stalin, who had a railroad built directly to the grounds, and a special bridge built across the river from the railroad to the front steps of the dacha. Today, Lekani is owned by the Georgian government, and it is used for government conferences as well as for official state visits.

The setting at Lekani is striking. The Romanov dacha itself is a spectacular example of late nineteenth-century architecture. It is a very large mansion, with big balconies and terraces, grand staircases and high ceilings. The grounds are as imperial as they can be, with marble fountains and statues. It is built in a valley near the river, surrounded by mountains covered with evergreens, and the ruins of an ancient castle rise along the ridge of one of the peaks. Standing on one of the balconies, looking out over the grounds and at the vista of the mountains across the river, it's easy to imagine Romanov princes and princesses strolling the grounds, czars hunting on horseback, or Stalin getting off the train, walking across the bridge and up the pathway through the gardens to take his room in the palace.

The Lekani complex of today, though, is itself a depiction of centuries of Georgian history. Alongside the grandiose Romanov dachas, across the river from the medieval ruins, are built monolithic Soviet-era facilities in concrete and glass. There are also smaller dachas, cafeterias, conference facilities, hotels, and office buildings, all of which have deteriorated like everything else in the former Soviet bloc. Giant eyesores of mid-seventies architecture, now unheated, without regular electricity, stand as crumbling monuments to the collapse of an empire.

I would usually make my way out to Lekani for training conferences with Georgia's ruling party, the Citizens Union of Georgia, one of the best organized, most western-oriented political parties in the former Soviet Union. Led by the president, Edward Schevardnadze (the famous former Soviet foreign minister), the CUG has gained the respect and confidence of the west. As a ruling party in a former soviet republic, however, the opportunity for corruption to take hold is ever present, a temptation that even the most conscientious of political leaders can sometimes fail to resist. This struggle is quite evident within the CUG, some of its leaders choosing to succumb to it, others struggling to contain it. A major feature of CUG seminars is the constant interruption from ringing mobile phones. In such a poor and collapsed country as Georgia, where the dollar value of a mobile phone would heat an apartment for a year, a roomful of government officials' mobile phones constantly ringing is a sure sign of something other than good government.

One of my visits to Lekani ended with a *supra* of enormous proportions, due to the attendance of many important leaders of the party. It was held in a drafty, cavernous, decrepit, and unheated cafeteria of one of the Soviet buildings, only because it was big enough to accommodate more than 100 people. Tables were set with the chipped dishes, plain glasses, and plastic table cloths you'd expect in a school cafeteria. Flimsy paper napkins had been unfolded and cut into four pieces to conserve the paper. The chairs were shaky, the tables rickety, and the room itself unwelcoming and chilly. I could well imagine that upon walking in, a first-time visitor might consider turning around and going back out.

But all this was offset by the incredible bounty of a traditional Georgian feast, one fit for a king and his court. Our plates were filled with chicken, lamb, bread, kebabs, *khachapuri* (a delicious Georgian cheese bread), cheeses, sausages, soups, fresh greens, and salads made of beets, walnuts, yogurt, and cucumbers. And of course, there was the wine. Servers carried giant pitchers of red and white wine around the tables, filling our short stubby glasses. As the meal got underway, a group of the men in one corner of the room began to sing.

There is nothing quite like a Georgian men's choir singing the traditional songs about Georgian soldiers, bravery, and tall tales, an a cappella mixture of deep medieval harmonies, echoing in the dank cafeteria as if it were a cathedral. I closed my eyes and felt transported back in time, to an age of castles and kings, knights and nobility. Instead of sitting in a cold, concrete, shabby, and crumbling 1970s Soviet cafeteria, I was sitting in a stone and wood castle, in a dining hall filled with festivity, around a massive fireplace, lit by candles, hundreds of years ago.

Then the toasts began and I returned to the present. The toastmaster, or *tamada* is appointed, usually the most important person at the table, or the host. Depending on the size of the gathering, the *tamada* might recognize one or two others who might be referred to as deputy *tamadas*, whose job it is to take requests from the people around the room who would also like to make toasts, and intercede for them to the *tamada*. Toasts are given in a traditionally recognized order, and each Georgian has a separate understanding of the order of the toasts; from what I've gathered, the consensus may be first, toast to God, second toast to Georgia, third toast to women. After that, there is much debate, leaving room for tailoring the toasts to the situation. In this fashion, a complex structure of toasting is set up controlled by the *tamada* and his deputies, particularly at a large *supra* like this one, which will result in enormous volumes of wine being consumed as the social order of the gathering is reinforced.

Thus, toasts at a Georgian *supra* can tell you a lot about the group of Georgians involved. This day, the *tamada* was one of the presidentially appointed governors who embody the worst of corruption in Georgian politics. He toasted to the new deputy chair of the party, someone perhaps twice as corrupt as himself. As the toasts continued, the *tamada* working his way from one corrupt official to another, I looked for the tables where the younger, anti-corruption leaders were sitting. They weren't even in the room; they'd left to return to Tbilisi before the *supra* had even started.

Their deputies, who remained behind, seemed to be enjoying their meals and their wine. But I knew they were observing the progress of the toasts, the unfolding of the *supra* and its unique internal political dynamic, and were sure to report to their superiors on what had happened. Here amidst powerful symbols of Georgian culture and history, a focal point of modern dictators, medieval myth, and imperial legend, they watched and wondered what these glasses of wine, raised in toast, might mean for them and their country.

Tim Russo has been working in the democracy development community throughout the former Soviet republics since 1997, and is currently working on a book about his adventures. Democracy work lends itself well to regular consumption of various local brews, including Armenian cognac, Russian vodka, and of course, Georgian wine.

PART FIVE

THE LAST WORD

JIM HARRISON

Wine

Wine can be muse, consort,
consolation—even savior.

I CONSIDER THE GREAT INVENTIONS OF THE PAST. NATURALLY ONE must include electricity and toilet paper, exclude computers of all varieties, but near the top of the products of the human imagination, like an ancient deity that is so omnipresent that it has become invisible, is the corkscrew.

Of course we all know that some vintners are so greedy that they would use old rags rather than the sacred cork tree, but then people of intelligence have had quite enough of this economic fascism, this sluice or trough of venality that is the global economy, and have resisted. The simple physical act of opening a bottle of wine has brought more happiness to the human race than all the collective governments in the history of Earth. Even organized religions are mere spiritual mousetraps compared to the "pop" of the cork, the delicious squeak when you loosen it from the firm grip of the corkscrew. And then the grandeur of the burble as we fill the glass, the very same sound we hear at the source, the wombs of all the rivers on earth.

That said, we must go to the particular; it is fruitless to keep chattering about women in general when they can be comprehended only on an individual basis, and then partially at best. Whether it is women or wine, our gifts of intelligence are limited, but it is this specific charm of the immutable that fuels our existence. Taste is a mystery that best finds its voice in wine.

At this very moment I'm a bit nervous because there is a gale on Lake Superior and the wind is so severe a large white pine tree has toppled in the backyard of my cabin. The marine forecast on the radio states that the waves will reach between twenty-two and twenty-four feet and the gale will last another full day. Stepping outside for a moment I can hear the roar of Lake Superior though it is three miles downriver from this cabin. What can I do about the forest surrounding me that is twisting in the wind? Why, have my first glass of wine of the day. I pull the cork of a Lirac, the gift of a friend. The cork sound counters the shuddering walls of the log cabin. As I drink the first glass rather quickly my metal Weber grill is blown over in the yard. The Lirac is very good, if a bit midrange, but such is its power that the storm becomes acceptable. At least I'm not in a boat. Another smaller tree falls and my dog barks. I'd offer her a glass but she doesn't care for wine. I read from a volume of Chinese poetry. The bottle slowly empties itself. Now the gale is only a gale. It's outside and I'm inside. Three blue jays at the feeder are ignoring the storm and its sixty-knot winds. If I went outside with a full glass there would be waves on the surface of my wine. Instead I prepare some duck confit for my dinner.

Acute fear is a peculiar emotion, always a surprise in its suddenness and power. Several years ago flying home from Montana with my wife, we boarded a small propeller plane in Minneapolis much delayed by thunderstorms. Finally the impatient pilot took off and halfway through the flight when we were over Lake Michigan we collided with the storm which couldn't be avoided by going north or south. The plane twirled on an invisible pivot, bucked like a rodeo horse, then stood on its tale with wings flapping like the rare Anhinga bird, which resembles an airborne serpent. The passengers moaned and hooted and vomited like doomed owls. I'd like to say I was fearless but it would be a pointless lie. I planned on strangling the impetuous pilot but when we reached Traverse City he emerged from the cockpit soaked with sweat and an utterly tortured expression of apology.

We reached home after midnight and my wife went promptly to bed. I was still trembling from having kissed death's ass and fetched two wines from the cellar, a Migoua and a Tourtine Bandol from Lulu Peyraud's Domaine Tempier. I slowly drank both of these superb bottles while meditating on the essential criminality of flight and how even birds have the wit not to fly into thunderstorms. After a short while this blessed Bandol began to take over and I again realized that we are only flowers for the void. Finally the wine swept me back to Provence in late April where I ate and drank so happily at Lulu Peyraud's house after we knelt in the courtyard by the grave of her husband Lucien who had created this splendid wine. By the time I went to bed the flight had become just another tidbit of horror to file in the brain, detoxified so nobly by the wine. Despite their frequent strikes, I fly Air France to Europe because it serves interesting wines, the only palliative for the essential blasphemy of flight.

Naturally we save our best bottles to celebrate or commemorate. Some twenty years ago by sheer luck I was able to buy a private collection for a modest price. A man had a liver problem but did not want to sell his wines to a restaurant for personal reasons. I heard about it and moved quickly and have put the experience up near funding my remote cabin in Michigan's Upper Peninsula, or our little winter *casita* near the Mexican border. And buying this collection, now mostly dissipated, allowed me to drink some wines that writers are rarely allowed to approach for financial reasons, also to treat friends. Guy de la Valdene, a dear friend and the main wine guide of my life, was at my house for bird hunting on the eve of going off for very serious surgery. We sat at my kitchen counter and gently drank two bottles of 1953 Richebourg. On another occasion when Guy made *salmi de becasse* we drank several bottles of Grands-Échézeaux, his father's favorite wine. And just a week ago, the night before Guy left after our annual grouse and woodcock hunt, we had a splendid 1967 Latour, the best Latour of my life except for the 1949 I shared with my daughter the night before she was married, along with the 1961 Lafite-Rothschild we had earlier with dinner.

Such bottles truly resonate in the memory, growing even more overwhelming as they distance themselves with the years. I close my eyes and let my taste memory become vivid somewhat like a sex fantasy that makes your hair stand on end and goose bumps arise on your arms. Now that I no longer write screenplays my tastes have had to become more modest, and I have to depend on the kindness of friends and strangers with bigger wallets. I have, in the past few years, developed a taste for about thirty different Côtes du Rhône, though naturally some of the most expensive ones like Crozes-Hermitage and Gigondas are the tastiest. Côte-Rôtie is of course off to the side, all by itself in lonely splendor. When my novel, *The Road Home,* had begun doing quite well in France I had several celebration bottles of old Côte-Rôtie with my friend and publisher Christian Bourgois. Success in itself can be quite disturbing, hard to accommodate, and I spent as much time as possible alone in my room where a number of good bottles consoled me including two Côte-Rôties sent over by Dominique Bourgois's father, and two bottles of a fine year of Château Beychevelle which were a gift from Jeanne Moreau whose gorgeous voice was obviously nurtured by wine.

Sometimes a humbler wine totally fits the situation. One day in Paris when I was angry from doing so many interviews I left the hotel lobby and walked over to the Select on the Boulevard du Montparnasse, a café I visit every day when in Paris, and had a simple but delicious bottle of Brouilly. My anger subsided when the resident cat allowed me to pet it, and by tilting my head I had a good look at a woman's legs in the corner. I shall ever after think of thighs when I drink Brouilly.

I have left out American wines because I can only think of one truly great one, the 1968 Heitz Martha's Vineyard, and I have no story attached to it. Doubtless there are some considerable American wines but most are too thickish and oaky for my taste.

I shouldn't forget how wine can assuage grief. Once my phenomenal bird dog, an English setter named Tess over whom I shot more than a thousand birds, got a stick caught in her throat and began to hemorrhage. After two trips to the veterinarian late at night she was finally pronounced out of danger. I had been so shattered I hadn't been able to eat dinner, and after she finally slept I remembered that that day a friend had sent a fresh *foie gras* from D'Artagnan. It was two o'clock in the morning when I finished steaming the *foie gras* over Sire de Gooderville cognac. I ate it with a baguette and my best remaining bottle of Margaux. I don't recall what year it was but I raised my glass to my sleeping dog who was nearly lost.

And lastly, but perhaps more important because we do not know what happens after death, I owe to wine the fact that I'm still alive. Several years ago I was in bad health and several doctors learned that I was utterly addicted to VO, a Canadian whiskey which, though delicious, is a poor substitute for water or wine. I explained the mortal problem to my friend Michael Butler, who works for the great importer of French wines, Kermit Lynch. We decided that some magnums of Châteauneuf-du-Pape Vieux Télégraphe might help me through the harrowing ordeal I was facing. One evening in our little *casita* I set out a bottle of the VO whiskey, and sat down in a rocker staring at this dread potion for four hours, drinking nothing but the spirits of denial. If I couldn't stop whiskey I'd have to give up alcohol altogether and what would become of the lonely bottles in my cellar? I rocked like an autistic child. Tears formed, but I won. I dumped the bottle of whiskey in the sink, had a glass of Vieux Télégraphe, petted my dog, and went to bed, a new man in an old bottle.

Jim Harrison is one of America's foremost writers, the author of seven novels, seven books of poetry, four volumes of novellas, two collections of nonfiction, and a number of major motion picture screenplays. He has been awarded a National Endowment for the Arts grant and a Guggenheim Fellowship, and his work has been published in twenty-two languages. His most recent books are The Raw and the Cooked, *a collection of essays originally published in* Esquire *and other magazines, and* The Beast God Forgot to Invent, *a novella.*

Recommended Reading

Asher, Gerald. *Vineyard Tales: Reflections on Wine*. San Francisco: Chronicle Books, 1996.

Aspler, Tony. *Travels with My Corkscrew: Memoirs of a Wine Lover*. New York: McGraw-Hill, 1997.

Brooks, Stephen (ed.). *A Century of Wine: The Story of a Wine Revolution*. London: Mitchell Beazley, 2000.

Conaway, James. *Napa*. New York: Avon, 1992.

Daley, Robert. *Portraits of France*. London: Arrow Books, 1992.

Fisher, M.F.K. *An Alphabet for Gourmets*. New York: Penguin, 1989.

Johnson, Hugh and Jancis Robinson. *The World Atlas of Wine* (5th ed.). London: Mitchell Beazley, 2001.

Lapsley, James T. *Bottled Poetry*. Berkeley: University of California Press, 1996.

Loftus, Simon. *Puligny-Montrachet: Journal of a Village in Burgundy*. New York: Alfred A. Knopf, 1993.

Lynch, Kermit. *Adventures on the Wine Route: A Wine Buyer's Tour of France*. New York: Farrar, Straus and Giroux, 1988; New York: Noonday Press, 1990.

MacNeil, Karen. *The Wine Bible*. New York: Workman, 2001.

Mayle, Peter. *French Lessons: Adventures with Knife, Fork, and Corkscrew*. New York: Alfred A. Knopf, 2001.

Peynaud, Emile. *The Taste of Wine: The Art and Science of Wine Appreciation*. New York: John Wiley & Sons, 1996.

Robinson, Jancis (ed.). *The Oxford Companion to Wine* (2nd ed.). New York: Oxford University Press, 1999.

Smith, Rod. *Private Reserve*. Stamford, CT: Daglan Press; Rutherford, CA: Beaulieu Vineyards, 2000.

Visser, Margaret. *The Rituals of Dinner: The Origins, Evolution, Eccentricities, and Meaning of Table Manners*. New York: Penguin, 1991.

Wilson, James E. *Terroir*. Berkeley: University of California Press, 1998.

Index

Index of Contributors

Acknowledgments

Immeasurable gratitude to Antonia Allegra, for starting me on the paths of essayist and wine journalist, and to my wife Antoinette von Grone, whose art inspires me every day.

"Sipping with the Gods" by Stephen Yafa published with permission from the author. Copyright © 2002 by Stephen Yafa.

"In the Valley of Beautiful Women" by Michelle Richmond published with permission from the author. Copyright © 2002 by Michelle Richmond.

"Arriving at Wine" by Karen MacNeil published with permission from the author. Copyright © 2002 by Karen MacNeil.

"The Angle and the Voice" by Steve Edmunds published with permission from the author. Copyright © 2002 by Steve Edmunds.

"A Harvest in Alsace" by Mike Steinberger published with permission from the author. Copyright © 2002 by Mike Steinberger.

"Exhilarating Virtues of Wine" by Emile Peynaud excerpted from *The Taste of Wine: The Art and Science of Wine Appreciation* by Emile Peynaud. Copyright © 1987, 1996 by Emile Peynaud. Reprinted by permission of John Wiley & Sons, Inc.

"The Passing of Butterflies" by Heidi Haughy Cusick published with permission from the author. Copyright © 2002 by Heidi Haughy Cusick.

"Etymology of a Wine Lover" by Jan Morris published with permission from the author. Copyright © by Jan Morris.

"Remembrance of Wines Past" by Gerald Asher excerpted from *Vineyard Tales: Reflections on Wine* by Gerald Asher. Copyright © 1996 by Gerald Asher. Reprinted by permission of Chronicle Books.

"Cellar Man" by Christopher Weir published with permission from the author. Copyright © 2002 by Christopher Weir.

"How to Conquer a Wine List" by Kit Snedaker published with permission from the author. Copyright © 2002 by Kit Snedaker.

"Among Flying Corks" by Peter Mayle excerpted from *French Lessons: Adventures with Knife, Fork, and Corkscrew* by Peter Mayle. Copyright © 2001 by Escargot Productions Ltd. Illustrations copyright © 2001 by Alfred A. Knopf, a division of Random House, Inc. Used by permission of Alfred A. Knopf, a division of Random House, Inc., and The Writer's Shop.

"Wine and Blood in Puligny-Montrachet" by Simon Loftus excerpted from

247

"Wine Country at the Crossroads" by Tim Russo published with permission from the author. Copyright © 2002 by Tim Russo.

"Wine" by Jim Harrison originally appeared in the October 28, 1999 issue of *Revue Des Deux Mondes*. Copyright © 1999 by Jim Harrison. Reprinted by permission of the author.

Additional Selections (arranged in alphabetical order)

Selection from *An Alphabet for Gourmets* by M.F.K. Fisher published by Penguin (1989).

Selection from *Bottled Poetry* by James T. Lapsley copyright ©1996 by The Regents of the University of California. Reprinted by permission of University of California Press, Berkeley.

Selection from *The Golden Bough* by James G. Frazer copyright © 1922.

Selection from *A Little Tour in France* by Henry James originally published by Riverside Press (1900).

Selection from *Notes on a Cellar-Book* by George Saintsbury originally published by MacMillan (1921).

Selection from *Private Reserve* by Rod Smith copyright © 2000. Reprinted by permission of Beaulieu Vineyard, Rutherford, California.

Selection from *The Rituals of Dinner: The Origins, Evolution, Eccentricities, and Meaning of Table Manners* by Margaret Visser copyright © 1991 by Margaret Visser. Published by Penguin Putnam USA.

Selection from *The Silverado Squatters* by Robert Louis Stevenson originally published in 1880.

Selection from "Taking the Plunge" by Catherine Fallis, M.S. published with permission from the author. Copyright © 2002 by Catherine Fallis.

Selection from *Terroir* by James E. Wilson copyright © 1998 by James E. Wilson. Published by the University of California Press in association with the Wine Appreciation Guild. Reprinted by permission.

About the Editor

Thom Elkjer is the versatile author of books, essays, journalism, criticism, and works for the theater. He is Wine Editor for *Wine Country Living* magazine, where he writes about wine, travel, and the arts. He has contributed to half a dozen Travelers' Tales anthologies, including the opening essays in the popular volumes *Paris*, *Italy*, and *The Road Within*. He is the author also of *Escape to the Wine Country* (Fodor's), a lyrical yet detailed travel guide to the premier wine regions of Northern California, photographed by Robert Holmes. Elkjer's award-winning first novel, entitled *Hook, Line and Murder*, sold through multiple printings in the late 1990s, and a sequel is planned. His book and music criticism appeared in the *San Francisco Chronicle*, *New Realities*, and other publications, and he has contributed feature articles and interview profiles to *Wine Spectator* in the U.S. and *WINE* magazine in the U.K. Before becoming an author and journalist, he worked professionally as a playwright, director, and actor in San Francisco, including celebrated, long-running performances at the Magic Theater and One Act Theater. He and his wife, the artist Antoinette von Grone, share a home in the California mission town of San Rafael and a farm in the wine country of rural Mendocino County.

TRAVELERS' TALES
THE SOUL OF TRAVEL

Footsteps Series

THE FIRE NEVER DIES
One Man's Raucous Romp Down the Road of Food, Passion, and Adventure
By Richard Sterling
ISBN 1-885-211-70-8
$14.95

"Sterling's writing is like spit-fire, foursquare and jazzy with crackle...."
—*Kirkus Reviews*

ONE YEAR OFF
Leaving It All Behind for a Round-the-World Journey with Our Children
By David Elliot Cohen
ISBN 1-885-211-65-1
$14.95

A once-in-a-lifetime adventure generously shared.

TAKE ME WITH YOU
A Round-the-World Journey to Invite a Stranger Home
By Brad Newsham
ISBN 1-885-211-51-1
$24.00 (cloth)

"Newsham is an ideal guide. His journey, at heart, is into humanity." —Pico Iyer, author of *Video Night in Kathmandu*

THE SWORD OF HEAVEN
A Five Continent Odyssey to Save the World
By Mikkel Aaland
ISBN 1-885-211-44-9
$24.00 (cloth)

"Few books capture the soul of the road like *The Sword of Heaven*, a sharp-edged, beautifully rendered memoir that will inspire anyone." —Phil Cousineau, author of *The Art of Pilgrimage*

LAST TROUT IN VENICE
The Far-Flung Escapades of an Accidental Adventurer
By Doug Lansky
ISBN 1-885-211-63-5
$14.95

"Traveling with Doug Lansky might result in a considerably shortened life expectancy...but what a way to go." —Tony Wheeler, Lonely Planet Publications

THE WAY OF THE WANDERER
Discover Your True Self Through Travel
By David Yeadon
ISBN 1-885-211-60-0
$14.95

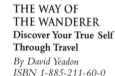

Experience transformation through travel with this delightful, illustrated collection by award-winning author David Yeadon.

KITE STRINGS OF THE SOUTHERN CROSS
A Woman's Travel Odyssey
By Laurie Gough
ISBN 1-885-211-54-6
$14.95 —★★★—

ForeWord Silver Medal Winner
— Travel Book of the Year

STORM
A Motorcycle Journey of Love, Endurance, and Transformation
By Allen Noren
ISBN 1-885-211-45-7
$24.00 (cloth)
—★★★—

ForeWord Gold Medal Winner
— Travel Book of the Year

Travelers' Tales Classics

COAST TO COAST
A Journey Across 1950s America
By Jan Morris
ISBN 1-885-211-79-1
$16.95

After reporting on the first Everest ascent in 1953, Morris spent a year journeying by car, train, ship, and aircraft across the United States. In her brilliant prose, Morris records with exuberance and curiosity a time of innocence in the U.S.

THE ROYAL ROAD TO ROMANCE
By Richard Halliburton
ISBN 1-885-211-53-8
$14.95

"Laughing at hardships, dreaming of beauty, ardent for adventure, Halliburton has managed to sing into the pages of this glorious book his own exultant spirit of youth and freedom."
— *Chicago Post*

THE RIVERS RAN EAST
By Leonard Clark
ISBN 1-885-211-66-X
$16.95

Clark is the original Indiana Jones, relaying a breathtaking account of his search for the legendary El Dorado gold in the Amazon.

THERE'S NO TOILET PAPER...ON THE ROAD LESS TRAVELED
The Best of Travel Humor and Misadventure
Edited by Doug Lansky
ISBN 1-885-211-27-9
$12.95

— ★★★ —
Humor Book of the Year
— Independent Publisher's Book Award

— ★★★ —
ForeWord Gold Medal Winner — Humor Book of the Year

TRADER HORN
A Young Man's Astounding Adventures in 19th Century Equatorial Africa
By Alfred Aloysius Horn
ISBN 1-885-211-81-3
$16.95

Here is the stuff of legends —tale of thrills and danger, wild beasts, serpents, and savages. An unforgettable and vivid portrait of a vanished late-19th century Africa.

UNBEATEN TRACKS IN JAPAN
By Isabella L. Bird
ISBN 1-885-211-57-0
$14.95

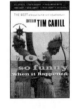

Isabella Bird was one of the most adventurous women travelers of the 19th century with journeys to Tibet, Canada, Korea, Turkey, Hawaii, and Japan. A fascinating read for anyone interested in women's travel, spirituality, and Asian culture.

Travel Humor

NOT SO FUNNY WHEN IT HAPPENED
The Best of Travel Humor and Misadventure
Edited by Tim Cahill
ISBN 1-885-211-55-4
$12.95

Laugh with Bill Bryson, Dave Barry, Anne Lamott, Adair Lara, and many more.

LAST TROUT IN VENICE
The Far-Flung Escapades of an Accidental Adventurer
By Doug Lansky
ISBN 1-885-211-63-5
$14.95

"Traveling with Doug Lansky might result in a considerably shortened life expectancy...but what a way to go."
—Tony Wheeler, Lonely Planet Publications

Women's Travel

A WOMAN'S PASSION FOR TRAVEL
More True Stories from A Woman's World
Edited by Marybeth Bond & Pamela Michael
ISBN 1-885-211-36-8
$17.95

"A diverse and gripping series of stories!"   —Arlene Blum, author of *Annapurna: A Woman's Place*

A WOMAN'S WORLD
True Stories of Life on the Road
Edited by Marybeth Bond
Introduction by Dervla Murphy
ISBN 1-885-211-06-6
$17.95

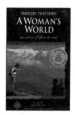

— ★*★* —

Winner of the Lowell Thomas Award for Best Travel Book—
Society of American Travel Writers

WOMEN IN THE WILD
True Stories of Adventure and Connection
Edited by Lucy McCauley
ISBN 1-885-211-21-X
$17.95

"A spiritual, moving, and totally female book to take you around the world and back." —*Mademoiselle*

A MOTHER'S WORLD
Journeys of the Heart
Edited by Marybeth Bond & Pamela Michael
ISBN 1-885-211-26-0
$14.95

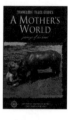

"These stories remind us that motherhood is one of the great unifying forces in the world"   —*San Francisco Examiner*

Food

ADVENTURES IN WINE
True Stories of Vineyards and Vintages around the World
Edited by Thom Elkjer
ISBN 1-885-211-80-5
$17.95

Humanity, community, and brotherhood comprise the marvelous virtues of the wine world. This collection toasts the warmth and wonders of this large, extended family in stories by travelers who are wine novices and experts alike.

FOOD (Updated)
A Taste of the Road
Edited by Richard Sterling
Introduction by Margo True
ISBN 1-885-211-77-5
$18.95

— ★*★* —

Silver Medal Winner of the Lowell Thomas Award for Best Travel Book—Society of American Travel Writers

HER FORK IN THE ROAD
Women Celebrate Food and Travel
Edited by Lisa Bach
ISBN 1-885-211-71-6
$16.95

A savory sampling of stories by some of the best writers in and out of the food and travel fields.

THE ADVENTURE OF FOOD
True Stories of Eating Everything
Edited by Richard Sterling
ISBN 1-885-211-37-6
$17.95

"These stories are bound to whet appetites for more than food."

—*Publishers Weekly*

Spiritual Travel

THE SPIRITUAL GIFTS OF TRAVEL
The Best of Travelers' Tales
Edited by James O'Reilly and Sean O'Reilly
ISBN 1-885-211-69-4
$16.95

A collection of favorite stories of transformation on the road from our award-winning Travelers' Tales series that shows the myriad ways travel indelibly alters our inner landscapes.

THE WAY OF THE WANDERER
Discover Your True Self Through Travel
By David Yeadon
ISBN 1-885-211-60-0
$14.95

Experience transformation through travel with this delightful, illustrated collection by award-winning author David Yeadon.

PILGRIMAGE
Adventures of the Spirit
Edited by Sean O'Reilly & James O'Reilly
Introduction by Phil Cousineau
ISBN 1-885-211-56-2
$16.95

— ✦ ✦ ✦ —

ForeWord Silver Medal Winner
— Travel Book of the Year

A WOMAN'S PATH
Women's Best Spiritual Travel Writing
Edited by Lucy McCauley, Amy G. Carlson & Jennifer Leo
ISBN 1-885-211-48-1
$16.95

"A sensitive exploration of women's lives that have been unexpectedly and spiritually touched by travel experiences.... Highly recommended."
— *Library Journal*

THE ROAD WITHIN
True Stories of Transformation and the Soul
Edited by Sean O'Reilly, James O'Reilly & Tim O'Reilly
ISBN 1-885-211-19-8
$17.95

— ✦ ✦ ✦ —

Best Spiritual Book — Independent Publisher's Book Award

THE ULTIMATE JOURNEY
Inspiring Stories of Living and Dying
James O'Reilly, Sean O'Reilly & Richard Sterling
ISBN 1-885-211-38-4
$17.95

"A glorious collection of writings about the ultimate adventure. A book to keep by one's bedside — and close to one's heart." — Philip Zaleski, editor, *The Best Spiritual Writing series*

Adventure

TESTOSTERONE PLANET
True Stories from a Man's World
Edited by Sean O'Reilly, Larry Habegger & James O'Reilly
ISBN 1-885-211-43-0
$17.95

Thrills and laughter with some of today's best writers: Sebastian Junger, Tim Cahill, Bill Bryson, and Jon Krakauer.

DANGER!
True Stories of Trouble and Survival
Edited by James O'Reilly, Larry Habegger & Sean O'Reilly
ISBN 1-885-211-32-5
$17.95

"Exciting...for those who enjoy living on the edge or prefer to read the survival stories of others, this is a good pick."
— *Library Journal*

Special Interest

365 TRAVEL
A Daily Book of Journeys, Meditations, and Adventures
Edited by Lisa Bach
ISBN 1-885-211-67-8
$14.95
An illuminating collection of travel wisdom and adventures that reminds us all of the lessons we learn while on the road.

THE GIFT OF RIVERS
True Stories of Life on the Water
Edited by Pamela Michael
Introduction by Robert Hass
ISBN 1-885-211-42-2
$14.95
"*The Gift of Rivers* is a soulful compendium of wonderful stories that illuminate, educate, inspire, and delight."
—David Brower, Chairman of Earth Island Institute

FAMILY TRAVEL
The Farther You Go, the Closer You Get
Edited by Laura Manske
ISBN 1-885-211-33-3
$17.95
"This is family travel at its finest." —*Working Mother*

LOVE & ROMANCE
True Stories of Passion on the Road
Edited by Judith Babcock Wylie
ISBN 1-885-211-18-X
$17.95
"A wonderful book to read by a crackling fire."
— *Romantic Traveling*

THE GIFT OF BIRDS
True Encounters with Avian Spirits
Edited by Larry Habegger & Amy G. Carlson
ISBN 1-885-211-41-4
$17.95
"These are all wonderful, entertaining stories offering a *bird's-eye view!* of our avian friends."
—*Booklist*

A DOG'S WORLD
True Stories of Man's Best Friend on the Road
Edited by Christine Hunsicker
ISBN 1-885-211-23-6
$12.95
This extraordinary collection includes stories by John Steinbeck, Helen Thayer, James Herriot, Pico Iyer, and many others.

THE GIFT OF TRAVEL
The Best of Travelers' Tales
Edited by Larry Habegger, James O'Reilly & Sean O'Reilly
ISBN 1-885-211-25-2
$14.95
"Like gourmet chefs in a French market, the editors of Travelers' Tales pick, sift, and prod their way through the weighty shelves of contemporary travel writing, creaming off the very best."
—William Dalrymple, author of *City of Djinns*

Travel Advice

SHITTING PRETTY
How to Stay Clean and Healthy While Traveling
By Dr. Jane Wilson-Howarth
ISBN 1-885-211-47-3
$12.95

A light-hearted book about a serious subject for millions of travelers— staying healthy on the road—written by international health expert, Dr. Jane Wilson-Howarth.

THE FEARLESS SHOPPER
How to Get the Best Deals on the Planet
By Kathy Borrus
ISBN 1-885-211-39-2
$14.95

"Anyone who reads *The Fearless Shopper* will come away a smarter, more responsible shopper and a more curious, culturally attuned traveler."
—Jo Mancuso, *The Shopologist*

GUTSY WOMEN
More Travel Tips and Wisdom for the Road
By Marybeth Bond
ISBN 1-885-211-61-9
$12.95

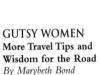

Second Edition—Packed with funny, instructive, and inspiring advice for women heading out to see the world.

SAFETY AND SECURITY FOR WOMEN WHO TRAVEL
By Sheila Swan & Peter Laufer
ISBN 1-885-211-29-5
$12.95

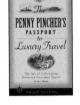

A must for every woman traveler!

THE FEARLESS DINER
Travel Tips and Wisdom for Eating around the World
By Richard Sterling
ISBN 1-885-211-22-8
$7.95

Combines practical advice on foodstuffs, habits, and etiquette, with hilarious accounts of others' eating adventures.

THE PENNY PINCHER'S PASSPORT TO LUXURY TRAVEL
The Art of Cultivating Preferred Customer Status
By Joel L. Widzer
ISBN 1-885-211-31-7
$12.95

Proven techniques on how to travel first class at discount prices, even if you're not a frequent flyer.

GUTSY MAMAS
Travel Tips and Wisdom for Mothers on the Road
By Marybeth Bond
ISBN 1-885-211-20-1
$7.95

A delightful guide for mothers traveling with their children— or without them!

Destination Titles:
True Stories of Life on the Road

AMERICA
Edited by Fred Setterberg
ISBN 1-885-211-28-7
$19.95

FRANCE (Updated)
*Edited by James O'Reilly,
Larry Habegger &
Sean O'Reilly*
ISBN 1-885-211-73-2
$18.95

**AMERICAN
SOUTHWEST**
*Edited by Sean O'Reilly
& James O'Reilly*
ISBN 1-885-211-58-9
$17.95

GRAND CANYON
*Edited by Sean O'Reilly,
James O'Reilly &
Larry Habegger*
ISBN 1-885-211-34-1
$17.95

AUSTRALIA
Edited by Larry Habegger
ISBN 1-885-211-40-6
$17.95

GREECE
*Edited by Larry Habegger,
Sean O'Reilly &
Brian Alexander*
ISBN 1-885-211-52-X
$17.95

BRAZIL
*Edited by Annette Haddad
& Scott Doggett
Introduction by Alex
Shoumatoff*
ISBN 1-885-211-11-2
$17.95

HAWAI'I
*Edited by Rick &
Marcie Carroll*
ISBN 1-885-211-35-X
$17.95

CENTRAL AMERICA
*Edited by Larry Habegger
& Natanya Pearlman*
ISBN 1-885-211-74-0
$17.95

HONG KONG
*Edited by James O'Reilly,
Larry Habegger &
Sean O'Reilly*
ISBN 1-885-211-03-1
$17.95

CUBA
Edited by Tom Miller
ISBN 1-885-211-62-7
$17.95

INDIA
*Edited by James O'Reilly
& Larry Habegger*
ISBN 1-885-211-01-5
$17.95

IRELAND
Edited by James O'Reilly,
Larry Habegger &
Sean O'Reilly
ISBN 1-885-211-46-5
$17.95

SAN FRANCISCO
Edited by James O'Reilly,
Larry Habegger &
Sean O'Reilly
ISBN 1-885-211-08-2
$17.95

ITALY (Updated)
Edited by Anne Calcagno
Introduction by Jan Morris
ISBN 1-885-211-72-4
$18.95

SPAIN (Updated)
Edited by Lucy McCauley
ISBN 1-885-211-78-3
$19.95

JAPAN
Edited by Donald W. George
& Amy G. Carlson
ISBN 1-885-211-04-X
$17.95

THAILAND (Updated)
Edited by James O'Reilly
& Larry Habegger
ISBN 1-885-211-75-9
$18.95

MEXICO (Updated)
Edited by James O'Reilly
& Larry Habegger
ISBN 1-885-211-59-7
$17.95

TIBET
Edited by James O'Reilly,
Larry Habegger, & Kim
Morris
ISBN 1-885-211-76-7
$18.95

NEPAL
Edited by Rajendra
S. Khadka
ISBN 1-885-211-14-7
$17.95

TUSCANY
Edited by James O'Reilly, &
Tara Austen Weaver
ISBN 1-885-211-68-6
$16.95

PARIS
Edited by James O'Reilly,
Larry Habegger &
Sean O'Reilly
ISBN 1-885-211-10-4
$17.95